Economic Policy in the European Union

This book is dedicated to the memory of

Petra Klosová
and
Elsa Di Bello

Economic Policy in the European Union

Current Perspectives

Edited by

Wim Meeusen

Professor of Economics, University of Antwerp (RUCA),

Belgium

Edward Elgar

Cheltenham, UK · Northampton, MA, USA

Published by
Edward Elgar Publishing Limited
Glensanda House
Montpellier Parade
Cheltenham
Glos GL50 1UA
UK

Edward Elgar Publishing, Inc.
6 Market Street
Northampton
Massachusetts 01060
USA

A catalogue record for this book
is available from the British Library

Library of Congress Cataloguing in Publication Data

Economic policy in the European Union : current perspectives / edited
    by Wim Meeusen.
    Includes index.
    1. Monetary unions—European Union countries. 2. Monetary policy-
    –European Union countries. 3. European Union countries—Economic
    policy. 4. Europe—Economic integration. I. Meeusen, Wim, 1945–
HG3942.E25 1999
338.94—dc21   99–17605
                                                                   CIP

ISBN 1 84064 036 7

Printed and bound in Great Britain by Biddles Ltd, Guildford and King's Lynn

Contents

PART II: PUBLIC POLICY ISSUES

List of Figures

List of Tables

List of Contributors

Nick Adnett
Economics Division
Staffordshire University Business
School
UK

Frank Barry
Department of Economics
University College Dublin
Ireland

Kristel Buysse
Department of Applied Economics
University of Antwerp (RUCA)
Belgium

Chris Coeck
Department of Applied Economics
University of Antwerp (RUCA)
Belgium

Sandra Coppieters
European Institute
University of Ghent
Belgium

Cláudia Costa
Banco de Portugal
Portugal

Paul De Grauwe
Centre for Economic Studies
University of Leuven
Belgium

Michel Dumont
Department of Applied Economics
University of Antwerp (RUCA)
Belgium

Herbert Glejser
Faculty of Economic, Social and
Management Sciences
University of Namur
Belgium

Stephen Hardy
Department of Social Work and Law
University of Salford
UK

Sonja Hellemann
Banque Paribas-London
UK

Luc Hens
Faculty of Economic, Social and
Political Sciences
Free University of Brussels (VUB)
Belgium

Wim Meeusen
Department of Applied Economics
University of Antwerp (RUCA)
Belgium

Roland Pepermans
Faculty of Psychology
Free University of Brussels (VUB)
Belgium

Geoff Pugh
Economics Division
Staffordshire University Business
School
UK

Blanca Sanchez-Robles
Department of Economics
University of Cantabria
Spain

Lukasz Tarnawa
Warsaw School of Economics
Poland

David Tyrrall
Accounting and Finance Division
Staffordshire University Business
School
UK

Anne-Marie Van den Bossche
European Court of Justice
Luxembourg

Daniel Van Den Bulcke
Institute of Public Administration
and Management
University of Antwerp (RUCA)
Belgium

Alain Verbeke
Faculty of Economic, Social and
Political Sciences
Free University of Brussels (VUB)
Belgium

José Villaverde
Department of Economics
University of Cantabria
Spain

(ξu)

BK Title:

1. Introduction and Outline

N / A

Wim Meeusen

Since the Treaty of Rome of 1957 few developments in the process of European integration have been so fundamental as the Maastricht 1992 decision to create a European monetary union before the turning of the century. It should therefore not come as a surprise that a relatively major part of the contributions to this book on current policy issues in European economic integration – those contained in Part I – deal with this subject.

In the logical order of things Geoff Pugh, David Tyrrall and Lukasz Tarnawa first try to answer the question whether exchange rate stability in its institutionalised form, of which the EMU is a radical manifestation, may at all be expected to promote stability and growth. The theoretical issue centres for a part around the argument of another contributor to this volume, Paul De Grauwe, who drew the attention of the profession to the ambiguous impact of exchange rate variability on international trade, even if traders would in majority be risk-averse (De Grauwe, 1988). The ambiguity would follow from the positive sign of the income effect of increased uncertainty on the trade of risk-averse firms: firms would increase international trade in order to offset a decline in expected utility. This positive effect may or may not dominate the negative substitution effect, depending on the degree of risk aversion of firms. The conclusion would seem to be that trade is only adversely influenced if traders are neither very nor only slightly risk averse or risk neutral. Add to this, on the one hand, hysteresis effects (see for instance Baldwin, 1988) and, on the other hand, the generalised practice of hedging short-run exchange rate variations, and the empirical scope for finding conclusive evidence for the negative effects of short-run exchange volatility becomes, not surprisingly, hard to find. Pugh and his co-authors' review of the theoretical and empirical literature on the subject lead them indeed to conclude that it is foremost long-run evidence that supports the case for a single currency. Perhaps one should add to the evident longer-run negative 'political economy' effects of exchange rate volatility – like the likelihood of adverse ratchet effects on the levels of trade protection − the long-run positive indirect economic effects of a monetary union on the entrepreneurial climate that explicitly pass through the political sphere. One thinks of the often cited beneficiary effect of the creation of an environment for investors where societal expectations stabilise and converge, and the boost that the monetary union may give – if all goes well, that is – to the European identity.

Whatever the result of this debate, 'alea jacta est', and the European Monetary Union has started on the 1st of January 1999. Other questions automatically arise, one of the most important and urgent being whether the need for further economic integration in different areas does not automatically arise. Cláudia Costa and Paul De Grauwe address this issue in a sweeping review of the different areas in chapter 3 of this volume. Their main thesis is that EMU will of course eliminate the exchange risk but will also create new risks which result from increased competition and the large economic disturbances that are bound to occur, and the ensuing restructurings that must follow. They successively deal with the effects of EMU on labour mobility, tax harmonisation, the concentration and localisation of industries, the organisation of the transport sector and the harmonisation of the various legal systems of protection against hostile take-overs.

They conclude that in all these areas, and in most of them sooner than later, integration will have to proceed, driven forward by the momentum created by the single currency. In their view the most fundamental issue will however be the political vacuum at the European level. This vacuum of course existed before the EMU, but, in the face of the declining possibility of the nation-states to soften the blows inflicted by the rapid transformations that are ahead, will only become more acute. Hence the necessity in the longer run of a real European government.

Frank Barry tackles another, closely related, important topic. If the EMU will boost economic growth and promote stability, will it also affect the cohesion process, i.e. bridge the gap in living standards separating the richer and poorer regions and member countries of the Union? Barry's analysis suggests that at least the economic union aspect of EMU has favoured cohesion, but that there is more ambiguity with respect to the monetary policy aspects. He sees two main mechanisms. Firstly, as a general rule, if the average rate of growth of the Union would increase, then cohesion is fostered since real convergence proceeds more rapidly during good than during bad times. Secondly, there is the issue of asymmetric (i.e. region-specific) shocks. If policy co-ordination, more precisely fiscal policy co-ordination, is further developed as a result of EMU, then the likelihood of these (demand) shocks diminishes. The matter is different with respect to supply shocks. Following the lead of Bayoumi and Eichengreen (1993, 1994) and of Krugman (1993), and in accordance with Costa and De Grauwe's analysis of the effects on industrial location of market integration, the author argues that the likelihood of adverse asymmetric supply-shocks may well increase with EMU, unless FDI inflows in the periphery countries turn out to be sufficiently important. In his view Ireland may in this respect perhaps be the only of the four periphery countries (Spain, Portugal, Greece and Ireland) which has moved out of the danger zone.

The fear that asymmetric supply-shocks, more precisely technological shocks, in an environment in the process of further economic integration may increase inequalities rather than decrease them, is substantiated by the contribution of José Villaverde and Blanca Sanchez-Robles. They studied the effects of the EU, and ultimately of the EMU, on regional convergence in Spain (chapter 5). Their interpretation of simulation results from a calibrated new growth theory version of the neo-classical model is, firstly, that there is a great deal of persistence in regional inequality and that Spanish regions presently are already close to their long-run equilibrium positions. An autonomous drive to more equality is therefore not to be expected. This at the same time means, this is their second point, that laggard regions not only are more exposed to adverse technological shocks produced by further European integration, but will also be slower to react. The authors expect most of a (national and European) policy aiming at making the flow of technological spillovers more easy. This point is taken up further in the contribution by Dumont and Meeusen in this volume.

The EMU starts in the beginning of 1999. But will it be successful and sustainable? Much will depend on popular support. It is perhaps good that professional economists are at times reminded of the fact that man is a cultural animal whose behaviour is not only determined by economic factors, but also by the national environment in which he lives. Roland Pepermans in the sixth chapter uses results obtained by a group of European sociologists and social psychologists who are doing empirical research on the national differences in attitude towards the euro (Müller-Peters *et al.*, 1998). The author uses national scores on Hofstede's cultural dimensions to identify clusters of countries. The exercise clearly shows that there is more between heaven and earth in euroland than what the main economic indicators tell.

The EMU part of this volume concludes with two contributions which are more theoretically oriented. In chapter 7 Sonja Hellemann and Luc Hens, by using the German mark as a proxy, try to anticipate on the elaboration in the future of a genuine exchange rate model for the euro-US dollar relation. Their analysis endeavours to show that the extended monetary model of Sarantis and Pu (1997), incorporating real variables like government spending and productivity, is superior to the traditional monetary model of exchange rate determination. They identify the remaining weaknesses of their approach as hints for future research : the handling of structural breaks in the data-series resulting from the introduction of the euro, and a better treatment in the model of speculative behaviour.

In chapter 8 Herbert Glejser takes a historical view. With spline regressions of export- and import-share equations in the post-war era he estimates the trade shocks that were produced by successive waves of European economic integration (the creation of the Benelux, the creation of the EEC-6 and after that the enlargement to the EEC-9). He confronts the observed trade shift with different trade models : (dynamic) comparative advantage, (dynamic) bilateralism and intra-industry trade. His conclusion is that it is most frequently induced comparative advantage effects that have dominated. On the basis of the results obtained he however expects, with respect to the present situation of new candidate members for the EU, that these effects of increased trade will appear in the first place between the latter countries, and less with the present members.

Part II of the book deals with more specific policy issues. In chapter 9 Dumont and Meeusen evaluate the results of the S&T policy of the EU, as implemented through its Framework Programmes. They concentrate on the European telecommunications industry and examine the rate with which, in the so-called 'pre-competitive' projects of the Framework Programmes, R&D partnerships between firms and laboratories in that industry and institutes of higher education evolved, first, into more 'near-market' forms of collaboration, such as organised within the EUREKA context, and later into strategic technological alliances between private firms. Although the EU policy undeniably contributed to transform the technological landscape in Europe, and, more in particular, helped to set up the network structure between firms that should enable the comparatively small average European firm to technologically compensate for its lack of sufficient scale, the authors find relatively little support for the so-called 'linear causal model'. Subsidies granted to pre-competitive projects in the telecommunication sector do not systematically seem to induce the same partner-firms to engage in more strategic forms of technological collaboration.

Chapters 10 and 11 deal with EU policy issues on the labour market. Daniel Van Den Bulcke reviews the process leading to the creation of European Works Councils. The story that is told is quite illuminating and probably representative for the way in which important new European policy initiatives are prepared and implemented in a context where strongly opposing interests are at stake. The story is an important one for another reason. The EWCs go to the heart of the matter of probably the highest hurdle to take if one wants European integration to continue to follow its historic course – the 'democratic deficit'. Van Den Bulcke goes so far as to suggest that the possible success of the EWCs may put pressure on multinational corporations to engage in similar exercises in democracy in non-EU countries where they operate.

Chapter 11 offers another example of the observed move towards more democracy in the European workplace. Hardy and Adnett discuss the European Commission's 1998 revision of the Acquired Rights Directive which, in comparison to the old ARD, by strengthening consultation rights and by requiring member states to introduce sanctions for non-compliance will achieve, in the view of the authors, not only more democracy, but also more efficiency. More particularly an inefficient tendering process in which efficient contractors suffer underbidding by those willing, under the previous ARD, to risk the (uncertain) consequences of non-compliance, can be more easily avoided. The authors illustrate the seriousness of this distortion with the results of a survey that they conducted with employers and employees in firms recently involved in business transfers occurring as a consequence of competitive tendering.

Kristel Buysse, Chris Coeck and Alain Verbeke discuss in chapter 12 European environmental policy issues. Their contribution is a plea for more co-ordination at the national and European level, possibly in combination with side payments. They substantiate their case with an illustration of the adverse effects of the unco-ordinated policies implemented by the Belgian regions to combat water pollution. They also suggest that a co-ordinated European and national policy may be beneficial for the development of 'green thinking', thereby entering a 'virtuous' circle.

In the last chapter of this book, chapter 13, Anne-Marie Van den Bossche and Sandra Coppieters ask the question how the European Union, with its accent on the strengthening of free market principles, deals with the problem of services of general interest and so-called universal service obligations, such as they arose in the historical development of the modern welfare state. Their approach is a legal one. They convincingly show that, as a result of a process of gradual legal and jurisprudential changes, culminating in the 1997 Amsterdam-revision of the EEC Treaty, and under the influence also of the emergence of the legal concept of the rights of consumers, a legal environment evolved in which the opening-up of more and more markets previously reserved for state monopolies does not prevent the latter companies, although exposed now to competitive pressure, to continue to provide universal services under acceptable conditions.

Their concluding statement that 'this element of European civilisation [i.e. the provision of services of general interest] is clearly not in danger' may, from a more generalised point of view, also be used as a conclusion with respect to the acceleration in the European economic integration process in this last decade of the 20th century. Impressive as the challenges lying ahead may be, the determination of the political class to succeed seems to be intact, and with the modest help of analytical efforts like the ones presented in this volume, there is room for moderate but healthy optimism.

REFERENCES

Baldwin, R. (1988), 'Hysteresis in Import Prices: the Beachhead Effect', *American Economic Review*, **78**, 773-785.
Bayoumi, T. and B. Eichengreen (1993), 'Shocking Aspects of European Monetary Integration', in F. Torres and F. Giavazzi (eds), *Adjustment and Growth in the European Monetary Union*, Cambridge: Cambridge University Press.
Bayoumi, T. and B. Eichengreen (1994), *One Money or Many? Analysing the Prospects for Monetary Unification in Various Parts of the World*, Princeton Studies in International Finance No. 76.
De Grauwe, P. (1988), 'Exchange Rate Variability and the Slowdown in Growth of International Trade', *IMF Staff Papers*, **35**, 63-83.
Krugman, P. (1993), 'Lessons of Massachusetts for EMU', in F. Torres and F. Giavazzi (eds), *Adjustment and Growth in the European Monetary Union*, Cambridge: Cambridge University Press.
Müller-Peters, A. *et al.* (1998), 'Explaining Attitudes towards the Euro. Design of a Cross-national Study', *Journal of Economic Psychology*, **19**, 663-680.
Sarantis, N. and Y. Pu (1997), 'Determination of ECU Exchange Rates, and Lessons for the Euro', London Guildhall Centre for International Capital Markets Discussion Paper, No. 97-05.

PART I

General Policy Issues of the Single Market, the
EMU and Beyond

F31

F32 F33

(EU)

2. Exchange Rate Variability, International Trade and the Single Currency Debate: a Survey

**Geoff Pugh, David Tyrrall and
Lukasz Tarnawa**

1. INTRODUCTION

Since the breakdown of the Bretton Woods system and the onset of generalised floating, international trade has been conducted in an environment of high exchange rate variability (Engel and Hakkio, 1993 and Hasan and Wallace, 1996). Yet there is still no consensus on the trade effects of exchange rate variability or on the appropriate policy response. Even in Europe several EU members, including the UK where a referendum is promised, have still to commit themselves to European Monetary Union (EMU). This chapter surveys the economic literature on this topic and assesses its relevance to EMU.

The European Commission (1994), Emerson and Huhne (1991), and Miles (1998) all support the case for the single currency with the argument that international trade benefits from the restriction of exchange rate movements, and that this benefit would apply *a fortiori* if such movements were eliminated altogether. Indeed, this has become the conventional wisdom. Campbell (1998), Director General of the Institute of Exports, maintains that '(T)here is one thing that exporters hate more than a strong currency: it is one that is bouncing all over the place'. Yet the academic literature is not so one-sided.

Section 2 discusses a variety of theoretical approaches, none of which concludes that exchange rate variability has unambiguously adverse trade effects. Section 3 surveys over thirty empirical papers using different data sets and modelling strategies, mainly published since the mid-1980s. Their results are far from unanimous, although the preponderance of evidence suggests that exchange rate variability over long periods is bad for trade. Surprisingly, even recent papers do not attempt to quantify the trade effects of a single European currency. Section 4 concludes and suggests directions for future research.

2. THEORETICAL APPROACHES

Short-run exchange rate fluctuations over periods up to a year are often distinguished from long-run fluctuations over periods beyond one year (Williamson, 1983; Bockelmann and Borio, 1990). These were noted as problems at different times and by different authors and, possibly, have different effects on trade. Section 2.1 discusses how exchange rate uncertainty arises from both short- and long-run variability. Section 2.2 goes on to demonstrate that the trade effect of uncertainty is ambiguous. Section 2.3 then discusses 'political economy' effects as an alternative theory of how long-run variability may exert an adverse effect on trade.

2.1. Exchange rate variability and uncertainty

Increased short-run variability under the floating regime was soon noticed. In 1976 McKinnon noted that 'current movements in spot exchange rates of 20 percent quarter-to-quarter, 5 percent week-to-week, or even 1 percent on an hour-to-hour basis are now not unusual, although they are very large by historical standards' (quoted in Hallwood and Macdonald, 1988, p. 85). By the mid-1980s it was recognised that long-run variability could have serious effects with 'persistent departure(s) of the exchange rate from its long-run equilibrium level' (i.e. from the rate compatible with simultaneous internal and external balance) (Williamson, 1983, p. 10).

Both short- and long-run variability are commonly supposed to increase the risks in international trade. If firms were able to predict the timing, direction and magnitude of rate changes, they would be unconcerned about them. However, the determinants and future course of exchange rates are not well understood. Since Meese and Rogoff (1983), the accepted view is that exchange rates essentially follow a random walk, implying that changes in exchange rates in the next period are unpredictable, and their 'fundamental' determinants continue to elude empirical research. Recent studies confirm that in the short run 'macroeconomic factors and their variation have difficulty in explaining the fluctuations and volatility of exchange rates' (Williams *et al.*, 1998). Similarly, the timing, duration, size and direction of long-run variations cannot be systematically explained and predicted (Frankel and

Rose, 1994; De Grauwe, 1996). Long-run purchasing power parity relations provide little help, because they gain significant explanatory power only over periods of five, ten, or more years (Taylor, 1995). Since neither short- nor long-run exchange rate variability can be predicted, export revenues and foreign investment suffer from more uncertainty than domestic revenues and investment (Perée and Steinherr, 1989; Ardeni and Lubian, 1991; Fisher and Park, 1991). Assuming risk aversion, then unpredictable *ex post* deviations of returns from their expected level will tend to cause a reallocation of resources from the export to the domestic sector, thus reducing the level and growth of international trade.

Most studies focus on the effects of short-run exchange rate movements on international trade. Here, the problem is the lag between the initiation of the purchase agreement and the actual payment/receipt of cash: 'While the price of a product is generally quoted when an order is first placed, the contract currency determines whether the buyer or seller is exposed to possible exchange rate losses within the contract period' (Akhtar and Hilton, 1984, p. 11). Unanticipated fluctuations in the exchange rate affect realised profits and, hence, the volume of trade. As compensation for bearing this risk, suppliers impose a premium that raises prices. Invoicing in the domestic currency transfers the risk but does not eliminate the effects of exchange rate variability from the trading system (Qian and Varangis, 1994; Stokman, 1995). Consequently, trade volume is likely to be reduced by exchange rate uncertainty (Akhtar and Hilton, 1984). However, short-run exchange rate variability can be, and frequently is, hedged (Stokman, 1995). Possibly for this reason, empirical studies have not always found it to constitute an obstacle to international trade.

The effects of long-run nominal exchange rate movements have been less frequently examined. Engel and Hamilton (1990, pp. 689-710) characterise these 'long swings (as a) sequence of stochastic, segmented time trends', which are 'likely to persist for several years', and cannot be related to economic fundamentals and are impervious to modelling. Krugman (1989) indicates that these nominal movements drive movements in real exchange rates, hence causing medium and long-term misalignments (also Taylor, 1995). De Grauwe (1996), Creedy *et al.* (1994), and Pentecost (1993) demonstrate that nominal exchange rate movements lack periodicity, and hence may be represented as chaotic. From either standpoint, long-run exchange rate movements cannot be anticipated and so create uncertainty for international trade. Long-run exchange rate movements are less subject to hedging (Bodnar, 1998). Consequently, realised profits from trade-related investment are subject to unpredictable fluctuations. For risk-averse managers, this reduces the incentive to invest in trade. Thus, uncertainty over long-run exchange rates also exerts an adverse effect on trade (Perée and Steinherr, 1989; De Grauwe and de Bellefroid, 1987; De Grauwe, 1988).

2.2. Trade effects of exchange rate uncertainty

Different theoretical approaches lead to different conclusions. Most theoretical studies have analysed the response of trading firms to exchange rate uncertainty by focusing on their degree of risk aversion.

On the one hand, expected profit increases with uncertainty (Varian, 1984). Assume a firm exports all of its output to a perfectly competitive market, at a given and constant world market price in foreign currency. The firm's output price in domestic currency is given by the exchange rate. When the domestic currency depreciates, the firm amplifies the rise in net income by increasing output. Conversely, when the domestic currency appreciates, it limits the decline in net income by reducing output. Accordingly, depreciation increases profit by more than a proportionately equivalent and equiprobable appreciation decreases profit. Hence, 'expected profits are an increasing function of exchange rate variability . . . where variability is interpreted as a mean preserving spread' (Gros, 1987, p. 5). On the other hand, uncertainty reduces the utility of expected profit.

Risk-averse traders, like any other, will be attracted by higher expected profits associated with exchange rate variability, but may attribute to these higher profits a lower utility because of their unpredictability. Accordingly, risk-averse traders may curtail investment in export capacity. In this case, if a sufficiently large proportion of traders is sufficiently risk averse, then trade may be a negative function of exchange rate variability. Conversely, risk-neutral traders care only about the expected rate of return, and are thus indifferent to the risks required to earn the return. Accordingly, if exchange variability increases expected profit and sufficient numbers of traders are risk neutral, or near risk neutral, then trade may be a positive function of exchange rate variability. Clearly, this applies *a fortiori* to risk-seeking traders.

De Grauwe (1988) elaborates the basic insight that exchange rate variability may have either a positive or a negative impact on trade according to the degree of firms' risk aversion. He argues that it is not only risk-neutral or near risk-neutral firms that may increase trade in response to exchange rate variability. There are two effects on risk-averse firms: a substitution effect, whereby greater uncertainty deters them from international trade, and an income effect, whereby they increase international trade to offset a decline in total expected utility. In the case of extreme risk aversion, the income effect dominates the substitution effect and increased exchange rate risk leads to increased rather than reduced international trade (De Grauwe, 1988). Dellas and Zilberfarb (1993) extend De Grauwe's theoretical model by introducing a forward market with transaction costs. Their conclusion is similar: the overall effect of increased uncertainty about future exchange rates depends on the magnitude of firms' risk aversion. Combining these approaches, it seems that if most firms are located at either end of the distribution of risk aversion – i.e., are either slightly or extremely risk averse – then exchange rate uncertainty is trade enhancing. Otherwise, risk aversion tends to depress trade.

Different approaches demonstrate that ambiguity over the trade implications of exchange rate variability does not depend upon the assumption of risk aversion. Dixit (1989a and 1989b), Baldwin (1988), Baldwin and Krugman (1989) and Krugman (1989) show how exchange rate fluctuations in the presence of sunk costs can lead risk-neutral competitive firms to make decisions about entry and exit into foreign markets that are not reversed when the exchange rate returns to its previous level. Ansic and Pugh (1998) find some empirical evidence for this *hysteresis* effect, whereby temporary exchange rate movements have persistent effects on trade decisions. However, while this literature also demonstrates that exchange rate uncertainty can affect trade behaviour, it still gives no clear predictions as to the net effect on trade volume or trade growth.

Viaene and de Vries (1992) develop a mean-variance model in which the net trade position of firms determines potentially positive or negative effects of exchange rate volatility.

Thus, a variety of theoretical approaches conclude that the effect of exchange uncertainty on the volume and growth of international trade is ambiguous.

2.3. The political economy of exchange rate variability

After analysing the ambiguity of uncertainty effects on trade, De Grauwe concludes 'if exchange rate variability has a negative effect on international trade, it must be through another mechanism … the political economy effect of exchange rate variability (1988, pp. 69-70).

Over-valuations tend to generate protectionist pressures, because loss of output and employment in the traded sector can be clearly related to international competitiveness. Moreover, protectionist pressures are asymmetric with respect to exchange rate variations, since it is unlikely that, when the currency returns from over-valuation to under-valuation, there will be offsetting pressure in favour of trade liberalisation. Consequently, exchange rate movements that entail a sequence of over-valuations and under-valuations, are likely to 'ratchet up the level of protection' and lead to reductions in the level and growth of international trade (Williamson, 1983, p. 45; see also De Grauwe, 1988, p.70).

The political economy of exchange rate movements had its point of departure in the spectacular rise of the US dollar in the 1980s (Destler, 1992). The dollar appreciation in the first half of the 1980s did generate 'record pressure on legislators': yet the 1980s as a whole saw no dramatic increase in the general level of US protection (Destler, 1992, pp. 109 and 207).

The economic literature conflates protectionist pressure and protectionist trade policy. Certainly, exchange rate movements are readily associated with protectionist pressure. Currency appreciation, both in the UK (late 1970s/early 1980s) and in the US (early/mid 1980s), fuelled demands for trade restrictions. However, protectionist pressure is mediated by political ideologies, institutions and processes that determine whether or not lobbying efforts are realised as actual trade policy. At the very least, the political process introduces lags between interest-group pressure and policy outcome.

Furthermore, in the US protectionist pressures were not asymmetric as hypothesised (Destler, 1992). Both business pressure groups and political institutions were divided on the protectionist issue. The Executive branch maintained its traditional opposition to protectionist measures. The Legislature was more responsive to the protection lobby, because of the intersection of concentrated producer interests with the role of personal coalition-building, rather than party endorsement, in the election of members of Congress. Countervailing pressures and delays in the system (e.g., due to presidential veto) allowed currency devaluation after 1985 to weaken the protectionist case. The Omnibus Trade and Competitiveness Act was not passed until 1988, and was only mildly protectionist.

In contrast, in the UK the Thatcher government inclined to trade liberalism. Executive domination of the legislature, party discipline, and membership of the EU ensured that trade policy pressure was resisted altogether. Thus, both in the US and the UK, similar economic processes and protectionist pressures intersected with different political systems that determined different, but generally non-protectionist, trade policy outcomes. Accordingly, exchange rate movements may give rise to protectionist *intent* with respect to trade policy, but not necessarily protectionist *results*.

2.4. Theoretical approaches: conclusion

Political economy effects of long-run exchange rate variability on trade are, if they operate, unambiguously negative. However, it is unclear whether they do actually operate. In contrast, uncertainty is a clear consequence of exchange rate variability in either the long or the short run, but its effect on trade is ambiguous. At a purely theoretical level, neither channel provides a determinate relationship between exchange rate variability and trade. Empirical investigation may resolve this issue.

3. EMPIRICAL APPROACHES

Section 3.1 reviews the extensive empirical investigations on the effect of short-run exchange-rate volatility on international trade flows. Different studies focus on aggregate or bilateral trade flows, on real or nominal exchange rates, use alternative measures of exchange rate volatility, in different time periods and different country groupings. Section 3.2 reviews the effect of long-run variability, which to date has been less extensively investigated. It includes our own recent work in this direction.

3.1. Trade effects of short-run variability[1]

In short-run studies, aggregate trade flow equations have been augmented with a measure of multilateral exchange variability. Among studies following this procedure, Akhtar and Hilton (1984), Kenen and Rodrik (1986), and Chowdhury (1993) observe significant negative quantity effects. However, Gotur (1985) finds flaws in Akhtar and Hilton's methodology. With small changes, their model generates only one negative significant effect and many positive effects. Cushman (1988, p. 318) points out that 'in a longer, unpublished version of their work, Kenen and Rodrik (1984) reported as many significant *positive* effects on aggregate exports . . . as significant negative effects'. In addition, papers by Bailey, Tavlas and Ulan (1986 and 1987) and Assery and Peel (1991) find no evidence of a negative effect of exchange rate volatility on trade.

A more disaggregated approach estimates bilateral trade flow equations augmented with bilateral exchange rate risk measures. Using this method, Hooper and Kohlhagen (1978) find no significant negative impact on trade volume. However, Cushman (1983 and 1988), using a real rather than a nominal measure of exchange risk, did observe significant negative effects. Abrams (1980) and Thursby and Thursby (1987), also report significant negative coefficients for exchange rate volatility. On the other hand, the IMF (1984) extended Cushman's sample period and added countries, and was able to reject the hypothesis that exchange-rate volatility has a systematically adverse effect on trade.

These 1980s studies are inconclusive. According to Kroner and Lastrapes (1993) and Arize (1997a), the mixed nature of this evidence arises from the use of inadequate measures of exchange-rate risk. Most of the earlier studies used unconditional measures of exchange rate uncertainty, typically a moving standard deviation of levels or changes in past exchange rates. Kroner and Lastrapes (1993, p. 299) criticise this approach for 'ignoring important information on the stochastic process generating exchange rates'. Recent studies use (generalised) autoregressive conditional heteroskedasticity —

(G)ARCH – models instead of simple unconditional measures to measure exchange-rate volatility.

By assumption, rational agents use all available information in making their decisions, including the expected mean and variance of exchange rate changes. Variances tend to cluster in short-run time series. Periods of turbulence (large changes in exchange rates) are typically followed by periods of tranquillity (small changes). This affects expectations. The 'GARCH model is […] particularly appropriate' as a proxy of exchange rate uncertainty (Caporale and Doroodian, 1994, p. 51), because the current variance of the error term is conditional on the variances of error terms in previous periods. In other respects, the GARCH studies differ in the same ways as those of the 1980s; for example, Pozo (1992) and Caporale and Doroodian (1994) use bilateral data, while Kroner and Lastrapes (1993), Holly (1995), and Arize (1995, 1996, and 1997a) use aggregate data. Unfortunately, these new techniques have so far yielded similarly inconclusive results. (G)ARCH studies from Pozo (1992), Caporale and Doroodian (1994) and Arize (1995, 1996 and 1997a) report coefficients on exchange rate volatility that are overwhelmingly negative and significant. Yet Holly's (1995) results suggest at most a weakly negative trade effect, Kroner and Lastrapes (1993) and Qian and Varangis (1994) results are inconclusive, while McKenzie and Brooks (1997) report an unambiguously positive effect of exchange rate volatility on trade.

Studies focusing on the sectoral effects of exchange rate volatility also point in different directions. Klein (1990) finds the impact of real exchange rate volatility on the value of US bilateral exports over the period 1978-1986 in specific commodity groups to have been mainly positive. Stokman (1995), however, finds the impact of nominal volatility on the export volumes of five EU economies to the EU area over the period 1980-1990 to have been overwhelmingly negative. Studies of the impact of exchange rate volatility on the trade of developing economies are similarly inconclusive.[2]

3.2. Trade effects of long-run variability

Most studies use standard deviation (SD) from the mean of either the level or percentage changes of whichever exchange rate series is subject to investigation (i.e., real or nominal, bilateral or effective). SD both measures variability and proxies exchange rate uncertainty (see Rana, 1981, IMF 1984, Perée and Steinherr, 1989, and Medhora, 1990). Brodsky (1984), Kenen and Rodrik (1986) and Boothe and Glassman (1987) elaborate the theoretical rationale for this practice, which has particular force when applied to longer-term movements. Unfortunately, there is no such consensus on the choice between nominal and real, or effective and bilateral exchange rates (Savvides, 1992 and McKenzie and Brooks, 1997). Although (G)ARCH models have become common in studies of short-run volatility, they are less appropriate to studies that use low frequency data. (G)ARCH allows for shocks to variance to be persistent, but their effect rapidly fades. Taking Holly's (1995) (G)ARCH estimates as representative, the effect of past shocks falls by a factor of 120 from the first to the sixth quarterly period back. Thus, the influence of shocks is negligible after only one year.

Like the short-run studies, the long-run studies use the framework of established trade models. There are two traditions in the modelling of international trade: the conventional utility maximising approach; and the 'gravity' approach. Table 2.1 below classifies the range of long-run studies according to the tradition and data type used.

De Grauwe and de Bellefroid (1987) study the impact of real exchange variability on average annual percentage trade growth during a 10-year fixed regime (1960-69) and a 12-year floating regime (1973-84) in 90 bilateral trade flows among 10 industrialised economies. They conclude, 'the variability of the exchange rates (especially . . . real exchange rates) had a significant negative effect on the growth rates of bilateral trade among the major industrialised countries' (p. 202). De Grauwe (1988) extends this study by introducing a relative price variable. This reduces both the size and the statistical significance of the trade effects of exchange rate movements, probably due to correlation between the relative price variable and the uncertainty proxy. He concludes that the hypothesised negative effect of exchange rate variability on trade cannot be rejected.

Table 2.1.   Empirical studies on the trade effects of long-run exchange rate variability

Type of Data	Utility Maximisation Model	Gravity Model
Time Series	Perée and Steinherr (1989) Arize (1996) Arize (1997b)	—
Cross Section	De Grauwe and de Bellefroid (1987) De Grauwe (1988) Savvides (1992)	Pugh *et al.* (1998b)
Pooled (Panel)	Pugh *et al.* (1998b)	—

Savvides (1992) analyses cross-section data from 62 industrial and developing countries during 1973-86, and finds that *unanticipated* real effective exchange rate variability inhibits the growth of aggregate real exports. Yet De Grauwe and de Bellefroid (1987, p.197) rejected attempts to distinguish between *ex post* (observed) and *ex ante* (forecast) exchange rate variability, because empirical studies suggest that 'most of the observed changes in the exchange rate were unanticipated . . . so that ex ante and ex post measures are highly correlated'. Savvides' results do not necessarily contradict this position. His results for the industrialised countries, which are those relevant to the present discussion, may reflect small sample size and consequent multi-collinearity. The results for the industrialised countries for the whole sample period (18 observations) show a statistically significant adverse trade effect of unanticipated exchange rate variability, but an insignificantly negative impact of anticipated variability. However, results from two sub-periods (1973-79 and 1980-86; hence, 36 observations) show not only significant unanticipated effects but also an anticipated effect with borderline significance at the 10 percent level. Moreover, in the all countries' sample (123 observations), the anticipated effect has not only similar size and sign to the unanticipated effect, but also borderline significance at the 5 percent level. Thus, larger samples seem to reveal adverse trade effects from both antici-pated and unanticipated variability. This is consistent with our earlier empha-sis on the inability to model and predict exchange rate movements.

Perée and Steinherr (1989) use annual data for the period 1960-85. Half their results (i.e., 9 from 20 time-series equations using aggregate trade data, and 9 from 16 bilateral equations using exports to the US) give statistically significant support to their conclusion that 'exchange rate uncertainty exer-cises negative effects on the volume of trade among industrial countries' (p. 1261). However, problems of misspecification, particularly with respect to residual autocorrelation, reduce the reliability of these results.

Arize's (1996) study of eight EU countries (four ERM and four non-ERM) over periods of five and eight quarters from 1973-94 is borderline between short and long periods. Arize proxies exchange rate uncertainty by the moving-sample standard deviation of the log real effective exchange rate. He overcomes the problem in previous time-series studies of inappropriate estimation of relationships between stationary variables by using multivariate cointegration and error-correction modelling. Nevertheless, for each country he finds 'a long-run relationship among real exports, foreign economic activ-ity, relative price and exchange rate volatility' (p. 193) and that the exchange rate volatility elasticities are negative and statistically significant. Moreover, his error-correction results confirm in each case that 'exchange rate volatility exerts a significant long-run effect on export volume' (p. 194). Arize (1997b) applies the same modelling strategy to the G-7 countries and achieves the same, similarly robust results.

The results of these studies are not overwhelming. The results of one time-series study are ambiguous, while De Grauwe and de Bellefroid recognise that cross-section results may suffer from multicollinearity. Moreover,

Arize's results arise from a limited sample of European countries, which excludes three of the four major EU economies, and are thus no more than suggestive with respect to monetary co-operation in Europe. Pugh *et al.* (1998b) attempt to generate results that are free of these sample limitations and specification problems (particularly multicollinearity) by using two different models; a panel model and a gravity model.

The panel model estimates the impact of exchange rate variability over three-, four-, five- and six-year periods on trade *growth* from 1980-92 among the industrialised OECD economies. A conventional import model, augmented to include real effective exchange rate variability, is analysed by applying an error-components model to panel data. The use of pooled data and panel techniques gives both time-series and cross-section variation in the data. The coefficients on real effective exchange rate variability are uniformly negative and statistically significant, with the consistent finding that exchange rate variability − measured over periods of 3, 4, 5 and 6 years − reduces the rate of trade growth by around one percentage point in ten.

The gravity model focuses on the *level* of intra-EU bilateral trade from 1984-90. The model is augmented by a measure of nominal exchange rate variability and analysed by applying OLS to cross-section data. In the tradition of gravity models, it is specified without a relative price variable and thus excludes a potential source of multicollinearity. The results consistently suggest that exchange rate variability has a negative effect on the level of intra-European trade. The negative trade effect is estimated to be about 7 times higher in the non-ERM group than in the ERM group (in line with Arize, 1996), even though most of the non-ERM group pegged their currencies to the German Mark. This suggests that commitment to institutionalised regime shift establishes greater credibility than managing a currency 'as if' it were subject to fixed parities, and that ERM members benefit from *both* reduced exchange rate variability *and* reduced sensitivity to variability. For the non-ERM group, reducing exchange rate variability to the average ERM level would yield a medium to long-term increase in the level of trade of about 30 percent. Similarly, transition from the ERM to a single currency could increase the level of trade by a further 10 percent.

4. CONCLUSION

4.1. Summary

The theoretical literature offers no conclusive guidance to the trade effects of exchange rate variability. The short-run empirical studies are also inconclusive. However, studies of longer-run variability more uniformly find adverse effects, perhaps because it is less easily hedged. Thus it is mainly the long-run evidence that supports the case for a single currency. Pugh *et al.* (1998b) find that trade benefits not only from reduced variability but also from institutionalised regime shift (i.e., from floating to fixed exchange rates and on to a single currency). If credibility is decisive in influencing firms' expectations, then trade benefits arising from the elimination of exchange rate variability by a single currency will be more secure than those arising from the suppression of exchange rate variability in a fixed rate regime prone to currency crises.

4.2. Directions for future research

Our thoughts here largely centre on the use of disaggregated data for a series of both theoretical and empirical reasons.

1) *Political economy effects.* Pugh *et al.* (1998b) exclude political economy effects in one of their models, by measuring trade flows within a free trade zone. Accordingly, it is not plausible to interpret adverse trade effects as driven by the protectionist consequences of exchange rate variability. This implies that political economy effects are not necessary for exchange rate variability to exert adverse effects on trade, and that uncertainty alone is a sufficient condition to depress foreign trade. Future study could isolate these effects differently in order to decide whether uncertainty is a necessary condition, or whether political economy effects alone would also suffice.

2) *Risk aversion:*
   a) *level and distribution.* Uncertainty is posited to depress foreign trade because of risk aversion. However, the effect on traders might vary, depending on their degree of risk aversion. Sitkin and Weingart (1995) imply that risk averse traders will weight the potential downside risk of exchange rate variability more heavily than the potential upside opportunity (cf. 2.2 above). The aggregate effect is dependent upon the level and distribution of risk aversion in the relevant populations, but we have found no direct estimates of these. Future research could combine literature on risk aversion and decision making with the work discussed in this paper.
   b) *mode of operation.* Risk aversion may be present in differing degrees, and have differing outcomes in the environments of small-, medium-, and large-sized firms. The dominant asset valuation models, CAPM and APT, hold that diversification should render investors, and hence managers, in listed companies, indifferent to diversifiable exchange rate risk. However, 'reward and punishment systems encourage open-

ness about loss and ... penalise concealment' and 'people hear bad news first and loudest' (Nicholson, 1998). Furthermore, security is a highly ranked job attribute among all levels of staff (Gallie and White, 1993). So perhaps it is not surprising that Caves' (1996) survey reports evidence of risk aversion in MNEs: for example, exchange rate variability promotes locating production abroad; managers display a stronger preference for avoiding losses than making gains; firms are particularly averse to firm specific risks (an effect which may be even stronger in smaller firms). An understanding of the distribution of risk aversion and its mode of operation on foreign trade could provide a motivational rationale for observed negative effects of exchange rate variability.

3) *Internal transfers:*
   a) *measurement.* A large proportion of international trade takes place as transfers within multinational enterprises (MNEs). Estimates of this proportion range from 30 percent upwards (for example, Plasschaert, 1979 and Rugman and Eden, 1985) and the proportion may be rising. These transfers are subject to ever more stringent and more widespread transfer pricing legislation as nations seek to protect their tax bases (Tyrrall, 1997). The 'arm's length prices' that are reported for these transactions owe at least as much to legislative control as market forces. This may raise time-varying measurement problems using aggregate data.
   b) *variability.* MNEs can at least partially shield intra-firm trade from exchange rate risk by offsetting transfers of real goods and services. The timing of related cash transfers can be separated from the real transfers by the central treasury function, which can manage around exchange rate variability to corporate advantage. Nevertheless, Rugman and Eden (1985) summarise a number of studies reporting that intra-firm trade is responsive to exchange rate movements and to differing levels of risk aversion. However, risk aversion could easily cause exchange rate variability to affect intra-MNE trade differently from trade with independent parties. More accurate estimates of the extent and variability of intra-firm trade would enhance understanding in the fields of both international trade and international taxation.

4) *Sample bias.* All the surveyed studies of the trade effects of exchange rate variability use aggregated trade data. Yet aggregated data includes only firms already engaged in international trade. It excludes risk-averse firms that eschew international trade because exchange rate variability exceeds their individual threshold level of acceptable risk. As indicated above, this may affect small- and medium-sized firms more than large firms (see also IMF, 1984). If so, aggregated data provides a biased sample yielding un-

derestimates of the trade effects of exchange rate variability. This might explain why the distaste for exchange rate volatility routinely reflected in business survey evidence (Emerson *et al.*, 1992; Stokman, 1995) is not overwhelmingly reflected in econometric results. Accordingly, future research is likely to be more fruitful if conducted at the level of the firm using techniques to correct for sample bias.

NOTES

1. All papers surveyed here are included in a table that summarizes their main features: sample period, countries, type of trade and exchange rate data used, the measure of exchange rate volatility, and their findings. The table is excluded for reasons of space but is available on request in Pugh *et al.* (1998a).
2. More details are available on request in Pugh *et al.* (1998a).

REFERENCES

Abrams, R. (1980), 'International Trade Flows under Flexible Exchange Rates', *Federal Reserve Bank of Kansas City Economic Review*, 65, 3-10.
Akhtar, M.A. and R.S. Hilton (1984), 'Effects of Exchange Rate Uncertainty on German and U.S. Trade', *Federal Reserve Bank of New York Quarterly Review*, 9, 7-16.
Ansic, D. and G. Pugh (1998), 'An Experimental Test of Trade Hysteresis: Market Exit and Entry Decisions in the Presence of Sunk Costs and Exchange Rate Uncertainty', *Applied Economics*, 30, forthcoming.
Ardeni, P. and D. Lubian (1991), 'Is There Trend Reversion in Purchasing Power Parity?', *European Economic Review*, 35, 1035-1055.
Arize, A.C. (1995), 'The Effects of Exchange Rate Volatility on US Exports', *Southern Economic Journal*, 62, 34-43.
Arize, A.C. (1996), 'Real Exchange-Rate Volatility and Trade Flows: The Experience of Eight European Economies', *International Review of Economics and Finance*, 5, 187-205.
Arize, A.C. (1997a), 'Conditional Exchange-Rate Volatility and the Volume of Foreign Trade', *Southern Economic Journal*, 64, 235-53.
Arize, A.C. (1997b), 'Foreign Trade and Exchange-Rate Risk in the G-7 Countries', *Review of Financial Economics*, 6, 95-112.
Assery, A. and D.A. Peel (1991), 'The Effects of Exchange Rate Volatility on Exports: Some New Estimates', *Economics Letters*, 37, 173-177.
Bailey, M.J., G.S. Tavlas and M. Ulan (1986), 'Exchange-rate Variability and Trade Performance: Evidence for the Big Seven Industrial Countries', *Weltwirtschaftliches Archiv*, 122, 466-477.
Bailey, M.J., G.S. Tavlas and M. Ulan (1987), 'The Impact of Exchange-rate Volatility on Export Growth: Some Theoretical Considerations and Empirical Results', *Journal of Policy Modelling*, 9, 225-43.

Baldwin, R. (1988), 'Hysteresis in Import Prices: the Beachhead Effect', *American Economic Review*, **78**, 773-785.

Baldwin, R. and P. Krugman (1989), 'Persistent Trade Effects of Large Exchange Rate Shocks', *Quarterly Journal of Economics*, **104**, 635-54.

Bockelmann, H. and C. Borio (1990), 'Financial Instability and the Real Economy', *De Economist*, **138**, 428-48.

Bodnar, G. (1998), 'Exchange Rate Exposure and Market Value', in *Mastering Finance*, London: FT Pitman.

Boothe, P. and D. Glassman (1987), 'The Statistical Distribution of Exchange Rates', *Journal of International Economics*, **22**, 297-319.

Brodsky, D.A. (1984), 'Fixed versus Flexible Exchange Rates and the Measurement of Exchange Rate Instability', *Journal of International Economics*, **16**, 295-306.

Campbell, I. (1998), *FT Exporter*, March, p. 7.

Caporale, T. and K. Doroodian (1994), 'Exchange Rate Variability and the Flow of International Trade', *Economics Letters*, **46**, 49-54.

Caves, R.E. (1996), *Multinational Enterprise and Economic Analysis*, 2nd ed., Cambridge: Cambridge University Press.

Chowdhury, A.R. (1993), 'Does Exchange Rate Volatility Depress Trade Flows?', *Review of Economics and Statistics*, **75**, 700-706.

Creedy, J., J. Lye and V.L. Martin (1994), 'Non-linearities and the Long-run Real Exchange Rate Distribution', Ch. 13 of *Chaos and Non-linear Models in Economics*, Cheltenham: Edward Elgar.

Cushman, D.O. (1983), 'The Effects of Real Exchange Rate Risk on International Trade', *European Economic Review*, **15**, 45-63.

Cushman, D.O. (1988), 'U.S. Bilateral Trade Flows and Exchange Rate Risk during the Floating Period', *Journal of International Economics*, **24**, 317-330.

De Grauwe, P. (1988), 'Exchange Rate Variability and the Slowdown in Growth of International Trade', *IMF Staff Papers*, **35**, 63-83.

De Grauwe, P. (1996), *International Money*, 2nd ed., Oxford: Oxford University Press.

De Grauwe, P. and B. de Bellefroid (1987), 'Long-run Exchange Rate Variability and International Trade', in S. Arndt and D. Richardson (eds), *Real Financial Linkages among Open Economies*, Cambridge, Mass.: MIT University Press.

Dellas, H. and B. Zilberfarb (1993), 'Real Exchange Rate Volatility and International Trade: A Reexamination of the Theory', *Southern Economic Journal*, **59**, 641-47.

Destler, I.M. (1992), *American Trade Politics*, 2nd ed., Washington: Institute for International Economics.

Dixit, A. (1989a), 'Hysteresis, Import Penetration, and Exchange Rate Pass-Through', *Quarterly Journal of Economics*, **104**, 205-227.

Dixit, A. (1989b), 'Entry and Exit Decisions under Uncertainty', *Journal of Political Economy*, **97**, 620-638.

Emerson, M. and C. Huhne (1991), *The ECU Report*, London: Pan Books.

Emerson, M., D. Gros, A. Italianer, J. Pisany-Ferry and H. Reichenbach (1992), *One Market, One Money*, Oxford: Oxford University Press.

Engel, C. and J.D. Hamilton (1990), 'Long Swings in the Dollar: Are They in the Data and do Markets Know It?', *American Economic Review*, **80**, 689-713.

Engel, C. and C. Hakkio (1993), 'Exchange Rate Regimes and Volatility', *Federal Reserve Bank of Kansas City Economic Review*, **1993**, 43-58.

European Commission (1994), *Factsheet 5*, http://www.cec.org.uk:80/pubs/facts/fact05.htm.

Fisher, E.O. and J.Y. Park (1991), 'Testing Purchasing Power Parity under the Null Hypothesis of Cointegration', *Economic Journal*, **101**, 1476-1484.

Frankel J. and A. Rose (1994), 'A Survey of Empirical Research on Nominal Exchange Rates', *NBER Working Paper*, No. 4865.

Gallie, D. and M. White (1993), *Employee Commitment and the Skills Revolution*, London: Policy Studies Institute.

Gotur, P. (1985), 'The Effects of Exchange Rate Volatility on Trade: Some Further Evidence', *IMF Staff Papers*, **32**, 475-512.

Gros, D. (1987), 'Exchange Rate Variability and Foreign Trade in the Presence of Adjustment Costs', *CEPS Working Papers* 8704, Université Catholique de Louvain.

Hallwood, P. and R. Macdonald (1988), *International Money*, Oxford: Basil Blackwell.

Hasan, S. and M. Wallace (1996), 'Real Exchange Rate Volatility and Exchange Rate Regimes', *Economics Letters*, **52**, 67-73.

Holly, S. (1995), 'Exchange Rate Uncertainty and Export Performance', *Scottish Journal of Political Economy*, **42**, 381-91.

Hooper, P. and S.W. Kohlhagen (1978), 'The Effect of Exchange Rate Uncertainty on the Prices and Volume of International Trade', *Journal of International Economics*, **8**, 483-511.

IMF (1984), 'Exchange Rate Volatility and World Trade', *IMF Occasional Paper* 28 Washington: International Monetary Fund.

Kenen P.B. and D. Rodrik (1986), 'Measuring and Analyzing the Effects of Short-term Volatility in Real Exchange Rates', *Review of Economics and Statistics*, **68**, 311-315.

Klein, M.W. (1990), 'Sectoral Effects of Exchange Rate Volatility on United States Exports', *Journal of International Money and Finance*, **9**, 299-308.

Kroner, K. and W. Lastrapes (1993), 'The Impact of Exchange Rate Volatility on International Trade', *Journal of International Money and Finance*, **12**, 298-318.

Krugman, P. (1989), *Exchange Rate Instability*, Cambridge, Mass.: MIT Press.

McKenzie, M. and R. Brooks (1997), 'The Impact of Exchange Rate Volatility on German-US Trade Flows', *Journal of International Financial Markets, Institutions and Money*, **7**, 73-87.

Medhora, R. (1990), 'The Effect of Exchange Rate Variability on Trade: the Case of the West African Monetary Union's Imports', *World Development*, **18**, 313-324.

Meese, R. and K. Rogoff (1983), 'Empirical Exchange Rate Models of the Seventies: Do They Fit Out of Sample?', *Journal of International Economics*, **14**, 3-24.

Miles, D. (1998), *Fundamental Economic Implications of EMU*, London: Merrill Lynch & Co., Global Securities Research & Economics Group and Imperial College.

Nicholson, N. (1998), 'How Hardwired is Human Behaviour?', *Harvard Business Review*, July-August, 134-47.

Pentecost, E. (1993), *Exchange Rate Dynamics*, Aldershot: Edward Elgar.

Perée, E. and A. Steinherr (1989), 'Exchange Rate Uncertainty and Foreign Trade', *European Economic Review*, **33**, 1241-1264.

Plasschaert, S. (1979), *Transfer Pricing and Multinational Corporations*, European Centre for Study and Information on Multinational Corporations.

Pozo, S. (1992), 'Conditional Exchange-rate Volatility and the Volume of International Trade: Evidence from the early 1990s', *Review of Economics and Statistics,* **74**, 325-329.

Pugh, G., D. Tyrrall and L. Tarnawa (1998a), 'Exchange Rate Variability, International Trade and the Single Currency Debate: a survey', *Staffordshire University Economics Division Working Paper*, 9810.

Pugh, G., D. Tyrrall, P. Rodecki and L. Tarnawa (1998b), 'Exchange Rate Variability, International Trade and Monetary Cooperation in Europe: Some Quantitative Evidence for the Single Currency Debate', *Staffordshire University Economics Division Working Paper*, 9809.

Qian, Y. and P. Varangis (1994), 'Does Exchange Rate Volatility Hinder Export Growth?', *Empirical Economics*, **19**, 371-96.

Rana, P.B. (1981), 'Exchange Rate Risk under Generalised Floating: Eight Asian Countries', *Journal of International Economics*, **11**, 459-466.

Rugman, A.M. and L. Eden (eds) (1985), *Multi-nationals and Transfer Pricing*, Australia: Croom Helm.

Savvides, A. (1992), 'Unanticipated Exchange Rate Variability and the Growth of International Trade', *Weltwirtschaftliches Archiv*, **128**, 446-63.

Sitkin, S.B. and L.R. Weingart (1995), 'Determinants of Risky Decision-making Behavior', *Academy of Management Journal*, **38**, 1573-1595.

Stokman, A.C.J. (1995), 'Effect of Exchange Rate Risk on Intra-EC Trade', *De Economist*, **143**, 41-54.

Taylor, M. (1995), 'Exchange Rate Modelling and Macro Fundamentals', *British Review of Economic Issues*, **17**, 1-42.

Thursby, M.C. and J.G. Thursby (1987), 'Bilateral Trade Flows, the Linder Hypothesis, and Exchange Risk', *Review of Economics and Statistics*, **69**, 488-495.

Tyrrall, D. (1997), 'The Tax Implications of International Transfer Pricing', *Journal of Applied Accounting Research*, **4**, 69-89.

Varian, H. (1984), *Microeconomic Analysis*, London: Norton.

Viaene, J.M. and C.G. de Vries (1992), 'International Trade and Exchange Rate Volatility', *European Economic Review*, **36**, 1311-1321.

Williams, G., A. Parikh and D. Bailey (1998), 'Are Exchange Rates Determined by Macroeconomic Factors?', *Applied Economics*, **30**, 553-567.

Williamson, J. (1983), *The Exchange Rate System*, Washington, DC.: Institute for International Economics.

For (EU) F33, F36

3. EMU and the Need for Further Economic Integration

Cláudia Costa and Paul De Grauwe[1]

1. INTRODUCTION

The European monetary union is now on track. Initially the reaction of economists towards the EMU-project was quite sceptical. The consensus was that the centralisation of monetary policies at the European level without integration in other fields of economic policy-making would create great risks. The major perceived risk was that the European Central Bank (ECB) would be called upon to solve problems that the nation states would not be able to solve anymore given that they had lost their monetary sovereignty. And the ECB would often not be able to deliver.

The attention of economists has been focused very much into devising rules for the conduct of fiscal policies. The latter will carry the full weight of dealing with idiosyncratic shocks hitting individual nations. This analysis, although very interesting, has not carried us very far. The stability pact which was proposed by the German Finance minister was mainly motivated by the need of the German government to pacify a sceptical German public. It has almost nothing to do with precepts that could be derived from economic analysis.

There are other areas, besides the budgetary one, that are in need of further integration. These other areas are described in this paper. We analyse why and how EMU will put further pressure on fostering co-operation and integration. We will deal with labour mobility, tax harmonisation, industrial location, transportation and the national legislation governing take-overs. In each case we ask the question how EMU will affect the issue at hand.

The paper is organised as a series of short sections describing these different areas in need of further integration. We will start with an introductory section analysing why it is difficult to quantify the costs and benefits of EMU.

2. THE COSTS AND BENEFITS OF THE EURO

The list of costs and benefits of a monetary union is relatively easy to establish. On the *benefit* side economists have identified the following items:

- EMU will eliminate *transactions costs* for firms and consumers who have to deal in different currencies.
- EMU will eliminate exchange risk. As a result, it will make it cheaper to make investment and production decisions within EMU.
- The elimination of national currencies will make it possible to have more price transparency, thereby stimulating further economic integration in Europe. The consumer should profit.
- The creation of one wide monetary area in Europe will stimulate the emergence of a European wide capital market. This has the potential of challenging the US capital markets, creating new benefits for Europe. This would also make it possible for the euro to become the major competitor to the dollar.

Whereas the benefits of EMU find their origin mostly at the micro-economic level, the *costs* originate at the macro-economic level. They arise because nations who join EMU lose an instrument of economic policy, i.e. their exchange rate. This instrument could be useful when the country is hit by a negative shock, e.g. a negative demand shock. In that case, a depreciation of the currency can be used to stimulate demand again. This option will be lost in a monetary union. Instead, in such a union, member countries will have to rely on more flexibility of wages and prices, and on labour mobility to absorb these asymmetric shocks. There is plenty of evidence that this flexibility is very imperfect in Europe today. Thus there are real costs to monetary union.

Most economists will agree with the previous analysis. The analysis remains qualitative however, so that it does not help countries to decide on the action to be taken. In order to make the cost benefit analysis of EMU operational, one would need to quantify these different benefits and costs for each country. Can this be done?

Some of the benefits can be given a monetary value relatively easily. This is the case for the transactions costs. The European Commission has estimated the elimination of the transactions costs to amount to ¼ to ½ of a percent of the EU-GDP.[2] In addition, this number tends be higher for smaller economies who have a high trade exposure.

For the other benefits and costs the precise quantification is much more difficult, if not impossible. In the remainder of this section we will illustrate this by analysing the most important benefits and costs of EMU.

EMU will eliminate exchange risk. The European Commission has attempted to quantify the benefits that will arise from the elimination of this risk. It has come to the following analysis. The lower exchange risk will lead to lower risk premia that are normally embodied in the long term real interest rates. This in turn will lower the long term real interest rate in EMU, thereby stimulating investment. EMU therefore will make it possible to stimulate economic growth in the European Union. Using a mathematical model, the European Commission has also quantified this economic growth effect of EMU. The result is that EMU could boost economic growth by 0.5 to 1 % per year.[3] If true, this would really be quite an achievement.

This attempt at quantifying the effects of the reduction of exchange risk has been met with great scepticism by economists. The main reason for being sceptical can be explained as follows. EMU will certainly reduce exchange risk. It is also certain, however, to create new risks, the quantitative importance of which we do not know today. These new risks are the following. EMU will make markets more transparent, thereby creating more intense competition. This is good news for consumers. At the same time, the increased intensity of competition in many markets will increase the penalty of those businesses that make wrong decisions. This increased risk from competition should be compared with the reduced risk from the elimination of exchange risk.

The upshot of all this is that we can certainly not conclude that because exchange risk will be eliminated in EMU, the systemic risk will decline. EMU will create new sources of uncertainty and risks that may fully compensate the elimination of exchange risk. As a result, we cannot be sure at all that the risk of doing business in Europe will decline in the future EMU. It follows that the claims that EMU will boost economic growth are highly speculative.

EMU will create macro-economic adjustment costs. There is no doubt that the absence of the exchange rate instrument and the limited flexibility of Europe's labour markets will make it more difficult for member countries to adjust to asymmetric shocks. As a result, EMU may increase unemployment.

The problem here also is to know what the quantitative importance of these adjustment costs will be. In order to answer this question several issues have to be resolved. First, there is the issue of the frequency of asymmetric shocks. Some economists argue that because of the increasing economic integration, EU countries will become more alike in their economic structures, so that asymmetric shocks will become less likely. Others argue that economic integration will lead to more regional concentration of economic activities, so that asymmetric shocks become more likely. The consensus today seems to be that even if the latter is true, these asymmetric shocks will increasingly be blind to national borders. For example, the automobile industry in the future may concentrate in particular regions of Europe. Chances are, however, that this concentration pattern will disregard national borders. To give an example, automobile production may concentrate in Southern Germany and Northern Italy. As a result, exchange rate policies may become quite ineffective in dealing with shocks hitting that particular sector. Put differently, shocks in the automobile industry will affect employment. But this would be the case whether or not these countries are in a monetary union.

A second issue is the effectiveness of exchange rates in dealing with shocks that hit a particular country. The consensus among economists today is that the exchange rate has only a limited effectiveness to deal with many asymmetric disturbances. This is so because a devaluation sets in motion a wage price spiral that can be difficult to control. The active use of the exchange rate can be a source of macro-economic stability.

All this leads to the view that the active use of the exchange rate as a macro-economic policy does not work well in many countries (especially the small ones). Therefore, the adjustment costs in a monetary union may not be much higher than outside a monetary union.

One big qualification should be added here, however, which makes it very difficult to quantify the adjustment costs in EMU. Although countries may not perceive it as a great loss that they lose the exchange rate to actively manage the economy, they still lose something valuable. Large and catastrophic economic shocks will hit particular countries. This will not happen frequently, but it will happen. It is then that the loss of the exchange rate instrument to correct for the disturbance will be felt most acutely. Examples of such events are the large decline in demand in Finland in the early 1990s due to the collapse of the Soviet market, or the Mexican debt crisis of 1994. In each of these cases, a devaluation of the national currency was an essential component of a successful recovery. In a monetary union this would not have been possible. If these countries had been in a monetary union, the adjustment costs they would have faced would certainly have been higher. This would also have created intense political conflicts between nations.

Thus nations do risk being faced by occasionally large adjustment costs in EMU. Since the events that trigger such costs are low probability events, we lack the data to compute their probabilities. As a result, the quantification of these costs is made difficult, if not impossible.

Conclusion

Economists know the nature of the costs and benefits of EMU relatively well. The problem, however, is that for most of these costs and benefits they find it nearly impossible to estimate their quantitative importance. The main reason we have identified here is that while EMU will eliminate the exchange risk, it will also create new risks in Europe. These have to do with the increased competition, and the ensuing restructurings, to which EMU will lead. It has also to do with the risk of large economic disturbances that are bound to occur infrequently. In the face of these large disturbances the absence of national instruments to deal with them will create the risk of structural adjustment problems. It may also create conflicts between nations about the appropriate policies to be conducted by the European Central Bank. Given their unique and unpredictable nature these risks cannot be quantified. As a result, economists will continue to disagree on the quantitative importance of the costs and benefits of EMU.

3. EMU AND LABOUR MOBILITY

When a country experiences an *asymmetric* shock (e.g. a decline in the demand for its products, or a loss of competitiveness) it needs some mechanism to adjust to this shock. If the country is in EMU, it cannot use the exchange rate (e.g. a devaluation) to deal with this shock. Instead it has to rely on other adjustment mechanisms. One such mechanism is labour mobility. In order to understand how it works, it is useful to start from an example. Suppose a country experiences a loss in demand for its products. If labour mobility exists, the decline in production will lead to emigration of workers who have lost their jobs. If mobility is non-existent, structural unemployment in the country experiencing the negative shock may be the outcome.[4] Labour mobility, therefore, appears to be important for the well-functioning of a monetary union. This then leads to the question of whether labour mobility is strong enough in Europe to guarantee the success of EMU.

3.1. The evidence about labour mobility

The empirical evidence we have today is that labour mobility between EU countries is weak. Several empirical studies have been undertaken illustrating that the inter-country labour mobility in the EU is considerably below the labour mobility within the US. The conclusion from these studies is that the EU countries that will participate in EMU, are less well-equipped than the US states to deal with asymmetric shocks in a monetary union.

This very general conclusion should be qualified, however. First, it appears that the mobility of labour in a number of 'peripheral' European countries (Portugal, Ireland, for example) is larger than in the core group of countries (Benelux, France, Germany). In the latter countries, the mobility of labour, and the willingness to emigrate because of negative economic developments, is very low. It is also much lower than in the past (say, fifty years ago), when workers were massively emigrating under economic hardship.

A second qualification is that there is an important difference between skilled and unskilled labour. The lack of labour mobility in the core countries is more pronounced among low-skilled labour than among highly skilled and professional workers. Whereas the mobility of low-skilled workers in the core countries has practically come to a standstill, this is not the case for highly skilled employees. This contrast between unskilled and skilled labour does not seem to be present in the 'peripheral' countries.

How can one explain these facts? The major factor explaining the starkly reduced degree of labour mobility in the core group of EU countries has to do with social security. It can now be said that the highly developed system of social security in the core EU countries has almost totally eliminated the financial incentives of low-skilled workers, who have lost their job, to incur the cost of moving so as to find a new job. When losing their job, these low-skilled workers fall in the unemployment trap which also implies that they become immobile. We show the nature of these financial incentives in Figure 3.1, which represents a hypothetical core EU country.[5]

On the horizontal axis we set out the income (skill) level of workers in this country, measured from 0 to 19. On the vertical axis we show the net earnings from work as a percent of gross wage cost. This net earning is defined as the net wage minus unemployment benefits. It can be interpreted as the (after tax) remuneration a worker obtains when he (she) decides to take a job instead of remaining unemployed. It can be seen that the financial incentives for low skilled workers to accept a job is extremely low. For the lowest-skilled workers it is often negative (as shown here for skill level 0). As a result, low skilled unemployed workers will have few incentives to take a job, especially if this requires him to move to another country. This incentive problem also explains why the mobility of unskilled workers *within* the core EU countries has become very low.

Figure 3.1. Net earnings from work as percentage of wage cost

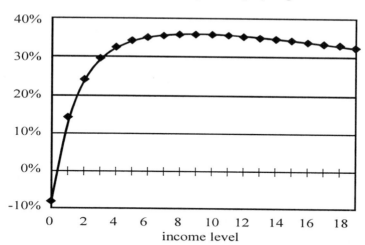

The figure also illustrates that job-searching, including moving elsewhere to find a new job, is financially much more rewarding for skilled workers than for low-skilled workers. This then also explains why the high-skilled workers in the core EU countries have maintained a relatively high degree of mobility.

The 'peripheral' EU countries have not experienced the same mobility problems as the core EU countries for two reasons. First, there is still a substantial wage differential with the core EU countries, stimulating outward mobility from the 'peripheral' countries. Second, the social security systems in the 'peripheral' countries are not as well developed as in the core and, therefore, do not create the same bias against mobility of low-skilled workers.

3.2. How to stimulate labour mobility?

From the preceding discussion one can conclude that policies aimed at stimulating labour mobility in Europe are quite complex and difficult to implement. The reason is that the financial incentives that have reduced labour mobility are grounded in the social security systems of the countries involved. Thus, policies aimed at increasing mobility require fundamental reforms of the social security systems. In particular, they require increasing the net wage relative to the unemployment benefits of low-skilled workers. But how to implement this? One way to do it would be to reduce unemployment benefits. The resistance against such cuts, however, is strong and understandably so. The only way out seems to be to reduce the taxes on labour income for the low-skilled workers. This is in fact being done in most core EU countries. There is a limit to what one can do here, because the lowering of the tax burden on low-skilled workers must be compensated by an increasing tax burden on high-skilled (and high-income) workers, which is also resisted.

The previous analysis leads to the view that the EU institutions are pretty powerless to stimulate across-country labour mobility in the EU, and will continue to be so. Since the lack of labour mobility of the core EU countries is the result of their social security systems, and since social security belongs to the sole responsibility of the member countries, the EU institutions can do very little. This is in fact a very general problem with employment policies. The latter require reducing taxes on labour and reforming social security and labour markets. All these things are national responsibilities, making it nearly impossible to devise European-wide employment policies.

It is sometimes said that EMU, together with the forces of globalisation, will put pressure on governments to reform social security so as to increase mobility. This is undoubtedly so, and in a number of countries (e.g. the Netherlands) this has already led to significant reforms. It is equally true, however, that the forces of resistance against the reform of social security and of the labour markets are also strong. The strength of this resistance is shown by the recent French experience, where changes have gone in the direction of making labour markets even more rigid. This resistance against reform is deep rooted for the simple reason that the changes that are needed to stimulate labour mobility imply that one reduces the degree of income protection of workers.

As argued earlier, the 'peripheral' EU countries have not experienced the same tendencies up to today. One may expect, however, that they may soon experience similar problems as the core countries. As they catch up, the wage differential with the core EU countries will narrow. In addition, the 'peripheral' countries are likely to institute similar systems of social security as in the core EU countries. This is likely to reduce their labour mobility in the long run.

3.3. Conclusion: how much does mobility matter for EMU?

The lack of labour mobility, and especially the near-absence of mobility of low-skilled workers in the core EU countries is certainly going to handicap EMU. The important issue, however, is how strong this handicap will be. Will it lead to a situation where EMU itself will be put into question? We do not believe so. The reason is the following. Most shocks that countries now experience are *symmetric*. They are the result of global changes in specialisation and technology, that work in all EU countries in much the same way. (This is why we call them symmetric shocks). These shocks are blind to political borders. As a result, the exchange rate has increasingly lost its effectiveness to deal with these shocks.

This does not mean, of course, that labour mobility is not desirable to deal with these disturbances. It certainly is. What it means is that labour mobility, and other forms of labour market flexibility, are necessary in all countries, whether or not they enter in a monetary union. Put differently, countries that stay out of EMU will equally need more labour mobility and flexibility of their labour markets as the countries that enter EMU. It would be an illusion to think that countries that keep their exchange rate can more easily confront the forces of change produced by globalisation and technological revolutions.

As was pointed out in our previous report, the only remaining risk for EMU-countries comes from the fact that large *social and political* disturbances in one country could arise. Because of the absence of the exchange rate instrument these shocks will be difficult to deal with in a monetary union. This is where the lack of labour mobility will prove to be an important handicap in EMU-countries hit by such a disturbance.

4. EMU AND HARMONISATION OF TAXES

EMU will intensify the process of market integration in the European Union. As a result, relatively small price differentials will set in motion strong movements of goods and services. In addition, factors of production are likely to become more sensitive to differentials in factor prices (wages and return on capital). In such an integrated union where most obstacles to the flow of goods and services will have disappeared, one of the most important factors causing differentials in prices will be the differences in taxation. As a result, increased pressures will exist to harmonise tax rates in EMU. Failure to do so will engender distortions in trade flows and in the flows of labour and capital, which will be deemed to be unacceptable by many governments. In this sense EMU will force governments to co-ordinate and to harmonise tax policies more than they have done in the past.

The impact of EMU on tax harmonisation, however, will not be uniform for all taxes. The reason has to do with *mobility*. In general, the pressure to harmonise tax rates increases with the mobility of the good and the factor that is taxed. This has important implications for the speed with which different taxes will be harmonised in the future EMU. Taxes on goods and on factors of production that are very mobile will be harmonised quickly, the other taxes will not be harmonised significantly in the foreseeable future.

Differences in the mobility of the taxable basis is important for another reason. It can lead to tax competition, i.e. countries reduce their tax rates on the mobile factors of production (mainly capital) in order to attract these; the ensuing shortfall in revenue then forces governments to raise taxes on the immobile factors (mainly labour). This can easily lead to a vicious circle where the immobile factor has to bear an increasing tax burden. This phenomenon will certainly add additional pressure on governments to harmonise taxes.

Before describing these different harmonisation processes it is useful to discuss the recent initiatives taken by the European Union.

4.1. Recent EU initiatives in tax harmonisation

Until today, the major stumbling block for progress in the field of tax harmonisation has been the fact that all EU decisions involving taxes must be made by unanimity. As a result, relatively little progress was made. The only exception was the harmonisation of VAT tax rates, where EU countries agreed to set some 'fork' within which these VAT-rates would be maintained.

Despite the political problem caused by the unanimity rule in tax matters, the pressure for tax harmonisation in anticipation of EMU has been strong enough to lead to an important new initiative. On December 1, 1997 the ECOFIN Council reached a landmark agreement on future taxation policies. The agreement consists of three parts.

- First, the member countries have agreed to a *Code of Conduct* governing corporate income taxes. According to this new *Code of Conduct*, member states agree not to introduce harmful new tax measures (the 'standstill' provision) and to eliminate existing harmful tax measures (the 'rollback' provision). A committee is created whose task it is to monitor whether countries abide by this new *Code of Conduct*.
- Second, a directive will be worked out on the taxation of savings. This should eliminate the anomaly whereby non-residents in the EU do not pay taxes on income from savings. An agreement in principle was reached based on the 'co-existence model': each member state will either use a withholding tax or provide information on savings income to other member states.
- Third, member states agree to discuss a directive making it easier for companies to transfer interest and royalties across borders without the risk of double taxation.

4.2. The complex dynamics of harmonisation

The December 1, 1997 ECOFIN agreement on tax harmonisation illustrates the general principle formulated in section 1 – progress in the field of harmonisation is dictated by the mobility of the taxable basis. It is no surprise, therefore, that the two areas in which speedy progress is likely, are the taxation of capital income (savings) and the taxation of corporate profits.

- Some harmonisation of the *taxation on capital (savings)* appears to be increasingly likely. The basic principle of the draft directive is that a European citizen will no longer be considered as a non-resident for tax purposes. The difficulty in applying this principle up to now was the fact that some EU countries apply a withholding tax on capital income, which is also a final tax, while other EU countries use a system where capital income is reported to the tax authorities and is added to the income tax declaration. (Table 3.1 gives an overview of the different systems). The breakthrough came because of the acceptance of the *co-existence principle* – instead of trying to enforce the same system (which would have been doomed), the two systems will co-exist. The practical implication is that countries will have the choice of either applying a withholding tax on non-residents capital income, or providing information on capital income of non-residents to the tax authorities of the other member states.
- Some progress in the harmonisation of corporate income tax is also likely. Corporations have a lot of possibilities to move the taxable basis (their profits). This mobility is likely to increase even further in EMU. The ECOFIN agreement to impose a *Code of Conduct* indicates the direction in which progress is likely to be made. In the future, member-states will be under much greater scrutiny regarding the new tax measures they take. If these are found to be harmful, i.e. to lead to displacement effects that hurt other EU countries, they could be pressured not to apply these measures. In addition, existing tax measures that are deemed to be harmful (using the same definition) may have to be rolled back. Ireland, for example, which applies a 10 % profit tax on manufacturing activities will come under increasing pressure to rescind this tax.

Table 3.1.   *Resident withholding taxes on interest and dividends in the EU*
              (1997)

	withholding tax		application
	interest income	dividends	
B	15	25	final
DK	RS	25	declared
D	25	25	declared
E	25	25	declared
F	15	25	final
I	12.5	12.5	final
IRL	26	0	final
L	0	25	declared
NL	RS	25	declared
AU	25	25	final
P	20	30	final
UK	20	0	declared

Note: RS means reporting system.

Source: Lannoo, 1998.

Much less harmonisation progress is likely to occur in other tax areas. The reason again has to do with the fact that the other taxes are applied on goods, services and labour that are much less mobile than financial capital and corporate profits. We discuss the different other forms of taxation:

- *Taxation on labour* (Income taxes and social security contributions). Very little progress in harmonisation should be expected here. As noted earlier in section 3, the mobility of labour is very small within the group of core EU member states. Some mobility exists between the South and the Core, but this is likely to be too weak to make much difference. As a result, the pressure on individual member states to bring their labour taxes in line with those of the other EU countries will continue to be weak even in EMU. There are some interesting examples that confirm this conclusion. Switzerland is a full scale monetary union. In addition, it is a small country. All this has not prevented income taxes being significantly different between the cantons. Switzerland appears to be able to live with these differences.
- *Indirect taxes*. In this area the future progress to be expected is mixed. As far as *VAT rates* are concerned, the existing differences between

EU countries have become relatively small, partly as a result of previous harmonisation efforts. A recent study performed by Professor Sijben Cnossen (1997) of the University of Rotterdam shows that the existing differences of VAT rates have very little impact on the flow of goods and services across borders. As a result, most EU countries can live with these differences. Things are different in the field of *excise taxes*. Here the differences across EU countries can be quite substantial. For example, excise taxes in Denmark on the sales of cars are such that they can double the price of some cars. Such differences are bound to have effects on trade flows when markets become more integrated. We should expect, therefore, that some of these excessively high excise taxes in some countries will have to be lowered.

5. EUROPEAN MONETARY UNION AND INDUSTRIAL LOCATIONS

Since Adam Smith it has been observed that an increase in the size of the market allows firms to better exploit economies of scale. The latter can take two forms. Individual plant size increases and small plants cluster together. These two phenomena lead to strong regional concentration of economic activities. This process has gone very far in the US. It is less the case in the EU today. The question is whether EMU and the continuing process of market integration will push the EU in the direction of US-type industrial concentration.

5.1. The facts

There is no doubt that the degree of regional concentration of industrial activities is more pronounced in the US than in the EU. This is illustrated by the regional shares of employment in three industries (automobile, textile and steel) in the US and the EU (see Table 3.2). It is striking that in the three industries the regional concentration of industrial activities tends to be stronger in the US than in the EU. This is especially the case in the automobile and textile industries. In the automobile sector the Midwest concentrates 65% of the US automobile activity. In the US textile industry this percentage is even higher: the US South takes 80% of the employment in that sector. In contrast with the US scene, the EU automobile and textile industries tend to be much more evenly spread across the continent.

Table 3.2.   Regional shares in the US (1990) and the EU (1995) in the textile, car and steel industry

	Textile industry	Car industry	Steel industry
US			
North-East	14.0	7.6	13.4
Mid-West	3.2	63.1	51.7
West	3.9	6.8	10.4
South	78.9	22.5	24.5
EU			
North	16.6	24.8	18.0
Core-West	14.2	21.4	22.8
Core-East	12.4	31.2	40.4
South	56.8	22.6	18.8

Source: Krugman and Venables, 1993; OECD, Database for Industrial Analysis, 1997.

5.2. Incentives for building 'industrial districts'

Economic geography stresses two kinds of forces that influence the location of industries: 'centripetal' forces tend to generate incentives for agglomerations, whereas 'centrifugal' forces break such agglomerations and put a limit to their size.

The centripetal forces are increasing in importance with economic integration. The latter increases market size As mentioned earlier, this allows firms to better exploit economies of scale. This in turn leads to two phenomena. First, in many industries, the optimal plant size increases. The dynamics of increase in plant size then necessarily leads to concentration as firms reduce the number of plants. A recent example of this effect was given by Renault's decision to close its Vilvoorde plant in Belgium.

A second consequence of increasing market size is that in many industries firms will have a stronger incentive to locate close to each other. When market size increases, the pool of local skilled labour expands together with local suppliers. These will tend to cluster together. In addition. low transportation costs generates an incentive for the producers to locate in the area of good access to market and suppliers. Factors of production, i.e. capital, labour and technology, are likely to concentrate at those places where the manufacturers are located. Hence, the interaction of all these factors generate agglomeration. This is sometimes called the 'Silicon Valley' effect: many small high-tech firms tend to cluster together to profit from a common pool of high-skilled labour, specialised suppliers and specialised knowledge.

Centrifugal forces are important too. Existence of formal and informal trade barriers, high transportation costs or the exchange rate uncertainty can easily put barriers to agglomeration. A manufacturer can prefer to locate in different countries to avoid uncertainties and formal trade barriers that may put obstacles to access markets and suppliers. On the other hand, natural borders created by the existence of different languages, cultures and life style may serve as an obstacle for an expansion of a particular industry beyond the national borders. Hence, incomplete integration of markets, both in the formal and informal sense, puts a limit to the existence and the size of the agglomerations.

There are still a lot of barriers to trade in the EU, thereby limiting the effect of the centripetal forces towards agglomeration. However, economic and monetary union which has been given a new impetus by the launch of the euro, will trigger a new dynamic towards the reduction of trade barriers. As a result, the centripetal forces will increase in intensity, leading to agglomeration and concentration of industrial activities in the EU. Put differently, EMU will lead Europe closer to the US model of concentration of industrial activities.

One can conclude that the future EU map of industrial activities will exhibit a stronger degree of concentration of industrial activities than the one existing today. What exactly this map will look like, however, is difficult to predict. For example, although we expect that the car industry will be more concentrated, we do not know where it will be concentrated. The exact location of industries quite often depends on historical accidents that are extremely difficult to forecast in advance.

6. EMU AND TRANSPORTATION

6.1. A new competitive environment in EU road transportation

The single market programme has introduced major changes in the workings of the European road transport market. Whereas prior to the start of the single market, most road transportation markets in the EU were protected from outside competition, this has changed drastically, especially since the early 1990s. One important change occurred on January 1993, with the adoption of regulation No. 881/92 which abolished all quantitative quota restrictions on international transport between Member States and eliminated border controls. As a result, road transportation in the European Union is now more subject to competitive forces than it used to be. Despite these major changes,

Economic Policy in the European Union

however, there are still important obstacles to the free movement of transport services in the EU.

These obstacles originate from the existence of different national regulations and taxation systems. It is useful to consider three types of *national regulations* that affect the free flow of services in the transport market:

- Government controls on prices (tariffs)
- Quantitative controls (licensing and permit systems)
- Qualitative standards (professional expertise, financial standing and reputation, environmental regulation).

In Table 3.3 we summarise the main differences between EU countries. Five countries (Germany, Greece, Spain, Italy and Portugal) still maintain control on market entry to their domestic markets by setting quotas. However, since 'cabotage'[6] was introduced in 1990, non-resident EU operators with a Community cabotage authorisation may operate national transport services without further quantitative restrictions. This has certainly increased competitive pressure in the domestic transport markets. Two countries (Italy and Spain) still maintain systems of price (tariff) controls.

Table 3.3.   Type of obstacles to European road transport

	Quantitative permits	Price controls	Qualitative standards
B			X
DK			X
D	X		
GR	X		X
E	X	X	X
F			X
IRL			X
I	X	X	
L			X
NL			X
P	X		X
UK			X

Source: European Commission, 1990.

In the field of qualitative standards, there still exist wide differences between Member States. For example, the financial conditions and the professional qualifications to obtain a permit vary widely between the Member States. Significant efforts have been made, however, to harmonise environmental regulations. For example, new common standards will be introduced on the emissions from diesel engines. Similarly, a new Directive of 1996 harmonises technical standards (weight and dimensions of vehicles).

In the field of *taxation*, significant progress has been made to harmonise the national systems. Important differences remain, however. The main taxation systems that matter for the road transportation business are the vehicle taxes, the excise duties on fuel (diesel), and the user charges for road infrastructure. Several Directives issued in the early 1990s have initiated a process of harmonisation. For example, the Directive of October 1993 (93/89/EEC) lays down minimum rates for annual vehicle taxes and harmonises toll and user charges for certain infrastructures. Following the adoption of this Directive, Germany, Belgium, Luxembourg and the Netherlands have introduced a common road user charge, the so-called *Euro-vignette*. Despite this progress, differences continue to exist. Some are due to the lack of implementation of the existing Directives into the national legislation.

6.2. The integration of the transport market and the workings of EMU

The internal market has had significant effects on the cost and price structure of road freight transport in the EU. Three opposing effects have been at work.

First, the *harmonisation* imposed by the single market has added to the cost of international transport. For example, the harmonisation of excise duties on diesel fuel has generally led to an increase in the duties. It has been estimated that the total effect of the harmonisation has been to increase the cost of a standard trip of 1,000 km by 8 to 12% depending on the individual Member State.[7]

Second, the *liberalisation* made possible by the internal market (e.g. elimination of border controls, introduction of cabotage) has led to a lowering of transport cost by 5 to 6%. Thus, the static effects of the single market have probably increased the cost of transporting goods across the EU. This, however, does not take into account the dynamic effects, that have to do with increased competition.

Third, by opening up national transportation markets, the single market program has certainly increased the *degree of competition* in the EU transport market. Thus, despite the increased costs produced by harmonisation, freight prices declined during the 1990s. This decline has been estimated to amount to 1 to 8% for cross-border transport.[8] As a result, profit margins declined, and the transport sector has undergone major restructurings, favouring a larger scale of the operations, and stimulating mergers. One should expect that these dynamic effects of increased competition will continue to operate and to reduce freight prices.

Thus, in the future, one should expect a further trend towards the lowering of freight prices. This could have important implications for the functioning of the EMU. Let us trace these effects. Economic theory tells us that, in general, the lowering of transport costs will induce regional concentration of economic activities. This is due to the fact that, with diminishing transport costs, locational advantages of particular regions become less important. As a result, it pays to concentrate production in fewer locations so as to fully exploit economies of scale. Put differently, the importance of production delocalisation becomes less relevant in the process of capturing distant markets.

In addition, economic theory predicts that this concentration of economic activities will be biased in favour of the centre and away from the periphery. This can be explained as follows. The centre typically has an advantage relative to the periphery mainly because of a superior economic infrastructure and better access to technology. Decreasing transport costs then have the effect of increasing the locational advantage of the centre relative to the periphery. This in turn leads firms to relocate some of their activities towards the centre.[9]

From the preceding analysis one may conclude that the functioning of the future EMU may be made more difficult. As the lowering of transport costs leads to concentration of economic activities, asymmetric shocks may become more prevalent within the EMU. Thus, it becomes more likely that while some regions or countries experience booming economic conditions, others confront a relative decline of economic activities. This will make the task of the European Central Bank to manage Europe's money more difficult. The ECB will have to find a difficult compromise between conflicting demands about how monetary policies should be conducted. The lowering of transport costs within the European Union may be a blessing in disguise for the smooth functioning of EMU.

7. ANTI-TAKE-OVER DEFENCES IN THE EUROPEAN UNION AND EMU

EU Member States have various systems of protection against hostile takeovers, reflecting different legal systems and traditions.

The Anglo Saxon tradition emphasises shareholder's value and the dynamic development of companies and markets. Therefore, anti-take-over defences favour the protection of shareholders' interests, avoiding shareholders' positions being excessively undermined.

In the Continental tradition the 'institutional' view of the company dominates. In this view, the interests of the company do not coincide with the shareholders' interests. As a result, continental anti-take-over defences emphasise the interests of the company and attach a great importance to the position of management. These defensive systems are influenced by the idea that management is better suited than shareholders to protect the long term interests of the company.

The main anti-take-over mechanisms existing in the EU Member States can be listed as follows:

1. *Procedures for appointing and for dismissing members of the company's management.* There are some statutory mechanisms which limit shareholders' influence on the appointment and dismissal of either the 'Supervisory Board' or the 'Board of Directors', namely:

- The requirement of a super majority (normally a 2/3 majority of votes) for dismissing or suspending members of the company's governing bodies (Germany, the Netherlands, Spain);
- The attribution of the right to appoint all or some of the managers to certain shareholders (so called 'stable shareholders') or to the employees (France, Germany);
- The binding character of the appointment of the managers (e.g., directors cannot be dismissed until their term of office has elapsed) (Germany, the Netherlands);
- The impossibility for the shareholders' general meeting of appointing directly the members of the Board of Directors. In this case shareholders can appoint only the members of the Supervisory Board who, in turn, appoint the members of the Board of Directors (Germany, the Netherlands).

2. *Measures for increasing the capital of the target company, when faced by a take-over.* Target companies can decide to increase their capital, through the issue of voting shares or convertible securities, in order to dilute the holding of the 'raider'. An increase in the capital can be accompanied by the withdrawal of the shareholders' right of pre-emption (priority purchase) of the new securities issued by the target company. This has the effect of excluding the 'raider' from the purchase. Germany, the Netherlands and Spain appear to have developed the strongest anti-take-over defences in this area.

3. *Issue of various kinds of shares.* In most EU member States, various kinds of shares can be issued as a means of defence against hostile take-overs, such as :

- Non-voting shares or comparable securities (e.g., certificates for shares), which represent capital but do not give any voting right (Germany, France, the Netherlands, Spain, Portugal);
- Multiple voting shares, which grant entitlement to more than one vote (France, Germany);
- Special shares, which grant some special rights like, for example, the right to appoint certain members of the management or to endorse some decisions of the shareholders' general meeting (Belgium, Germany, the Netherlands).

4. *Procedures for exercising voting-rights and limitations on voting.*
- Statutory limitations on voting. In many EU countries, statutes of companies frequently lay down that each shareholder may not cast more than a given percentage of the total number of votes attached to his shares or of the total number of votes that all shareholders can cast (France, Belgium, Germany, the Netherlands, Spain, Portugal).
- Proxies' (proxy votes). The delegation of shareholders' votes, namely when it is solicited for by the management of the company, favours a major control on the exercise of the voting rights (France, Belgium, Germany, the Netherlands, Spain).
- Voting agreements between shareholders (so called 'syndicate agreement'). Under these agreements some shareholders agree to fix their voting-patterns in advance. Syndicate agreements are usually accompanied by 'pre-emption agreements', under which the members of the 'syndicate' cannot sell their shares until they have first offered them to the other members of the 'syndicate'. In most EU countries voting agreements can be declared null and void by the judicial courts if they entirely restrict the shareholder's will or prevent him from taking part in the decision-making process of his company (France, Belgium, Germany, the Netherlands, Spain, Portugal).

Conclusion
The continental European countries surveyed in this section have developed a whole battery of defences against hostile take-overs. These defences have been influenced by the idea that management is better placed than the shareholders to serve the long term interests of the company. This continental model of corporate governance is in stark contrast with the Anglo-Saxon model. Whether the continental European model will be able to survive in a world where the Anglo-Saxon model increasingly dominates remains to be seen.

There is no doubt that there exists a continental European model of corporate governance. At the same time, however, there are large national differences in the implementation of this model. Germany and the Netherlands are the countries that stand out as having erected the strongest barriers against hostile take-overs. In general, the differences in the institutional detail are baffling. This will make the development of a unified euro stock market difficult. As long as these differences will exist, the valuation of companies and thus the pricing of their shares in different countries will follow a different dynamic, preventing a complete integration of the euro equity markets. This will be a handicap for the euro if it wants to become an international currency on equal footing with the dollar.

8. GENERAL CONCLUSION

Monetary unification is likely to change Europe's economic landscape in a fundamental way. In general, it will intensify the process of economic integration. In this paper we analysed some of the channels through which this integration process will occur. First, by intensifying the process of economic integration EMU will lead to regional specialisation and to agglomeration effects. In other words, EMU will move Europe in the direction of American-type specialisation and concentration. Second, EMU will force further institutional integration. We identified several ones. Some forms of taxation (e.g. taxation of savings, indirect taxes) will increasingly be harmonised. Labour taxes, however, will not be harmonised soon. Transportation costs will also be reduced, not only because of technological changes, but also because EMU will further open up markets thereby speeding up the move to larger scale in the European transport sector. Finally, EMU will put pressure on the existence of financial barriers, thereby stimulating the emergence of one large capital market.

Modern welfare states of the European type are based on the idea that a central government must be ready to soften the blows that are inflicted on individuals and groups of individuals as a result of rapid economic changes. During the post-war period these European welfare states have been relatively successful in doing so. Monetary unification, however, presents new challenges in Europe. On the one hand, by further opening up markets, it will speed up economic transformation. As a result, individuals and groups of individuals are likely to be hit more often by economic disturbances. On the other hand, EMU is being launched with a huge political vacuum at the European level. The brute fact is that there will be no European government that takes over the role of softening the economic blows inflicted by the existence of a monetary union. The responsibility of providing shock absorbers remains firmly in the hands of the nation states. EMU, therefore is a risky undertaking. Will the nation states be able to deal with their traditional responsibility as shock absorbers? We tend to think that the answer to this question is negative. This then is likely to lead to intense conflicts between national governments and the European Central Bank. These conflicts can only be reduced by creating a European government with similar responsibilities as the national ones. Failure to do so creates the risk of a break-up of the monetary union.

NOTES

1. The authors are grateful to Yunus Aksoy for research assistance and to Dante Storti for advice on the last section.
2. See European Commission (1990).
3. *Ibid.*
4. It should be noted that if real wages are sufficiently flexible we may not need labour mobility to adjust to the negative shock. In that case, real wages will go down in the country hit by the shock. This will then reduce the unemployment problem. The issue here is whether real wages are sufficiently flexible in Europe to eliminate the need for labour mobility.
5. Actually, the graph broadly corresponds to the Belgian case. It can be said that it has a similar shape in the other core EU countries.
6. 'Cabotage' is the permission given to a country to perform inland transport services in another country.
7. See European Commission (1997).
8. *Ibid.*
9. It should be noted that the monetary union in itself tends to have opposite effects on the location of economic activities as between the centre and the periphery. In a previous report we have analysed these effects of EMU on foreign direct investments, and we came to the conclusion that the EMU would probably increase FDIs towards the periphery.

REFERENCES

Cnossen, S. (1997), 'VATs in CEE Countries: a Survey and Analysis', Research Memorandum 9711, Centre for Economic Policy, Erasmus University Rotterdam.
Lannoo, K. (1998), 'Taxation of Capital Income', CEPR, Brussels.
European Commission (1990), 'One Market, One Money', *European Economy*, **44**, October 1990.
European Commission (1997), 'Road Freight Transport', *Single Market Review – Subseries 2: Impact on Services*, Luxembourg.
Krugman, P. and A.J. Venables (1993), 'Integration, Specialization and Adjustment', CEPR Discussion Paper 886, London.

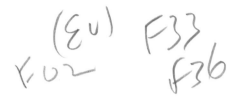

4. EMU and the Cohesion Process

Frank Barry[1]

'Cohesion' in the EU context refers to the bridging of the gap in living standards that separates the poorer and richer regions of the Union. The EU committed itself to this goal in the Single European Act and the Maastricht Treaty. As part of this commitment the allocation of Structural Funds was doubled for the 1994-99 period.

The aim of the present paper is to study the impact of economic and monetary union on the cohesion process, and specifically on the four cohesion countries – Greece, Spain, Portugal and Ireland. Section 1 reviews the cohesion experience and notes a number of structural similarities between the cohesion countries. Section 2 looks at the impact of economic union on cohesion; economic union is interpreted to mean continuing trade integration, as the EU proceeds towards the goals of the Single Market. Section 3 looks specifically at the monetary aspects of EMU, asking how the adoption of a single currency will affect cohesion.

1. THE COHESION PROCESS AND COHESION COUNTRIES

The cohesion process is illustrated in Figure 4.1 below, which depicts per capita GDP of the cohesion countries as a proportion of that of the EU15. The slow pace of real convergence for all four economies over most of the period depicted is clear, as is Ireland's impressive performance in recent years.

Neo-classical growth theory suggests that poorer economies should grow more rapidly than rich ones, and this holds true for Western European economies over the period 1950-1985. The four cohesion countries grew less rapidly than would have been expected on the basis of convergence theory

however (Ó Gráda and O'Rourke, 1996).[2] This suggests that it may be fruitful to ask whether there are structural characteristics that these economies
share that might inhibit their growth.[3]

*Figure 4.1.   Cohesion-country GDP per capita (plus GNP per capita ad-
justed for the terms of trade, for Ireland); EU15=100*

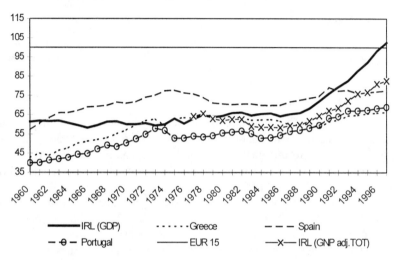

One shared characteristic is the high proportion of GDP accounted for by
agriculture. Ó Gráda and O'Rourke find that this variable accounts substantially for Ireland's poor performance in the 1950-85 period.[4]

A further shared characteristic is that within industry in the cohesion
countries the sub-sectors that exhibit increasing returns-to-scale (IRS) are
relatively underrepresented. In the economic geography model of Krugman
and Venables (1990) this indeed defines peripherality; expansion of the IRS
sectors would raise living standards towards levels prevailing in the core. In
fact many IRS sub-sectors are also R&D-intensive.[5] In endogenous growth
models such as Grossman and Helpman (1992), expansion of these sectors in
the periphery would also hasten real convergence.

A further shared characteristic is that enterprise size is relatively small in
the countries of the EU periphery, while one that will clearly have a bearing
on the costs and benefits of EMU is that their financial systems are also relatively underdeveloped (Larre and Torres, 1991).

Characteristics such as industry structure, enterprise size and the level of
development of the financial system will influence how economies respond
to economic and monetary union.

2. ECONOMIC UNION AND COHESION

The ambitious Single European Market programme aimed at the integration of the segmented national markets of the EU member states over the eight years to 1992. The Cecchini Report, details of which are provided in Emerson *et al.* (1988), predicted an increase of 4.5 percent in EU GNP and an extra 1,840,000 EU jobs as a result of market integration.

A recent European Commission publication, Monti (1996), charts the progress that has been achieved so far towards these goals. The Single Market programme is estimated to have knocked more than 5 billion ECUs a year off the costs of European traders and road hauliers, it almost doubled the share of public sector purchases from other member states between 1987 and 1994, and it reduced the variance of EU prices for identical consumer goods from 26 percent in 1980 to 19.5 percent in 1993, and from 18 percent to 14.5 percent for identical equipment goods.

In overall macroeconomic terms, however, achievement of the Cecchini goals remains some distance away. Recent estimates of the consequences of the Single Market suggest that it has increased output in the EU by a little more than 1 percent, and has raised the level of employment by between 300,000 and 900,000 jobs (Monti, 1996). It is also noted that small and medium-sized companies thus far have benefited less than larger companies which were better positioned to exploit new opportunities. In line with the analysis of Barry *et al.* (1997b) however, Monti argues that the process has allowed the poorer member states to grow faster than the richer ones, and so has promoted cohesion.

The study of Barry *et al.* (1997b) starts from the position that the processes underlying the development of the EU periphery might be quite different from those underlying the development of the 'core' economies upon which the Cecchini analysis had been based. For example, Krugman and Venables (1990) show that, in contrast to traditional trade theory, the net effect of the sectoral gains and losses associated with trade liberalisation can be negative for peripheral economies, because their increasing-returns sectors may be wiped out.

In forming a view as to which sectors would gain and which would lose, Barry *et al.* (1997b) made use of the analysis of Buigues *et al.* (1990b) which identified 40 out of about 120 NACE 3-digit manufacturing sectors as being likely to be affected by the Single Market. On the basis of the individual country studies presented in that document these 40 sectors in each periphery country were grouped into those that were predicted to do well in the individual countries, (the S or 'successful' sectors) and those that were predicted to do badly (the D or 'declining' sectors). Buigues *et al.* argued that the 'revealed comparative advantage' (RCA) methodology could be used to determine this. Barry *et al.* (1997b) worked on the premise that while RCA might represent an appropriate methodology for predicting developments in sectors which are not dominated by footloose MNCs, developments in sectors which are open to strong FDI flows must instead be analysed on the basis of the attractiveness of each periphery country to multinational investors. The first-round output shock of the Single Market measures will be related, they argued, to the data in Table 4.1 (which refer to sectors in which MNC activity is not very strong), supplemented by information on FDI flows.

Table 4.1.   Share in Manufacturing Output of S and D categories

	Share of S_i in Y_M	Share of D_i in Y_M
Ireland	23.6	2.7
Spain	6.5	7.3
Portugal	20.4	6.0
Greece	2.5	9.6

Note: S_i: sectors that are, and are likely to remain, indigenous-dominated, and that are predicted to be successful; D_i: sectors that are, and are likely to remain, indigenous-dominated, and that are predicted to decline. Y_M is manufacturing output.

Table 4.1 shows that Irish indigenous firms on average are predicted to do well from continuing trade integration. Spain has a fairly even spread between *S* and *D* sectors. Portugal is predicted to do better than Spain since many of the sectors that the RCA methodology would predict to decline can actually expand if the country is successful in attracting FDI. Greece is predicted to do poorly however because it has a revealed comparative disadvantage in a group of sectors that do not appear capable of attracting FDI.[6]

The predicted expansion of the *S* sectors and the contraction of the *D* sectors entail a combination of beneficial and adverse shocks. The raw sectoral predictions in Table 4.1 must then be translated into macroeconomic shocks, while the macroeconomic effects of such shocks will depend on the endogenous response of each economy. How these issues are dealt with is discussed fully in the 1997 study.

The completion of the Single Market, proxied by the output shocks implied by the data in Table 4.1 alongside a number of other Single Market-related shocks, are predicted to have the following medium-term effects on Cohesion country GDP (see Table 4.2, column 2, 'no FDI effects').

Table 4.2. *Single market effects on cohesion country GDP,
          % above baseline*

	No FDI effects	FDI effects included
Ireland	7.2	–
Spain	-0.7	7.1
Portugal	4.3	6.9
Greece	-0.9	–
'Cecchini'	4.5	

Column 2 reveals that before account is taken of the increased FDI flows associated with trade integration, both Spain and Greece are predicted to suffer output losses, confirming the pessimistic possibilities alluded to by Krugman and Venables (1990). Ireland and Portugal are both predicted to gain however, because their indigenous firms have a revealed comparative advantage in the sectors that will be affected by further trade integration.

These predictions on the performance of indigenous industry, based on comparative advantage, must be supplemented by an analysis of the ability of each country to attract footloose foreign industry.

US FDI inflows into Europe expanded quite dramatically in the late 1980s, and the US Department of Commerce *Survey of Current Business* (March 1991) attributes much of this to the Single Market initiative. US inflows to the periphery increased more than those going to the core. Furthermore, Monti (1996) points out that 'the smaller Benelux countries in the geographical core of the EU, and Ireland, Spain and Portugal on its periphery, were the main gainers of foreign investment coming from other EU states' (p. 85).

The OECD *International Direct Investment Statistics Yearbooks* reveal that real FDI inflows into Spanish and Portuguese manufacturing did indeed increase dramatically from the late 1980s onwards; as mentioned above there is strong evidence that this happened also for Ireland.[7] The Greek position however appears to have remained relatively static. Barry et al. (1997b) include the effects of the increased FDI inflows into Spanish and Portuguese manufacturing that the OECD identifies, and this transforms the outcome to that reported in column 3 of Table 4.2. Full implementation of the Single Market is now predicted to raise Spanish GDP by a little over 7 percent in the medium term, rather than falling by 0.7 percent as was predicted in the absence of increased FDI inflows. Portuguese GDP now rises by almost 7 percent rather than the 4.3 percent that was predicted before the increased FDI inflows were taken into account.

Comparison of the numbers in the third column of Table 4.2 with the 4.5 percent increase that the Cecchini Report predicted for the core EU econo- mies reveals that the periphery may well benefit more than the EU core from fuller economic union. Only Greece appears vulnerable, because the weak- ness of its indigenous industry is not being compensated for by increased FDI inflows, presumably because of macroeconomic instability and poor infra- structure.

3. MONETARY UNION AND COHESION

Part of the rationale for the near doubling of Structural Fund allocations in 1989 and their further doubling in 1994 was the belief that continuing trade integration and movement towards monetary union could widen regional disparities within the EU. We have argued that trade integration is unlikely to have widened disparities between Ireland, Portugal and Spain, on the one hand, and the EU core on the other, largely because it stimulated further FDI flows to these countries. As Monti (1996) points out, trade integration is still proceeding, so that many of the gains discussed above have yet to be real- ised, for both core and periphery. The implications of monetary union may be less benign however. We are concerned in this section not with attempting to address the broad question of the costs and benefits of monetary union for Europe, on which see Barry (1998), but with the question of how the periph- ery is likely to fare relative to the core.

One way to proceed in exploring the effects of alternative exchange rate arrangements on cohesion would be to determine whether the pace of real convergence differed between eras of exchange-rate stability and eras of ex- change rate volatility. A difficulty with this strategy, though, is that turbulent world conditions tended to be associated with exchange-rate volatility pre- cisely because they brought to an end the stable exchange-rate regimes – e.g. World War I and the end of the first Gold Standard, the Great Depression and the end of World War II, the huge monetary expansion of the Vietnam War era and the end of Bretton Woods, the first oil crisis and the demise of the Snake. It is therefore difficult to disentangle the effect of world turbulence from that of exchange-rate volatility.

It appears preferable to explore the impact of exchange rate arrangements on the various strands of the cohesion process separately. This is done in the following six sub-sections.

3.1. Growth in the encompassing European economy and the cohesion process

While the underlying causes are not fully understood, it is well established that real convergence proceeds most rapidly when the wider encompassing (world) economy is performing well (Williamson, 1995). This is exemplified by the rapid pace of convergence in the 1960-73 period seen in Figure 4.1. If EMU is indeed beneficial for the core European economies, therefore, this will automatically strengthen the tendency towards real convergence. If monetary union proves to have been inadvisable, of course, the opposite conclusion emerges.

3.2. The relationship between nominal and real convergence

Fischer (1993) explores the role of macroeconomic stability in the growth process. The following findings are of particular relevance:

> The strongest result . . . is the consistent negative correlation between inflation and growth. Inflation is negatively associated with both capital accumulation and productivity growth. There is a strong positive correlation between the budget surplus and growth, with the evidence suggesting some influence of the surplus on capital accumulation and a stronger effect on the rate of growth of productivity. (p. 502).

Again convergence is likely to be hastened if further expansion in the overall EU economy is promoted by the lower inflation and reduced budget deficits that appear likely under EMU. Note though that the greatest gains from nominal stability will go to those countries that have traditionally been furthest from fulfilling the Maastricht criteria, and this category includes all the cohesion countries, as seen in Table 4.3.

Table 4.3.   *Positions in regard to the Maastricht criteria, 1981-90*

	CPI inflation 1981-1990	Av. Net borrowing by govt. as % of GDP, 1981-90
Greece	18.3	8.7
Portugal	17.3	6.1
Spain	9.3	4.5
Ireland	7.1	8.4
Italy	10.0	11.2
EU15	6.5	4.1*

Note: * excludes Luxembourg.

Source: European Commission (1997)

It was partly in recognition of the dangers of fiscal cutbacks for public investment in the periphery that Structural Funds allocations were increased as part of the Maastricht agreement.[8]

3.3. Interest rates, investment and periphery growth

De Long and Summers (1992) identify interest-sensitive equipment investment as crucial for growth, so that if real interest rates fall for those periphery economies participating in EMU, growth should be stimulated.[9] Table 4.4 reveals that real interest rates have tended to be high in the periphery when account is taken of the distorting effects of the very high inflation that prevailed in Greece and Portugal during the 1980s.

Table 4.4.   Real interest rates, 1981-90

	Real short-term interest rates
Greece	-0.9
Portugal	-0.1
Spain	5.6
Ireland	5.5
Italy	5.0
EU15	4.2

Note: Nominal rates as in European Commission (1997), less CPI inflation.

Also, as mentioned earlier, periphery financial markets tend to be underdeveloped relative to those of the core, and since periphery enterprises tend to be small they provide a captive market. EMU is likely to rectify these problems through integrating European financial markets, and so periphery investment may receive an especially strong stimulus.

3.4. Exchange-rate arrangements, trade and FDI

Since trade tends to be more important to smaller economies, the savings in transactions costs for Ireland and Portugal will be larger than average.[10] Small average enterprise size will also raise transactions cost savings.[11]

Many economists argue that trade promotes growth. Hence it is important to ask whether the reduction in exchange rate variability entailed by EMU will stimulate trade. The issue has been studied by De Grauwe (1988) and Frankel and Wei (1993) among others. The general consensus is that the possibility afforded by forward markets to hedge against currency risk means that this uncertainty has only modest effects on trade volumes.

Since many investments are too long-term to be adequately hedged, though, it is possible that the adverse effects of exchange rate uncertainty might be more dramatic in the case of FDI. Morsink and Molle (1991) report such effects for FDI between EU economies. It has been argued on the other hand though that exchange risk can induce international diversification of production, in that firms with liabilities in several different currencies have an incentive to hold assets also in these currencies; some evidence of this is reported by Cushman (1988). The overall consensus from studies such as Campa and Goldberg (1995) and Huizinga (1994) is that there are statistically significant but economically minor effects of exchange rate volatility on investment.

This leads Obstfeld (1995) to conclude that 'it is not clear that exchange rate volatility *per se* has had an economically important dampening effect on trade in goods and services or capital flows'.

Some further perspective is provided by the results of surveys of the views of foreign MNCs located in Ireland. These reveal that 'the majority of companies interviewed (by the Industrial Development Agency) did not see EMU membership as being an important location determinant but, of those who saw it making an impact, the vast majority were of the view that it would encourage facilities in Ireland'.[12] Thus, even if aggregate FDI flows into Europe are affected to only a small extent, as Obstfeld posits, the effects may be particularly important for the periphery, where FDI inflows are high relative to GDP. These FDI inflows in turn play an important role in the process of real convergence (Barry and Bradley, 1997c).

3.5. Labour-market structures in the periphery

The exchange rate is a particularly useful instrument when labour markets operate inflexibly or when the migration option is not available, and the costs of entering EMU may be high under these circumstances. The European Commission (1990) argues that 'wage discipline will be more effective in a credible EMU' so that EMU will itself tend to increase labour market flexibility. It goes on to argue that 'wage adjustments are likely to come faster than otherwise' if domestic fiscal policy is no longer available to bail out a region suffering an adverse shock' (p. 149). These arguments are controversial however. Blanchard and Muet (1993), for example, found little evidence of increased wage flexibility in France as the Franc-DM peg gained in credibility.

How do core and periphery compare in terms of labour-market flexibility? Greece and Portugal have traditionally had unemployment rates below the

EU average, indicating greater labour market flexibility, even if only because of relatively underdeveloped social welfare systems and large informal or rural economies capable of expanding to take up labour market slack in the formal economy. Ireland represents an intermediate case; while Irish emigration has been high historically, the traditionally high unemployment rate would suggest an inflexible labour market.[13] The policy followed over the course of the 1990s however of unions accepting low rates of pay increase in return for tax reductions may have made the Irish labour market more flexible.[14] There is a limit to how far this process can go, however, and the fact that unions refused to countenance nominal reductions in the wake of sterling's departure from the ERM suggests that rigidities remain. With Spanish unemployment still the highest in the EU, Spain must certainly be judged to have an inflexible labour market.[15]

3.6. The structure of trade and industry in cohesion countries and the likelihood of asymmetric shocks

Small open economies clearly tend to be more specialised in production than larger economies. This may make them more vulnerable to asymmetric (region-specific) shocks.

There is a debate however over whether asymmetric shocks are largely the result of a lack of policy co-ordination (in which case the likelihood of such shocks should be diminished within EMU) or instead arise because of different trade and industry structures. Evidence on this can be gleaned from the work of Bayoumi and Eichengreen (1993, 1994) who distinguish between demand shocks, which are assumed to reflect monetary and fiscal policy, and supply shocks, which are largely independent of macro policy. For supply shocks none of the cohesion countries are identified as being suitable for monetary union with Germany. This suggests then that the periphery will continue to be hit with asymmetric shocks even if macro policies are completely harmonised across participating countries.

The European Commission (1990) suggests however that the Single Market process will cause production structures to become more similar across the EU, since 'the removal of barriers obstructing the exploitation (of economies of scale and the potential for product differentiation) will increase intra-industry integration' (p. 142). This would mean that sectoral shocks resulting from changes in tastes and technology would be less region-specific than before, reducing the usefulness of the exchange rate as an instrument of adjustment.

Krugman (1993) argues that trade integration is more likely to cause regional concentration of industrial activities however.[16] He points to car production, which is much more highly concentrated in the US, with its long history of free internal trade, than it is in Europe.

Brülhart (1998b), in a survey of the evidence on trade integration and industrial location, notes the importance of distinguishing between increasing-returns (IRS) sectors, which are the topic of the debate between Krugman and the European Commission, and constant-returns sectors, the location of which is more likely to be driven by factor costs and comparative advantage.

As Ireland is by far the most open of the economies of the EU periphery we can perhaps draw some implications from its recent history for future developments elsewhere in the periphery. FDI inflows into Ireland have tended to be in modern sectors characterised by some degree of increasing returns. For this reason, and because the strength of the inflows contributed to the crowding-out of traditional industry, the economy's production structure has been substantially modernised and become more similar to that of the EU core.[17] This reduces the likelihood of asymmetric sectoral shocks.[18]

Note though that traditional trade theory predicts that trade integration will cause core and periphery to specialise in different types of industries, and that this has indeed been happening in sectors whose location depends primarily on factor cost. Thus Brülhart (1998a) notes that the strongest increase in concentration in the EU has been in labour-intensive sectors, which have been shifting to peripheral regions other than Ireland.

Trade integration therefore generates two opposing pressures on production structures in the periphery. The first is the standard trade liberalisation effect that favours the geographical concentration of traditional industries, and that will make regions more prone to asymmetric shocks; this effect appears likely to dominate at low levels of FDI. The second force we might term the FDI effect.[19] Once the FDI presence in a peripheral economy passes some critical level, further integration appears likely to harmonise factor endowments and production structures across core and periphery, reducing the excessive vulnerability of the periphery to sector-specific shocks.[20] Somewhat paradoxically though this increases the country's vulnerability to a different set of shocks: those that change the relative attractiveness of different regions as bases for FDI inflows. Economic union then is reducing Ireland's vulnerability to one set of shocks and increasing it to another, while increasing the vulnerability of Greece, Spain and Portugal to asymmetric sectoral shocks.

4. CONCLUSIONS

Our analysis suggests that the economic union aspect of EMU promotes, rather than inhibits, cohesion. Recent trade integration appears to have

favoured the periphery more than the core; firstly because indigenous industry in a number of the periphery countries was favourably positioned in many
of the sectors that integration was deemed likely to affect, and secondly (and
more importantly) because the periphery countries have increased their
shares of FDI inflows. Of the four cohesion countries, only Greece appears to
face the possibility of divergence rather than convergence from continuing
trade integration. This appears to be due to macroeconomic instability and
inadequate infrastructure.[21]

Structural Funds allocations were almost doubled from 1988 and doubled
again from 1994. In part this was because of fears that trade integration and
monetary union would inhibit real convergence. We have argued that trade
integration is unlikely to have done so. What of monetary union? We summarise the general relationship between monetary union and cohesion first
and then discuss some particular details that arise in the cases of Ireland and
Greece.

The first general point to make is that if monetary union is successful, as
its protagonists clearly expect, then cohesion is likely to be promoted, because real convergence proceeds more rapidly during good times than bad.
Furthermore, the periphery countries, during the 1980s at least, showed
themselves to be less disciplined with respect to inflation and budgetary policy than the core countries, and so have more to gain from the imposition of
external discipline that EMU entails. Real interest rates also tended to be
higher and financial structures less developed than in the core, so again on
both these grounds the periphery may gain relatively more from EMU.

The effects are more ambiguous when we come to consider the issues that
arise in the optimal currency area literature. We know that maintaining the
exchange rate as an instrument of economic policy is less important if labour
markets are flexible. Greece and Portugal have traditionally had unemployment rates below the EU average, which would suggest considerable labour
market flexibility, though the formal sector could still suffer from the loss of
the exchange rate instrument. The Irish labour market might traditionally
have been classified as inflexible on the basis of the country's high unemployment. That may now be changing, though there are reasons for suspect-
ing that that judgement may be premature. The Spanish labour market appears to remain inflexible. On this issue the differences between periphery
countries may be greater than the similarities.

The other important issue is the vulnerability of the various economies to
asymmetric shocks. We referred to the work of Bayoumi and Eichengreen
which finds that cohesion-country supply shocks tend to be uncorrelated with
those of Germany. While giving up the exchange rate under these circumstances may not matter too much for Portugal, if its labour market is indeed

very flexible, it may represent far greater problems for Ireland and more particularly for Spain.

The fact that production structures are asymmetric between core and periphery, and that shocks to sectors in which the core is specialised are more likely to be met by a monetary-policy response, means that periphery economies are more vulnerable to shocks within EMU. They have more to gain then from increased labour-market flexibility or from a move towards fiscal federalism.

Is the process of economic union likely to increase or reduce the extent of asymmetries between core and periphery? Traditional trade theory suggests the former. For example, the migration of factor-cost-sensitive sectors to the periphery would increase the asymmetry of production structures still further. The implications of 'new' trade theory, on the other hand, can go in either direction. The Irish experience suggests though that if FDI inflows are sufficiently strong then asymmetries between core and periphery may be reduced. Our tentative conclusion is that Ireland has surpassed the critical level of FDI presence in the economy for economic union to shift its industrial structure closer to that of the EU core. While this reduces the vulnerability of the economy to asymmetric sectoral shocks, it increases its vulnerability to shocks affecting FDI location decisions. For the rest of the EU periphery, on the other hand, economic union under current circumstances appears likely to increase its vulnerability to asymmetric sectoral shocks. This could present special difficulties for Spain, given the labour-market rigidities prevailing there.

Finally we come to the particular circumstances of Ireland and Greece. Ireland suffers two adverse effects if its single major trading partner, the UK, fails to adopt the single currency. Firstly it means that the transactions-cost savings for Ireland of adopting the euro are substantially reduced, and secondly it raises considerably the vulnerability of the economy to asymmetric shocks, since sterling-euro fluctuations that violate PPP represent such a shock. These effects must reduce considerably the benefits to Ireland of adopting the euro.

Greece, of course, is in a different position altogether since it is excluded from EMU participation at present. While it could possibly be argued that this is appropriate for Greece, given the extent of its trade with non-EMU economies, it seems clear from our analysis that Greece is losing out on many of the benefits of EU membership through macroeconomic instability. This manifests itself particularly through its negative impact on FDI inflows, which reduces the tendency towards real convergence and leaves the economy more vulnerable to sector-specific shocks. Greece would have much to gain therefore from subjecting itself to the externally-imposed discipline associated with the Maastricht criteria and EMU participation.

NOTES

1. Helpful discussions with Marius Brülhart are gratefully acknowledged.
2. The cohesion-country convergence line lies to the left of that representing the other economies, even when human capital is controlled for.
3. Data on the shared characteristics of cohesion countries is presented in Barry, Bradley and Duggan (1997a).
4. Matsuyama (1992) presents a theoretical model consistent with this.
5. IRS sectors are identified in Barry (1996).
6. These predicted first-round effects are broadly consistent with those reported in Bliss and Braga de Macedo (1990). In that study Viñals *et al.*, for Spain, and Katseli, for Greece, predict strong increases in imports with less favourable effects for exports, while Braga de Macedo is more optimistic with respect to the Portuguese position.
7. Data on FDI flows are notoriously unreliable. Although it does not show up in the OECD data, US FDI flows to Ireland certainly increased dramatically from the early 1990s, while Monti (1996) asserts that the same hold true for intra-EU FDI.
8. The severe restrictions on deficit spending imposed by the Stability Pact however will impact on the financing of public investment projects. This could have serious consequences for the periphery countries, which have relatively poor infrastructure and high rates of return on investment in human capital.
9. Baker, Fitz Gerald and Honohan (1996) argue that there will be real interest gains, for Ireland at least, because pre-EMU Irish pound interest rates were on average much higher than needed to compensate for actual exchange rate declines. They argue that these 'excess returns' will fall in EMU, either as a credibility bonus or through the removal of the premium required for the risk and unfamiliarity of dealing in a small currency.
10. Greece, as a small economy, is unusual in that exports and imports combined comprise only 42 percent of GDP, compared to an EU average of 59 percent. Ireland and Portugal stand at 134 and 75 percent respectively, while Spain stands at 53 percent; European Commission (1997).
11. For Ireland these effects will be substantially reduced if the country's major trading partner, the UK, does not adopt the single currency, particularly since it tends to be relatively smaller exporters that concentrate on UK markets.
12. Private communication to the author from Forfás, the Policy and Advisory Board for Industrial Development in Ireland.
13. Honohan (1992) finds the equilibrium gap between Irish and UK unemployment rates to be 4 percentage points; when Irish unemployment is higher by this amount there is no net flow of migrants between the two jurisdictions.
14. An alternative view is expressed by Fitz Gerald (1998) who argues that the fact that Irish wages caught up to British levels over the course of the 1980s removed much of the upward pressure that had been driving them.
15. Estimated Phillips curve coefficients, representing the percentage change in wages that results from a 1 percentage point increase in unemployment, do indeed differ across the various periphery economies, and suggest a similar picture to that described in the text; Barry *et al.* (1997b).
16. As Bayoumi and Eichengreen (1994) note however, this does not necessarily reduce the desirability of EMU, since a high degree of specialisation implies that floating exchange rates may be very disruptive of living standards!
17. This applies to services as well as manufacturing. Keeble, Offord and Walker (1988) note the distinction between core and periphery in terms of the ratio of producer-services employment to consumer-services. Developments in both Irish sectors are detailed in Barry, Bradley and Duggan (1997a).
18. This conclusion should not be overstated however. Strong FDI flows into Chemicals and Metals and Engineering have shifted Ireland's industrial structure towards that of the core,

but the economy has become overspecialised (relative to the core) in Office Machinery and Instrument Engineering (O'Malley, 1992; Barry, 1996).
19. The author's current research confirms that Spain and Portugal follow the Irish pattern in this regard; i.e. that the FDI inflows cause the sectoral structure of their manufacturing industries to become more similar to that of the core.
20. Dumais *et al.* (1997) find that the decrease in average industry concentration in the US between 1972 and 1992 is mainly due to new plants locating in the periphery.
21. Though Greece's infrastructure in 1986 was rated more highly than Portugal's, Barry *et al.* (1997b) find that CSF spending has had more beneficial effects in Portugal.

REFERENCES

Baker, T., J. Fitz Gerald and P. Honohan (1996), *Economic Implications for Ireland of EMU*, Dublin: Economic and Social Research Institute.

Barry, F. (1996), 'Peripherality in Economic Geography and Modern Growth Theory: Evidence from Ireland's Adjustment to Free Trade', *World Economy*, **19**, 345-365.

Barry, F. (1998), 'Does EMU Make Sense for Europe?', in J. Bradley (ed.), *Regional Economic and Policy Impacts of EMU: The Case of Northern Ireland*, Belfast: Northern Ireland Economic Council; also available as Working Paper 97/25, University College Dublin.

Barry, F., J. Bradley and D. Duggan (1997a), 'Economic Structure and Structural Change in the EU Periphery', in B. Fynes and S. Ennis (eds), *Competing from the Periphery*, Dublin: Oaktree Press.

Barry, F., J. Bradley, A. Hannan, J. McCartan and S. Sosvilla-Rivero (1997b), *The Single Market Review: Aggregate and Regional Impact – The cases of Greece, Spain, Ireland and Portugal*, London: Kogan Page in association with the European Commission.

Barry, F. and J. Bradley (1997c), 'FDI and Trade: the Irish Host-Country Experience', *Economic Journal*, **107**, 1798-1811.

Bayoumi, T. and B. Eichengreen (1993), 'Shocking Aspects of European Monetary Integration', in F. Torres and F. Giavazzi (eds), *Adjustment and Growth in the European Monetary Union*, Cambridge: Cambridge University Press.

Bayoumi, T. and B. Eichengreen (1994), *One Money or Many? Analysing the Prospects for Monetary Unification in Various Parts of the World*, Princeton Studies in International Finance No. 76.

Blanchard, O. and P. Muet (1993), 'Competitiveness through Disinflation: An Assessment of the French Macroeconomic Strategy', *Economic Policy*, **16**, 11-56.

Bliss, C. and J. Braga de Macedo (eds), *Unity with Diversity in the European Economy*, Cambridge: Cambridge University Press.

Brülhart, M. (1998a), 'Trading Places: Industrial Specialisation in the European Union', *Journal of Common Market Studies*, **36**, 319-346.

Brülhart, M. (1998b), 'Economic Geography, Industry Location and Trade: The Evidence', *World Economy*, forthcoming.

Buigues, P., F. Ilzkovitz and J.-F. Lebrun (1990), 'The Impact of the Internal Market by Industrial Sector', *European Economy*, special edition.

Campa, J. and L.S. Goldberg (1995), 'Investment in Manufacturing, Exchange Rates and External Exposure', *Journal of International Economics*, **38**, 297-320.

Cushman, D. (1988), 'Exchange Rate Uncertainty and Foreign Direct Investment in the United States', *Weltwirtschaftliches Archiv*, **124**, 322-336.

De Grauwe, P. (1988), 'Exchange Rate Variability and the Slowdown in the Growth of International Trade', *International Monetary Fund Staff Papers*, **35**, 63-84.

De Long, J. and L. Summers (1992), 'Equipment Investment and Economic Growth: How Strong is the Nexus?', *Brookings Papers on Economic Activity*, **1992**, 157-199.

Dumais, G., G. Ellison and E. Glaeser (1997), 'Geographic Concentration as a Dynamic Process', *NBER Working Paper*, No. 6270.

Emerson, M., M. Aujean, M. Catinat, P. Goybet and A. Jacquemin (1988), *The Economics of 1992: The E.C. Commission's Assessment of the Economic Effects of Completing the Internal Market*, Oxford: Oxford University Press.

European Commission (1990), 'One Market, One Money: An Evaluation of the Potential Benefits and Costs of Forming an Economic and Monetary Union', *European Economy*, No. 44.

European Commission (1997), 'Statistical Annex', *European Economy*, No. 63.

Fitz Gerald, J. (1998), 'Wage Formation and the Labour Market', in F. Barry (ed.), *Understanding Ireland's Economic Growth*, London: Macmillan, forthcoming.

Fischer, S. (1993), 'The Role of Macroeconomic Factors in Growth', *Journal of Monetary Economics*, **32**, 485-512.

Frankel, J. and S.J. Wei (1993), 'Trade Blocs and Currency Blocs', in G. de la Dehesa *et al.* (eds), *The Monetary Future of Europe*, London: CEPR.

Grossman, G. and E. Helpman (1991), *Innovation and Growth in the Global Economy*, Cambridge, Mass.: MIT Press.

Honohan, P. (1992), 'The Link between Irish and UK Unemployment', *Quarterly Economic Commentary*, Economic and Social Research Institute, Spring, 33-44.

Huizinga, J. (1994), 'Exchange Rate Volatility, Uncertainty and Investment: An Empirical Investigation', in L. Leiderman and A. Razin (eds), *Capital Mobility: The Impact on Consumption, Investment and Growth*, Cambridge: Cambridge University Press.

Keeble, D., J. Offord and S. Walker (1988), 'Peripheral Regions in a Community of 12 Member States', Brussels: European Commission.

Krugman, P. (1993), 'Lessons of Massachusetts for EMU', in F. Torres and F. Giavazzi (eds), *Adjustment and Growth in the European Monetary Union*, Cambridge: Cambridge University Press.

Krugman, P. and A. Venables (1990), 'Integration and the Competitiveness of Peripheral Industry', in C. Bliss and J. Braga de Macedo (eds), *op. cit.*

Larre, B. and R. Torres (1991), 'Is Convergence a Spontaneous Process? The Experience of Spain, Portugal and Greece', *OECD Economic Studies*, **16**, 169-198.

Matsuyama, K. (1992), 'Agricultural Productivity, Comparative Advantage and Economic Growth', *Journal of Economic Theory*, **58**, 317-334.

Monti, M. (1996), *The Single Market and Tomorrow's Europe: A Progress Report from the European Commission*, London: Kogan Page in association with the European Commission.

Morsink, R. and W. Molle (1991), 'Direct Investment and Monetary Integration', *European Economy – Reports and Studies*, No. 1, 36-55.

Obstfeld, M. (1995), 'International Currency Experience: New Lessons and Lessons Relearned', *Brookings Papers on Economic Activity*, **1995**, 119-220.

Ó Gráda, C. and K. O'Rourke (1996), 'Irish Economic Growth, 1945-88', in N. Crafts and G. Toniolo (eds), *European Economic Growth*, Cambridge: Cambridge University Press.

O'Malley, E. (1992), 'Industrial Structure and Economies of Scale in the Context of 1992', in J. Bradley *et al.* (eds), *The Role of the Structural Funds: Analysis of Consequences for Ireland in the Context of 1992*, Dublin: ESRI.

Williamson, J.G. (1995), 'The Evolution of Global Labor Markets since 1830: Background Evidence and Hypotheses', *Explorations in Economic History*, **32**, 141-196.

5. The European Union and Regional Convergence in Spain: a New Approach

José Villaverde and Blanca Sanchez-Robles[1]

1. INTRODUCTION

The economic and institutional features of Spain have experienced deep changes in the last decades. These changes made the catching up process with other Western European countries possible. The Spanish real per capita GDP has increased from 57.2 per cent of the European Union average in 1960 to 76.2 per cent in 1996 (Fundación Banco Bilbao-Vizcaya, 1997). Predictions for the near future may be regarded as optimistic: although the connection between nominal convergence and real convergence is not straightforward, depending on the type of shock impinging on the economy (Viñals, 1994), it is expected that the fulfilment of the Maastricht criteria and the subsequent future integration of Spain in the EMU will draw Spanish per capita output still closer to average European levels.

Monetary integration is however, more specifically, looked upon with a certain amount of concern by both national policymakers and population, since the impact of the single currency on regional disparities in Spain is not clear at all. As is well known, from a theoretical approach it is not possible to quantify accurately the net benefits and costs that the integration process entails for a particular country or region.

This chapter intends to shed some light on this issue by exploring the recent performance of the Spanish regions, in order to characterise their convergence pattern and get some insights about the long run equilibrium position to which they are possibly heading. The analysis is pursued in the framework provided by a stylised dynamic growth model. Some preliminary conclusions about the main determinants of the current relative positions of the regions, together with predictions for the near future, will be inferred with the help of it.

The structure of the chapter is as follows: section 2 gives a brief overview of the Spanish evolution in the last four decades. In section 3, some theoretical considerations about the relevant concept of long run equilibrium, which will be the basis of the empirical part of the chapter, are provided. Section 4 comments on the data used and describes the empirical estimates of the dynamic steady state that have been obtained. Section 5 summarises some implications of the results, and finally section 6 offers some concluding remarks.

2. THE RECENT SPANISH PERFORMANCE: SOME FACTS

2.1. The global evolution of the Spanish economy

It may prove useful to place the regional analysis that will be performed later on in the broader framework of Spanish global performance.

As it was said above, the last 40 years have seen a progressive narrowing of the distance between Spain and most advanced European countries; this process, however, has neither been uniformly distributed over time nor did it relate equally to the whole of the Spanish territory.

As regards the time profile of this convergence to the leader countries, it could be stated that the bulk of the post-war catching up process of the Spanish economy took place before the mid-1970s, while the relative distance between Spanish per capita GDP and the European average increased during the recession that followed both oil shocks. This divergent trend reverted in the mid-1980s, when the gap started to decline again, although at a lower rate that in the 1960s and early 1970s. A thorough analysis of the evolution over time of the Spanish economy is beyond the scope of this chapter, but some ideas may nevertheless be provided succinctly in order to help understand this growth process both at the aggregate and regional levels

According to some recent contributions, the main factors that explain the Spanish growth process in the second half of the 20th century are the following:

- An intense pattern of investment, considered in a broad sense: i.e. not only in physical but also in public and human capital (De la Fuente and Da Rocha 1994; Argimón *et al.*, 1994). Both public and human capital endowments at the beginning of the 1960s were comparatively low, and have been considerably increased; thus, they now exhibit levels that are more comparable to those achieved in other advanced European countries.

- A technological catching up process with the leader countries (Cuñado, 1997).
- A progressive tendency towards the internationalisation and liberalisation of the economic and institutional set-up (in areas such as trade and financial services) and the pursuit of macroeconomic stability (Raymond, 1995; Bajo and Sosvilla-Rivero, 1995; Sanchez-Robles, 1997, 1998).

Several empirical analyses developed within the growth accounting framework convey similar messages, attributing the main contribution to GDP growth to total factor productivity growth (the so-called Solow residual) and, to a lesser extent, to capital accumulation (Suárez, 1992; Nicolini and Zilibotti, 1996).

The gradual process towards the economic integration of Spain in Europe is confirmed by some basic indicators: the evolution of the ratio '(exports + imports)/2GDP' has increased from 17.9 in 1988 to 26 in 1996 (Villaverde, 1997). Intra-industry trade, as captured by an aggregate index, has also increased for the same period (Carrera and Villaverde, 1998).

From the theoretical point of view, the impact of economic integration on economic growth is still controversial, and therefore predictions about its benefits or its drawbacks will generally differ on the basis of the underlying theoretical models which are considered. Generally speaking, neo-classical models predict that the integration will modify only the steady state per capita income (*level effect*) and therefore the impact of the integration will be modest. In contrast, endogenous growth models – through a relaxation of one or more neo-classical features of the economy – may imply larger effects of integration, and could conceivably alter the rate of growth of output in the steady state (*growth rate effect*).

Different explanations may account for this greater impact in the context of endogenous models. The most obvious one is that integration will promote international trade among the members of the agreement. Thus, larger markets will allow the exploitation of scale economies while more dynamic competition will foster gains in efficiency and in competitiveness.[2] Another rationale is provided by Rivera-Batiz and Romer (1991), who show how trade between countries or regions of similar features – this is, in fact, the case of an economic integration *stricto sensu* – will allow exploitation of increasing returns associated with the R&D sector.[3]

Indeed, one feasible mechanism by which integration may foster growth is through the appearance of externalities. If externalities indeed appear foremost at the national or local level, then it is conceivable that they may induce faster growth only in some countries or regions, since firms will tend to concentrate in those areas in which the spillover effects of knowledge (Romer, 1986), infrastructure (Barro, 1990) or a large demand due to agglomeration (Krugman, 1991) are more noticeable. Other areas, instead, may suffer from stagnation and diverge from the leaders.

However, if externalities operate mainly at the international level (Coe and Helpman, 1995), then integration may foster growth even in relatively laggard countries or areas. This last assertion may be combined with the technological diffusion mechanism (as designed, for example, by Barro and Sala i Martin, 1997). Accordingly, this last channel may be regarded as a *contagion* force (Baumol, 1994) promoting convergence among countries or regions. The rationale underlying this process is easy to grasp: since it is cheaper to imitate than to innovate, laggard countries may benefit from their relatively backward position and grow even faster than the technological leaders, although this process is not automatic if there is some degree of persistence in technology leadership in particular products (see Meeusen and Rayp, 1998). Imports of intermediate capital goods that incorporate new technology may, in turn, be a specific way by which these links operate (Lee, 1995).[4]

From a theoretical approach, therefore, the impact of integration on a particular country or region is not unambiguously determined. Empirical evidence on the links between economic integration and growth is not conclusive at this stage either, but there are already some studies that suggest a positive and significant effect of European integration on growth at the national level (see, for example, for the Spanish and the French cases Cuñado, 1997, and Coe and Moghadam, 1993, respectively). In particular, the beneficial integration-effect for the Spanish economy can be attributed to the catching up process that has been facilitated by technological diffusion. This insight will be further considered below.

2.2. Some considerations at the regional level

The empirical analysis of regional convergence has gained some momentum in the last few years, since the, at least expected, homogeneity in parameters and data across regions allows circumvention of some practical problems that arise in cross-country convergence studies. The Spanish case has not been an exception in this regard, and therefore much research effort has been already devoted to this issue. Many questions remain still unanswered, and some results are not, by any means, clear-cut. Nonetheless, we aim to survey here some – in our opinion – relevant results.

First, most recent contributions state that the convergence of Spain to other advanced countries has been accompanied by a reduction of the re-

gional disparities within Spanish regions, as measured by the evolution of the
σ-convergence indicator (Villaverde, 1997). However, the dispersion among
Spanish regions has not decreased steadily, but only until the early 1980s, to
stagnate thereafter. Figure 5.1 shows a plot of the distribution of output per
worker in two selected years, 1980 and 1992. Productivity levels are considered relative to the Spanish average. The distribution is slightly smoother in
1992 for the poorer regions but steeper for the last deciles (richer regions),
pointing to a reduction of the disparities at the bottom of the income distribution and to an increase of inequality in the upper third.

Figure 5.1.   Relative output per worker, 1980 versus 1992

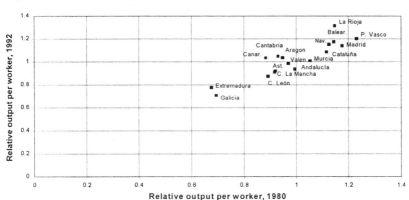

In this regard, some authors (De la Fuente, 1996; García, Raymond and
Villaverde, 1995) have suggested that the forces of convergence among
Spanish regions are exhausted, since the various regions may already be close
to their steady state. This issue has important practical consequences since it
could be interpreted as suggesting the future persistence of regional inequalities unless important structural reforms are carried out.

Some contributions (Sala i Martín, 1996; Mas *et al.*, 1995a) have however
provided evidence about the existence of absolute β-convergence among
Spanish regions. Other empirical studies (Canova and Marcet, 1995; Dolado
et al., 1994; De la Fuente, 1996) instead have dismissed the hypothesis of
absolute β-convergence of Spanish regions and provinces, suggesting instead
that conditional convergence is a more accurate description of the long run
evolution of these units. This assertion is also supported by Villaverde and
Sanchez-Robles (1998), who have found different convergence clubs within
Spanish regions for some selected periods. This result implies, in turn, that
Spanish regions are headed towards different steady states, and therefore that
they are not expected to reach a common level of per capita income auto-

matically by the sole action of traditional convergence mechanisms such as the diminishing marginal productivity of capital.

Some studies have pointed to a set of variables that seem to have had relevance in conditioning the convergence process and therefore in determining the steady states levels of output and productivity of the various regions. Some of the variables are public capital (Mas *et al.*, 1995a), technological catching up and re-allocation among sectors (De la Fuente, 1996), human capital (De la Fuente and Vives, 1995; Dolado *et al.*, 1994) and migrations (García, 1997).

Part of the regional inequality in Spain is also reflected in the behaviour of unemployment rates (De la Fuente and Vives, 1995), the dispersion of which has increased during the 1980s (Villaverde, 1997). This fact, in turn, may be related to severe rigidities in the labour market and in the bargaining process, resulting in uniform rates of growth of wages across the nation despite regional differentials in productivity. As Faini (1995) argues convincingly, there seems to be scope for regional measures oriented towards the removal of distortions in goods, services and labour markets in specific geographical units. These measures should complement other traditional instruments of regional policy such as the provision of human and public capital.

Two empirical questions arise at this point: first, taking into account its recent evolution, how will the pattern of Spanish regional convergence or divergence look like in the following years? Second, which are the main factors – including international considerations and, in particular, European monetary integration – determining the steady state to which a specific region converges? The rest of the chapter will deal with these issues, but first it may be useful to clarify the particular steady-state concept used.

3. THE STEADY STATE: A THEORETICAL FRAMEWORK

In growth models, the steady state or long run equilibrium roughly corresponds to a situation in which the relevant variables of the economy grow at a constant rate.

In practical terms, it is not easy to estimate the steady state to which a particular economy is converging, especially because of the difficulty of figuring out the correct model underlying its dynamic behaviour. Nonetheless, Jones (1997) has devised a useful procedure in order to overcome this problem and obtain an approximation to the steady state. He has applied this method to a set of developed and developing countries. The implicit assumption in his analytical and empirical apparatus is that long run values of per capita income may be inferred from recent past data, since a country's fundamentals regarding preferences and technology show strong persistence over time. We shall apply this insight to the Spanish regions.

As far as the theoretical framework of this technique is concerned, the starting point is the neo-classical growth model as used by Mankiw, Romer and Weil (1992) (equation 5.1).

$$Y(t) = K(t)^{\alpha} \left[A(t) H(t) \right]^{1-\alpha}$$
$$0 < \alpha < 1 \tag{5.1}$$

Y is output, A is the level of technological progress – proceeding at a constant rate g – and α is the share of capital in production. We assume for simplicity that the technology is the same in all sectors of the economy, and that there is perfect competition in product and factor markets. The restriction of α being strictly less than one is in accord not only with the conventional presentation of these models but also with some empirical evidence: Cuñado (1997) has shown that the marginal productivity of physical capital in Spain is decreasing, this result being robust to alternative definitions of capital accumulation.

H is human capital or skilled labour. The production function in this model, while keeping the main neo-classical features (non-increasing returns of reproducible inputs) captures also an important feature of the new growth models, by means of the introduction of human capital H. We can assume (as in Lucas, 1988), that human capital is a rival and excludable good that accumulates by means of education. A straightforward way to capture this idea is to model it as follows:

$$H(t) = e^{\phi m(t)} L(t) , \tag{5.2}$$

in which m stands for the number of years devoted to education, ϕ is the rate of return to education investment and L is the total of employed population (raw labour input).

In order to alleviate notation, we suppress the time argument and divide by L so that lowercase letters represent per worker variables, i.e.:

$$y \equiv \frac{Y}{L} .$$

This last procedure has the useful advantage of providing a direct interpretation of the results in terms of productivity.

If the economy is assumed (for now) to be closed and without public sector, then the dynamics of the capital-labour ratio are of course described as follows:

$$\dot{k} = sy - (\delta + n)k \quad , \tag{5.3}$$

where δ is the depreciation rate, n stands for population growth and s is the (constant) share of output devoted to gross investment.

As is common in this kind of model, in the steady state the growth rate of the capital-labour ratio is equal to the rate of technological progress g. Simple algebraic manipulation in equation 5.3 allows to compute the long run equilibrium growth path of labour productivity, y^*, as equation 5.4:

$$y^* = \left(\frac{s}{n+g+\delta} \right)^{\frac{\alpha}{1-\alpha}} Ah \quad , \tag{5.4}$$

where the expression for the level of human capital per worker is obtained from equation 5.2 and yields

$$h = e^{\phi m} \quad .$$

As equation 5.4 shows, the steady state level of output per worker depends on the level of saving, technology and human capital, and on the rate of technological progress, population growth and depreciation, together with the elasticity of output with respect to capital, α. This equation will be the benchmark of our empirical analysis.

4. DATA AND EMPIRICAL RESULTS

4.1. Data

The empirical part of this chapter carries out basically the estimation of equation 5.4, first in a baseline case and afterwards specifying several alternative assumptions.

We have used data for the 17 Spanish regions, in the period 1980-92. Output series have been obtained from the GAV (Gross Added Value) data at constant prices published by the Ministry of Economy. Total and employed population series have been taken from the TEMPUS database (INE), and physical and human capital from Fundación Banco Bilbao-Vizcaya (1996) and Mas *et al.* (1995b).

In order to construct the series of human capital, and according to some recent studies (Psacharopoulos, 1994), we have taken the value 0.1 as the rate of return to a year of schooling (ϕ in equation 5.2). The number of years devoted to education have been approximated by the fraction of the employed population that have completed studies at a Bachelor's level. According to Jones (1997), the proportion of the population with a certain level of studies may be an acceptable forecast of the future level of human capital.

The levels of A have been computed as labour-augmenting total factor productivity (Solow's Residual), from a traditional growth accounting exercise applied to the production function in equation 5.1, written in per worker magnitudes.

Finally, other parameters have been given standard and constant values across regions, such as $\alpha = 1/3$ (in accord with De la Fuente, 1996) and $g+\delta = 0.075$ (following Jones, 1997).

4.2. Empirical estimates of the steady state

4.2.a. Baseline case

As it was stated above, some authors have argued that Spanish regions seem to be already rather close to their steady state values of per capita income and productivity. De la Fuente (1996) goes one step further and provides some estimates of the steady state levels of productivity that – interestingly – display values that are not far from the levels that were reached in 1991. Agreeing with the results of this research, we have assumed that the values of some relevant variables in 1992 may be used in order to calculate the steady state of the Spanish regions. Therefore, we have estimated the steady state level of productivity by means of computing equation 5.4, with the values of A, s and h that correspond to 1992 levels. As the rate of population growth, though, the average for the 1980-92 period has been used. All computations have been made in relative terms with respect to the national average.

Figure 5.2 shows the predicted steady state distribution, which is not very different from the one implied by Figure 5.1: disparities tend to decrease in the lower part of the distribution (poorer regions) but increase for the richer regions. The value of the dispersion of productivity that corresponds to this distribution is 0.19, which is indeed very close to the figure of 0.20, around which σ-convergence has tended to stagnate from the mid-1980s onwards. The relative position of the various regions is rather similar for 1992 and the predicted steady-state values.

Figure 5.2.   Steady-state distribution, baseline

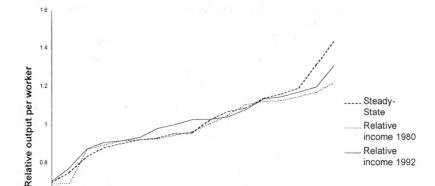

Table 5.1 displays the values of R^2 obtained from a linear regression of the 1992 level of productivity on its steady-state level. The interpretation of this figure should be made with caution, however, since it may be argued that the correlation between both productivity levels may be an artefact of the procedure followed in order to estimate the steady state level. In any case, the high value (0.87) of the coefficient of determination confirms the message conveyed by the σ–convergence indicator, in the sense that regions in 1992 were already near their long run equilibria.

Finally, the table also reports the σ–values corresponding to the consumption per worker distribution, where consumption has been computed as one minus the savings rate times output per worker. Its dispersion is slightly smaller than the one corresponding to productivity in each scenario, as reported in the last column of Table 5.1. This may be explained by the fact that consumption is more related to disposable income than to productivity. According to some estimates (Villaverde, 1997), regional disposable income disparities in Spain are lower than those of productivity, due to the redistribution policies implemented by the state.

Table 5.1.   *Regional productivity and distribution of consumption:*
alternative scenarios

Scenario	GDP		Consumption	
	Sigma	R^2	Sigma	R^2
Data for 1980	0.155	–	0.157	–
Data for 1992	0.156	–	0.135	–
Steady-state distributions:				
(1) Base model	0.194	0.872	0.164	0.877
(2) $A \geq 1$	0.132	0.460	0.112	0.521
(3) Same A	0.056	0.135	0.029	0.226
(4) $A \geq 1$, same h	0.128	0.424	0.108	0.487
(5) Same n	0.193	0.900	0.162	0.900
(6) Open economy	0.219	0.918	0.189	0.936

4.2.b. Alternative steady-state scenarios

The steady-state distribution may be estimated under different assumptions concerning the values of the relevant parameters. This exercise – the construction of fictitious or *virtual* economies, in the terminology of Marimón and Zilibotti (1996) – may shed some light on the reasons that are behind the persistence of regional disparities. Case number 2 assumes a more rapid process of technological diffusion among regions. This feature is captured by means of letting those regions that are below the national average catch up with that value. The more productive regions, however, keep their positive differences with regard to the average. In this particular instance the estimated dispersion diminishes to 0.13 (Table 5.1, row 4).

Case 3, in turn, allows for perfect technological diffusion and considers the same A for all regions. The predicted distribution is characterised by a process of homogenisation among regions which is almost perfect. The dispersion of productivity decreases to 0.056. Not surprisingly, in this case the coefficient of determination displays a lower value (0.135).

It is interesting to compare the predicted outcomes of these two last virtual economies. The main message that this comparison conveys is that the relative reduction of the divergence – as measured by the standard deviation of productivity – is smaller if it is especially the group of relative laggard regions which converge fast. The estimated σ is not very different from the baseline case in scenario 2, implying that most of the divergence is the result of the distance of the richer regions from the average. The dispersion decreases dramatically, though, if all regions converge in productivity (scenario 3) while maintaining their differences regarding saving habits, population growth and human capital.

Case 4 considers a slight variation of case 2: the assumption regarding technology flows replicates case 2, but human capital is considered to be the same across regions. In this scenario the dispersion does not decrease significantly (the estimated value is 0.12). We have tried to disentangle the impact of human capital from technology, by means of estimating also a small modification of case 4. Accordingly, we have assumed that all regions maintain their technological advantages (differences in A) while imposing the restriction of having the same human capital. The outcome, however, is similar to the one obtained in case 4. These exercises imply that human capital differences do not seem to be crucial to regional disparities, at least at this stage. Indeed, our data show that autonomous communities in Spain have already reached rather similar levels of human capital (the dispersion of human capital endowments in 1992 is only 0.007).[5] Notwithstanding this fact, we should not forget that most of the analysis in this chapter conveys information about the *level effect* of the various factors that are relevant for the dynamics of the economy. As Serrano (1998) points out, human capital may also induce a *rate effect* by enhancing activities of innovation or imitation that, in turn, accelerate technical progress. In addition, high endowments of human capital in a particular area may induce further accumulation of physical capital or even attract investment from other regions, refuting the neoclassical prediction that investment should flow to those regions characterised by sparser capital endowments and larger rate of returns.

In case 5 all regions are supposed to exhibit the same population growth rate. The standard deviation for this case is 0.19, very close to the one of the baseline model.

Finally, case 6 explicitly shows the pattern of behaviour following complete monetary integration. A single currency should bring about, at least theoretically, perfect capital mobility and therefore a tendency towards the equalisation of interest rates across the countries that are in the monetary union.[6] It could be argued, however, that such an equalisation should be already apparent in the Spanish economy, since – at least presumably – factors are already mobile. Surprisingly, this is not the case: the computed marginal productivities of capital have a sizeable variance across regions, as well for the reference years 1980 and 1992, as for the predicted value in the steady state baseline case. In this last scenario, the standard deviation of the return to capital is 0.017. In particular, it is higher in the more developed autonomous communities.[7] Moreover, the difference between the return to capital in the region exhibiting its maximum (Canarias) and its minimum (Castilla La Mancha) is 0.056. Hence these data provide evidence in favour of the assertion that a further increase in the mobility of factors, and in particular capital, is still feasible within the Spanish regions,[8] therefore supporting the case for further liberalisation in specific markets.

The calculations for steady state distribution corresponding to this last case are shown in the last row of Table 5.1. The dispersion of estimated productivity is the highest of all the scenarios analysed, amounting to 0.21.

The comparison of all cases suggests that allowing for technological catching up, totally or partially, induces the largest changes with respect to the relative productivity distribution prevailing in 1992, whereas to permit equalisation of the growth rate of population, human capital or the marginal productivity of capital does not change the existing *statu quo* very much.

5. A PRELIMINARY INTERPRETATION OF THE RESULTS

The main ideas suggested by the preceding analysis may be summarised as follows:

1. The use of Jones' (1997) methodology has allowed us to confirm a prediction already pointed out by previous research: Spanish regions seem indeed to be very close to their steady state. The relative position of the 17 autonomous communities in the steady state – as captured by labour productivity – is similar to the one prevailing in recent years, with dynamic areas, such as La Rioja or Navarra, at the top of the distribution and traditionally backward areas, such as Galicia or Extremadura, at the bottom. This ranking is also in accord with the division of Spanish areas in 'convergence clubs' that was obtained in Villaverde and Sanchez-Robles (1998).

2. Technological catching up seems to be the most important factor influencing regional disparities, since allowing for complete convergence in technology levels (case 3) yields the smallest dispersion in productivity. At the same time, this scenario seems relatively far away from the present situation, according to our 1992 productivity levels, and its low correlation with the predicted steady state levels in case 3 (R^2 is 0.13). This means that there are significant differences among technology levels of the Spanish regions.

The importance of technology in determining the long run equilibria of Spanish regions agrees with other contributions (De la Fuente, 1996; Cuñado, 1997), and in our view points to the existence of externalities in the R&D sector. The results in this chapter, however, are too explorative to ascertain the exact geographical nature of these spillover effects (international or domestic) and their origin (agglomeration effects, infrastructure, localisation or technological diffusion). The conjecture can be made, however, that further integration, by fostering these kind of externalities, will not necessarily reduce regional disparities. Instead, the differences in human capital or in population growth do not seem to be that important for the relative position of Spanish regions.

3. The open economy scenario (Spanish integration in the EMU) has yielded the largest value of dispersion in productivity. This is, at first sight, a perplexing result. There is a possible explanation, though, which is consistent with the assumption of decreasing marginal productivity of physical capital: poorer regions are still able to exploit decreasing returns of capital and have therefore a potential to converge to the leaders through this mechanism. If however this is suppressed by the assumption of perfect capital mobility, the only convergence mechanism remaining is contagion by technology diffusion, which benefits precisely the most advanced regions if – as seems to be the case – technology displays noticeable spillover effects.

4. Nonetheless, the message conveyed by this chapter as regards Spanish integration in the EMU is not as dismal as one could think at first sight. It is true that our results do not point to a reduction of regional disparities within Spain as a consequence of integration. However, we do think that the integration will enhance Spanish growth globally and hence will draw Spanish regions nearer to average European living standards. Summarising, we – tentatively – forecast a twofold process of convergence whereby the gap of Spanish autonomous communities with Europe will decrease, on the one hand, while we are sceptic about further homogenisation of living standards within Spanish geographical units.

6. CONCLUSION

This research has been carried out in order to get some insights into the present and future situation of regional inequalities in Spain. Our basic findings suggest that there is a remarkable degree of persistence in geographical disparities, as implied by the fact that Spanish regions seem already to be approaching their long run equilibrium. Although the estimated dispersion in productivity in the steady state does not yield an outrageous value, it nevertheless generates a certain amount of concern. This discomfort is especially acute due to the fact that future monetary integration will not presumably smooth these differences if, as we think, the process of technological diffusion and other spillover effects associated with knowledge are a crucial factor influencing regional dynamism.

Regional policy implications are not easy to formulate. On the one hand, we support the frequent call in favour of further liberalisation and removal of distortions from those markets in which they hinder efficiency. These measures will entail gains in productivity. On the other, we advocate more serious support to R&D activities on the part of economic agents: the allocation of more resources to this strategic sector is compelling, moreover, for the laggard regions if they want to catch up with the leaders in the near future.

NOTES

1. The research assistance provided by M. Angeles Llamas is gratefully acknowledged. The authors would also like to acknowledge the financial aid of the Caja de Ahorros de Santander y Cantabria and of the Spanish Ministry of Education (project PB 97-0351).
2. The links between international trade and growth have spurred a vast amount of contributions in recent years. For surveys, see Edwards (1993) and Raymond (1995). Although the general consensus today seems to be that international trade enhances economic growth (in contrast with structuralist contributions of the 1950s), this assertion is not easily proved by empirical research due, among other factors, to reverse causation between exports and growth.
3. This conclusion, however, does not necessarily carry over to the case of trade between countries with different production features (Grossman and Helpman, 1990).
4. The assessment of the benefits and costs of integration may also be understood by an approach that focuses on the theory of optimal currency areas. Seminal contributions are Mundell (1961), and McKinnon (1963). For an update, see Villaverde (1997).
5. Nonetheless, we cannot discard the possibility of measurement error in the series of human capital that we used; unfortunately more accurate descriptions of the human capital endowment of the different regions are not available yet.
6. The technology assumed in the chapter is homogeneous of degree one in reproducible factors, and therefore the price of factors should equalise their marginal productivity.
7. This effect is similar to the main prediction of the Balassa-Samuelson model, whereby more developed countries exhibit higher price levels than developing ones. The feasibility of explaining differentials in the marginal productivity of capital across Spanish regions by such a mechanism will be explored in further research.
8. A similar reasoning may be applied to the case of labour. See García (1997) and Villaverde (1997).

REFERENCES

Argimón, I., J.M. Gonzalez-Paramo, M.J. Martin and J.M. Roldan (1994), 'Productividad e Infraestructura en la Economía Española', *Moneda y Crédito*, **198**, 207-252.

Bajo, O. and S. Sosvilla-Rivero (1995), 'El Crecimiento Económico en España, 1964-93: algunas regularidades empíricas', Documento de Trabajo n. 95-26, FEDEA.

Barro, R. (1990), 'Government Spending in a Simple Model of Endogenous Growth', *Journal of Political Economy*, **98** (part 2), S103-S125.

Barro, R. and X. Sala i Martin (1997), 'Technological Diffusion, Convergence and Growth', *Journal of Economic Growth*, **2**, 1-26.

Baumol, W. (1994), 'Multivariate Growth Patterns: Contagion and Common Forces as Possible Sources of Convergence', in W. Baumol, R.R. Nelson and E.N. Wolff (eds), *Convergence of Productivity. Cross-National Studies and Historical Evidence*, New York: Oxford University Press, pp. 62-85.

Canova, F. and A. Marcet (1995), 'The Poor Stay Poor: Non-Convergence across Countries and Regions', Economic Working Paper nr. 137, Universidad Pompeu Fabra, Barcelona.

Carrera, G. and J. Villaverde (1998), 'Unión Monetaria Europea, Comercio Intra-industrial y Regiones Españolas: una primera aproximación', *Cuadernos de Información Económica*, **131**, 50-56.

Coe, D. and E. Helpman (1995), 'International R&D Spillovers', *European Economic Review*, **39**, 859-887.

Coe, D. and R. Moghadam (1993), 'Capital and Trade as Engines of Growth in France', *IMF Staff Papers*, **40**(3), 542-566.

Cuñado, J. (1997), *Crecimiento y Convergencia de la Economía Española con los Países Líderes*, PhD. dissertation, Universidad de Navarra, Pamplona.

De la Fuente, A. (1996), 'On The Sources of Convergence: A Close Look at the Spanish Regions', mimeo, Instituto de Análisis Económico, Barcelona.

De la Fuente, A. and J.M. Da Rocha (1994), 'Capital Humano, Productividad y Crecimiento', in J.M. Esteban and X. Vives (eds) (1994), *Crecimiento y Convergencia Regional en España y Europa*, Instituto de Análisis Económico, Barcelona .

De la Fuente, A. and X. Vives (1995), 'Infrastructure and Education as Instruments of Regional Policy: Evidence from Spain', *Economic Policy*, **80**, 13-51.

Dolado, J.J., J.M. Gonzalez-Paramo and J.M. Roldan (1994), 'Convergencia Económica entre las Provincias Españolas: evidencia empírica', *Moneda y Crédito* **198**, 81-119.

Edwards, S. (1993), 'Trade and Growth in LDCs', *Journal of Economic Literature*, **31**, 1358-93.

Faini, R. (1995), 'Discussion', in A. De la Fuente and X. Vives (1995), 'Infrastructure and Education as Instruments of Regional Policy: Evidence from Spain', *Economic Policy*, **80**, 13-51.

Fundacion Banco Bilbao-Vizcaya (1996), *El 'Stock' de Capital en España y sus Comunidades Autónomas*, Bilbao.

Fundacion Banco Bilbao-Vizcaya (1997), *Renta Nacional de España y su Distribución Provincial. Síntesis*, Bilbao.

Garcia, B. (1997), *Distribución de Renta, Crecimiento y Convergencia Regional en España*, PhD. dissertation, Universidad Complutense, Madrid.

Garcia, B., J.L. Raymond and J. Villaverde (1995), 'La Convergencia de las Provincias Españolas', *Papeles de Economía Española*, **64**, 38-53.

Grossman, G. and E. Helpman (1990), 'Comparative Advantage and Long Run Growth', *American Economic Review*, **80**, 796-815.

Jones, C. (1997), 'Convergence Revisited', *Journal of Economic Growth*, **2**, 131-153.

Krugman, P. (1991), 'Increasing Returns and Economic Geography', *Journal of Political Economy*, **99**(3), 483-499.

Lee, J.W. (1995), 'Capital Goods Imports and Long Run Growth', *Journal of Development Economics*, **48**, 91-110.

Lucas, R. (1988), 'On the Mechanics of Economic Development', *Journal of Monetary Economics*, **22**, 3-42.

Mankiw, N.G., D. Romer and D.N. Weil (1992), 'A Contribution to the Empirics of Economic Growth', *Quarterly Journal of. Economics*, **107**, 407-437.

Marimón, R. (ed.) (1996), *La Economía Española: una Visión Diferente*, Barcelona: Bosch and CREI.

Marimón, R. and F. Zilibotti (1996), '¿Por qué hay menos empleo en España? Empleo 'real' vs. Empleo 'virtual' en Europa', in R. Marimón (ed.), *op.cit.*

Mas, M., J. Maudos, F. Perez and E. Uriel (1995a), 'Public Capital and Convergence in the Spanish Regions', *Entrepreneurship and Regional Development*, 7, 309-327.

Mas, M., F. Perez, E. Uriel and L. Serrano (1995b), *Capital Humano, series históricas 1964-1992*, Valencia: Fundación Bancaixa.

McKinnon, R. (1963), 'Optimum Currency Areas', *American Economic Review*, 53, 717-725.

Meeusen, W. and G. Rayp (1998), 'Patents and Trademarks as Indicators of International Competitiveness: the ECM versus the Hysteresis Approach', CESIT-paper 98-04, University of Antwerp.

Ministerio de Hacienda. Direccion General de Analisis y Programacion Presupuestaria (1997), *Evolución de las Economías Regionales en los primeros 90*, Madrid.

Mundell, R.A. (1961), 'A Theory of Optimum Currency Areas', *American Economic Review*, 51, 657-665.

Nicolini, J.P. and F. Zilibotti (1996), 'Fuentes de Crecimiento de la Economía Española', in R. Marimón (ed.), *op.cit.*

Psacharopoulos, G. (1994), 'Returns to Investment in Education: A Global Update', *World Development*, 22, 1325-1343.

Raymond, J.L. (1995), 'Exportaciones y Crecimiento Económico', Documento de Trabajo nr. 115, Fundación FIES, Madrid.

Rivera-Batiz, L. and P. Romer (1991), 'Economic Integration and Endogenous Growth', *Quarterly Journal of Economics*, 106, 531-555.

Romer, P. (1986), 'Increasing Returns and Long Run Growth', *Journal of Political Economy*, 94, 1002-1037.

Sala i Martin, X. (1996), 'Regional Cohesion: Evidence and Theories of Regional Growth and Convergence', *European Economic Review*, 40, 1325-1353.

Sanchez-Robles, B. (1997), 'Financial Efficiency and Economic Growth in Spain, 1962-1995', *International Advances in Economic Research*, 3, 333-351.

Sanchez-Robles, B. (1998), 'Macroeconomic Stability and Economic Growth: the Case of Spain', *Applied Economic Letters*, 5, 587-591.

Serrano, L. (1998), 'Capital Humano, Estructura Sectorial y Crecimiento en las Regiones Españolas', Documento de Trabajo nr. 98-04, IVIE, Valencia.

Suarez, J. (1992), 'Economías de escala, poder de mercado y externalidades: medición de las fuentes del crecimiento español', *Investigaciones Económicas*, 16, 411-441.

Villaverde, J. (1997), *Convergencia Regional y Unión Monetaria. ¿Dónde estamos? ¿A dónde vamos?*, Servicio de Publicaciones, Universidad de Cantabria, Santander.

Villaverde, J. and B. Sanchez-Robles (1998), 'Convergence Clubs in Spanish Regions, 1955-95', paper presented at the Atlantic Economic Association Annual Conference, Rome, March 14-19.

Viñals, J. (1994), '¿Es posible la convergencia en España?: En busca del tiempo perdido', Banco de España, Servicio de Estudios, Documento de Trabajo nr. 9430.

F33 (Europe)   FO2
Z13

6. Hofstede's Cultural Dimensions and a Psychological Perspective on European Countries Awaiting the Euro

Roland Pepermans[1]

1. INTRODUCTION

In this chapter, attitudes towards the euro in the countries of the European Union are linked to a number of psychological constructs, under the hypothesis that the latter could explain national differences in attitudes.

With the help of multidimensional scaling five country regions and two unclustered countries (United Kingdom and Ireland) are represented in three dimensions: 1) *national economic pride and satisfaction*; 2) *self-confident open-mindedness*; 3) *progressive non-nationalism*. Country attitudes towards the euro are then related to national scores on Hofstede's cultural dimensions, indicating that favourable euro-attitudes can be expected in those cultures that are oriented towards central control institutions.

2. THE ISSUES

A major objective of the introduction of the single European currency – the euro – is to take a further step towards greater unification among the 15 countries in the European Union (EU). The aim is that the EU would consolidate and increase its economic power in the global competition, positioned between the economic blocks of the dollar and the yen. However, it has often been debated among economists and in the press whether this ultimate goal is realistic given the diversity of national cultures (and subcultures) derived from various experiences in different social, political and economic situations. A purely economic or political approach to the pros and cons of

European Monetary Union (EMU) (e.g. Crawford, 1993; Currie, 1997; Pitch-ford and Cox, 1997) presents only part of the picture. Policymakers and re-searchers require an additional psychological approach that copes with the reasons why citizens in different countries possibly take different positions towards the euro (Pepermans, Burgoyne and Müller-Peters, 1998). So far, only a few studies have concentrated on this issue, and then only partially (Hewstone, 1986; Cinnirella, 1997), while the Eurobarometer, an initiative of the European Commission (Reif and Inglehart, 1991), presents only descrip-tive data and does not explain why national differences exist.

As supported by Hofstede (1991), different socialisation processes and experiences in the past – within the national boundaries – may lead to differ-ent cultures, and these encompass different ways of thinking, feeling and acting (Schwartz, 1997). Therefore, it may be assumed that specific national features and their perception by citizens have an impact on the way individu-als may deal with the forthcoming EMU in general, and with the change of currency in particular. Katona (1951) showed more than 40 years ago that economic life depends in an important way on the attitudes of people, on their optimism and trust. Moreover, national differences – social and cultural traditions – were shown to play a significant differential role (Katona, Strumpel and Zahn, 1971). Therefore, the first question that will have to be dealt with in this chapter is the existence of differences in attitudes towards the euro in the 15 EU countries and how country differences, as related to a number of psychological, cultural and social constructs, can be used for mapping these countries.

A second objective of this chapter is to relate country differences in euro-attitudes to cultural differences as presented by Hofstede (1980). Years ago, Hofstede started highlighting the subject of differences between countries, albeit from an organisational perspective. He has mainly focused on how different cultural values influence management and business practices. Since his landmark study a lot of related studies have been carried out (e.g. Laurent, 1983, Ronen and Shenkar, 1985, Trompenaars, 1993), which come up with comparable country classifications. Hofstede (1980) was able to de-fine four major dimensions that distinguish national cultures:

- *Power Distance*, which associates with centralisation of authority and autocratic leadership. In fact, this dimension stresses that an unequal distribution of power in institutions and organisations is accepted.
- *Masculinity*. So-called 'male' values, i.e. acquisition of goods and money, assertiveness, competitiveness, dominate. Gender-roles are rigidly defined. Femininity is the opposite side of this dimension.
- *Individualism*, which refers to the degree of integration of people in groups. Individualistic people primarily prefer to take care of them-

selves and their immediate families; they emphasise self-respect highly. On the opposite side, collectivist values stress group membership throughout life.

- *Uncertainty Avoidance*. The higher a country scores on this dimension, the more its people prefer control of situations. They feel uneasy when facing ambiguous and unstructured situations and aim for 'law and order'.

In view of the research around these dimensions (e.g. Hofstede, 1984; Hoecklin, 1995), the four cultural dimensions of Hofstede may have different applications, also in a non-organisational environment. Therefore, we shall attempt to link them to national differences in attitudes towards the euro, with the following hypotheses:

- H_1: Since EMU will perform as a central European control unit governing the different countries' financial and economic situation, it is expected that country attitudes towards the euro will be positively related to *Power Distance*.
- H_2: Since EMU may be seen as emphasising Europe as a collective unit facing other economic blocks in a globalised world, it is expected that country attitudes towards the euro will be negatively related to *Individualism*.
- H_3: Since EMU is not seen as altering male/female gender roles, it is expected that country attitudes towards the euro will not be related to *Masculinity*,
- H_4: Since EMU will install new financial and economic control devices for countries to adhere to, it is expected that country attitudes towards the euro will be positively related to *Uncertainty Avoidance*.

This chapter will therefore explore how country-related psychological characteristics, as perceived by the citizens of a nation, can be related to attitudes towards the euro, and how Hofstede's cultural dimensions can further help document those country differences.

3. METHOD

The data were collected as part of a broader project on the Psychology of the European Monetary Union during the summer of 1997 (Müller-Peters, Pepermans and Kiell, 1998). It involved the 15 countries of the EU, with a

Table 6.1.   Psychological constructs, their averages and correlations
*   with MDS-dimensions*

Psychological Constructs	Short explanation	Average across countries[a]	Dim. 1 ([b])	Dim. 2 ([b])	Dim. 3 ([b])
Involvement and knowledge					
• Subjective involvement	Personal importance of the euro.	2.98	-0.73 ***	0.06	-0.05
• Subjective level of information	How well informed does the respondent feel?	2.58	0.30	0.35	0.58 **
• Objective level of information	Level of knowledge, measured by six knowledge questions.	1.45	0.60 **	0.74 ***	0.09
Life satisfaction and values					
• Personal satisfaction	How satisfied is the respondent with life in general?	3.47	0.81 ***	-0.10	0.38
• Satisfaction with one's own country	How satisfied is (s)he with his/her country, and how proud is (s)he of the political and economic system in which (s)he lives?	2.91	0.85 ***	-0.16	0.33
• Self-transcendence	To what extent is self-transcendence (e.g. broad-mindedness) seen as a central value in life?	5.94	0.18	0.36	0.07
• Conservatism	To what extent is conservatism (e.g. respect for traditions) seen as a central value in life?	5.47	0.22	-0.09	-0.50 *
• Wealth	To what extent is wealth seen as a central value in life?	4.83	-0.64 ***	0.44 *	-0.44 *
National identity and pride					
• Nationalism	To what extent does the respondent tend to derogate other collectives in order to upgrade his own ?	2.99	-0.04	-0.35	-0.69 ***
• National patriotism	To what extent does the respondent feel attached to his/her home country?	3.87	0.16	-0.72 ***	0.22
• European patriotism	To what extent does (s)he feel attached to Europe?	3.19	-0.22	0.30	0.06

Table 6.1.   (continued)

• Pride in cultural and historical symbols	To what extent is the respondent proud of cultural and historical symbols related to his/her country?	3.88	-0.61 **	-0.67 ***	-0.12
• Pride in the national currency	To what extent does (s)he feel pride in the national currency?	3.42	0.73 ***	0.02	-0.32
Motivation to control and economic expectations					
Micro-control					
• Ease of adaptation	To what extent does (s)he consider the adaptation to the new currency easy?	3.26	0.51 *	0.55 **	0.03
• Necessity of preparatory activities	To what extent does (s)he consider preparatory activities necessary?	3.98	-0.62 **	-0.66 ***	-0.22
• Easier travel	Does (s)he expect travelling to become easier?	4.02	-0.15	-0.64 ***	0.56 **
Macro-control					
• Political independence	To what extent does (s)he consider the loss of national sovereignty in the process of integration as negative?	2.33	-0.68 ***	0.48 *	0.16
Economic expectations	Are the macro- and micro-economic expectations positive or negative?	2.84	-0.76 ***	-0.17	0.389
Equity/Fairness	Is the process of introduction in one's own country seen as fair or unfair? (also including procedural and distributive justice questions)	2.22	-0.70 ***	0.00	0.30
Attitudes towards the euro	7-item index to be answered on a 5-point scale	3.19	-0.71 ***	0.06	0.48 *

Notes:

a. All scores on a 5-point scale (1 to 5), except 'Objective level of information' (min. 0, max. 6) and 'Self-transcendence', 'Conservatism' and 'Wealth' (7-point scale, 1 to 7).

b. * means $p \leq .10$; ** means $p \leq .05$; *** means $p \leq .01$.

total of 15,088 respondents. The final questionnaire included six semantic differential type measures of attitudes towards the euro and one question also used in the Eurobarometer ('Are you for or against the European Union having one European currency in all member states, including [COUNTRY]? That is, replacing the [CURRENCY] by the European currency?').[2] The answers to these seven questions could be combined into a single index (5-point scale). This was justified by high values of internal consistency in all countries (see Müller-Peters *et al.*, 1998). A number of psychological constructs that hypothetically relate to the attitudes were also operationalised through various questions. These constructs were the result of a number of discussions between the researchers in the international research group mentioned above, after initial literature research, open-ended interviews and pre-testing had taken place (Müller-Peters *et al.*, 1998). Constructs that were included were either proximal and directly linked to EMU or the euro (e.g. involvement, knowledge, micro- and macro-economic expectations, fear of losing control, fairness and equity), while others were more distal to EMU (i.e. life satisfaction, values and national identity). Most constructs have been measured using different sets of questions to be answered on 5-point scales, although some also involved 7-point scales. Sampling and measurement specifics have been described in Müller-Peters *et al.* (1998). An overview of the constructs, a short indicative explanation and average scores across countries can be found in Table 6.1.

As could be expected, given the large sample sizes, all variables showed significant differences between countries. For this chapter, country averages were computed for each of the psychological constructs (variables)[3], and multidimensional scaling (MDS) (Young and Hamer, 1987) was applied, treating countries as single respondents. This method determines a spatial structure that will represent the countries in a minimal number of dimensions, and will allow for a structural and/or regional interpretation (Shepard, 1962; Levin, Faraone and McGraw, 1981). Similarity measures are computed using Euclidean distances between the different countries based on the average scores for the psychological constructs.[4] Through an iterative process, empirical similarities/dissimilarities are represented in a way that the predicted proximities/distances (projected data) would yield the 'best' monotonic relationship to the empirical data. This transformation was carried out using the ALSCAL-algorithm in the SPSS-programme. Given the assumed interval scaling for the psychological concepts, further analyses were performed under the interval option. Several measures of goodness-of-fit can be computed to assess whether the derived metric configuration matches the empirical data configuration (Cliff, 1972). Kruskal's *stress* is among the most popular. The smaller the index (between 0.00 and 1.00) the better the monotonic relationship (Spence and Ogilvie, 1973). Also the RSQ-value (squared correlation) has been computed as a goodness-of-fit index.

In order to test our four hypotheses relating attitudes towards the euro to the Hofstede dimensions, the country scores for each of these dimensions were introduced and correlated with the average country attitudes as well as with the country scores for the MDS-dimensions.[5]

4. RESULTS

The measure for attitudes towards the euro (5-point scale, from 1 to 5) indicated significant country differences ($p < 0.01$) as shown in Table 6.2.

Table 6.2.   Attitudes towards the euro in the 15 EU countries

	Sample size	Attitudes towards the euro [*]
Austria	534	3.15
Belgium	721	3.47
Denmark	1167	2.77
Finland	1079	3.03
France	526	3.42
Germany	1046	2.74
Greece	643	3.29
Ireland	396	3.66
Italy	4707	3.71
Luxembourg	301	3.33
The Netherlands	762	2.98
Portugal	504	3.37
Spain	410	3.77
Sweden	1152	2.64
United Kingdom	1140	2.55

Note: [*] :   Attitude-measure as an index of 7 questions: min. = 1, max. = 5

MDS produced, after 9 iterations, a spatial structure with an acceptable fit to the observed data in three dimensions (Kruskal's 'stress' = 0.109; RSQ = 0.902). This is displayed in Figure 6.1.

The figure can be seen as a representation of the EU countries based on their average country specific psychological stand on EMU (rotation of the axes does not affect the goodness-of-fit of an MDS-solution). It proved possible to label each of the dimensions as displayed, based on information provided by the correlation coefficients between the average values for the psychological constructs and the dimensional co-ordinates for all 15 countries (see Table 6.1):

Figure 6.1.   Representation of EU countries after multi-dimensional scaling

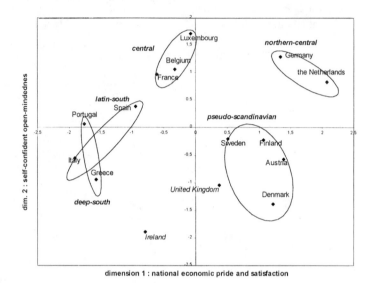

- *National economic pride and satisfaction.*
  This dimension explains most of the variance among the 15 countries. It is heavily determined by the way citizens perceive and appreciate their national economic and political systems, hence the name of the dimension. Citizens in the Netherlands, Austria, Germany, Denmark and Finland score high on this dimension. On the other hand, countries such as Italy, Portugal and Greece express their national pride through cultural and historical achievements, and much less through economic and political factors. This dimension is highly negatively correlated with the average attitudes of the country towards the euro: $r = 0.708$ ($p < 0.01$).

- *Self-confident open-mindedness.*
  This dimension differentiates between countries where the average citizen has high vs. low knowledge about Europe. Luxembourg, Germany, Belgium, the Netherlands and France are high on this dimension. They have higher correlations between the constructs *national* and *European patriotism* ($r \cong 0.200$) than low-scoring countries (Ireland, Denmark, the United Kingdom and Greece), and their citizens see relatively fewer problems in personal adaptation and say that they require fewer preparatory activities. This fact, interpreted as a feeling of confidence about the introduction of the euro, together with a more open attitude to other nationalities, helped us decide on the name of this dimension. Moreover, it can be seen that high-scoring countries favour wealth as a life value relatively more than low scoring countries.

- *Progressive non-nationalism.*
  This dimension is of a more personal and subjective nature than the two others. It emphasises differences between EU countries related to an average score on the nationalism-construct that makes them, at the same time, focus on potential positive effects of open borders. High-scoring countries (Spain, Ireland, Italy) consider themselves to be well-informed and expect travel to become easier. They also tend to have a higher degree of personal satisfaction and higher positive economic expectations. Citizens in countries that have a low score (Portugal, the United Kingdom, Germany and Greece) are more 'nationalistic' and have higher levels for the *conservative* and *wealth* values, hence the name of this dimension. It needs to be said too that this third dimension does not only split the southern countries into two clusters, but also that the Netherlands and Germany show rather different scores on this dimension. This third dimension also links positively to attitudes towards the euro ($r = 0.483$, $p < 0.10$).

An alternative way of inspecting the MDS-map is through a regional interpretation of the three-dimensional space. A region represents a group of countries with a rather homogeneous set of scores on the psychological constructs. Support for this regional interpretation was found after applying a hierarchical cluster analysis.[6] As a result of it, five regions were defined, covering 13 of the 15 countries; the two remaining countries are presented separately (see Figure 6.1):

- Northern-Central region: Germany and the Netherlands.
  This region contains two countries with prosperous economies with, on average,[7] negative attitudes towards the euro, i.e. 2.86.
- Pseudo-Scandinavian region: Austria, Denmark, Finland and Sweden.
  This region contains the three Scandinavian countries, plus Austria, hence the region label. One also notices that it clusters the three countries that last joined the EU and Denmark. The latter and Sweden have negative attitudes towards the euro (average = 2.70), while Austria and Finland have moderate positive attitudes (average = 3.09). The average euro-attitude for the four countries is 2.90.
- Central region: Belgium, France and Luxembourg.
  This region is geographically central in Europe and countries have positive attitudes towards the euro, i.e. 3.41.
- Latin-South region: Italy and Spain.
  This region contains two countries from Southern Europe, mainly different from the other Southern countries on the dimension 'Progressive non-nationalism'. Their average attitudes towards the euro are highly positive, i.e. 3.74.
- Deep-South region: Greece and Portugal.
  Here we find two southern countries with less dominant economies, with on average positive attitudes towards the euro, i.e. 3.33.
- United Kingdom.
  Average attitudes towards the euro = 2.55.
- Ireland.
  Average attitudes towards the euro = 3.66.

The average country attitude and the scores of the different countries on the three dimensions were then correlated with the country scores on the Hofstede cultural dimensions. This result is displayed in Table 6.3.

Euro-attitudes correlate positively and significantly with *Power Distance* and *Uncertainty Avoidance*, hence confirming H_1 and H_4. Also H_3 is not rejected, since no significant relationship has been found between the average euro-attitudes of the countries and *Masculinity*. However, H_2 could not be confirmed: the correlation between attitudes and *Individualism* is negative, as predicted, but not statistically significant.

Table 6.3.   *Correlations between euro-attitudes, MDS- and Hofstede dimensions for the 15 EU countries*

	Euro-attitude	MDS-dim1	MDS-dim2	MDS-dim3
Power Distance	.535**	-.694***	.487*	-.141
Masculinity	.336	-.287	-.163	-.062
Individualism	-.346	.466*	.013	.355
Uncertainty Avoidance	.581**	-.587**	.431	-.239

Note :   *** means $p < .01$; ** means $p < .05$; * means $p < .10$.

Considering the relationship between the Hofstede dimensions and the MDS-dimensions (in Table 6.3) a somewhat expected pattern arises, knowing that it is the first MDS-dimension (*National Economic Pride and Satisfaction*) that correlates negatively and significantly with the euro-attitude. Incidentally, *Individualism* is now correlating significantly with *National Economic Pride and Satisfaction*.

Applying stepwise multiple regression analyses on the data for the 15 countries, with attitudes towards the euro being the dependent variable and the Hofstede and MDS-dimensions being the independent variables,[8] results in a highly significant model ($R^2_{adj} = 86.2$ %; $F_{3,10} = 27.980$, $p < 0.001$):

Attitudes towards the euro =   - 0.475 *(National economic pride and satisfaction)* +0.614 *(Progressive non-nationalistism)* +0.449 *(Uncertainty Avoidance)* +2.781 .

All standardised β are significant at $p < 0.01$.

5. DISCUSSION

There exist clear differences in attitudes towards the euro between the EU countries. Moreover, similar average attitudes in two or more countries are not necessarily related to similar positions on a number of psychological, social or cultural variables.

The MDS-map reveals the most important dimension to differentiate between countries to be *National Economic Pride and Satisfaction.* Southern European countries (in both the Latin-South and the Deep-South region) seem to express their national pride through cultural and historical achievements, while others, especially the countries in the Northern-Central region, find pride in their national economic situation. This could be seen in accordance to social identity theory (Tajfel and Turner, 1986; Barnum, 1997): groups (here, nations) are thought to define their social identity on dimensions in which they fare well, compared to relevant others. This helps to explain why the countries that are, on average, proud of their culture and history are more likely to favour the euro. It may be assumed that the introduction of a single European currency, and the economic change involved, is not much of a threat to their national pride. But citizens in countries that feel pride in their currency and who are satisfied with their political and economic achievements might fear a loss of their national self-esteem through EMU. Since this first MDS-dimension also correlates with involvement and knowledge variables, it may also be assumed that especially because of a relatively higher level of knowledge in these countries (average = 2.04),[9] citizens in the Northern-Central region fear their national independence to be threatened by further European integration. But at the same time, more information may bring them to the expectation that personal adaptation will not be too difficult (average = 3.73).

High-scoring countries on the second dimension (*Self-confident Open-mindedness*), i.e. countries in the Central region, see fewer problems in personal adaptation and require less by way of preparatory activities. This may be explained by their somewhat higher levels of objective information about the euro (compared to the European average) (Müller-Peters, Pepermans and Kiell, 1998). This knowledge-related MDS-dimension is also negatively related to cultural and historical pride, as if being proud about such issues may prevent one from becoming better informed. Especially citizens in Central region countries favour *wealth* as a value, which may be due to the fact that they have gained insights (through more/better information?) which leads them to believe that materialistic prosperity will result from the EMU. However, this statement certainly needs further confirmation.

The third MDS-dimension (*Progressive Non-nationalism*) is especially relevant for differentiating between the two Southern regions. High scores coincide with valuing certain positive personal outcomes of the advent of the euro, but also relate to their subjective level of information (although not to objective knowledge). Ireland demonstrates more positive personal expectations too, maybe because they have so far largely benefited from the EU as well. Countries that score higher on *conservative* and *wealth* values (e.g. Germany and the United Kingdom) expect negative personal effects, as if they perceive the changeover to the euro as a threat to their personal comfort. Furthermore, it can be noticed that this third dimension also differentiates, in a way, the two countries in the Northern-Central region.

The Pseudo-Scandinavian region is the least homogeneous region in the MDS-mapping. The four countries can even be split into two subclusters according to their attitudes towards the euro. Compared to the 15 countries, citizens in Denmark score lowest (except Ireland) on the dimension *Self-confident Open-mindedness*, and within this cluster, Swedish citizens score low on *National Economic Pride and Satisfaction* (Müller-Peters, 1998). Not by coincidence, these countries demonstrate negative attitudes towards the euro. Citizens in Austria and Finland, who are on average more in favour of the euro, show a higher level of *National Economic Pride and Satisfaction*, and are generally more positive on all three dimensions of the MDS.

The United Kingdom can be considered to be in a unique position, if only by its most negative attitudes towards the euro. Its citizens show the most nationalistic and conservative feelings among the EU countries, while taking a rather middle-of-the-road position on the other dimensions. The idea of living on an island with no real need for European ties was already clear in the study by Hewstone (1986). However, in recent research, It can be shown that it is not the EU that the British disfavour, but rather the euro (Burgoyne and Routh, 1998).

The other English speaking country, Ireland, is the other outlier in the MDS-analysis. Being somewhat less proud of their economic and political system, and feeling less self-confident and open-minded, the Irish show a favourable attitude, probably influenced by their relatively non-conservative and non-nationalistic opinions. They seem to be more open to the economic changes and believe they gain relatively more personally, as well as at macro-level. The MDS-mapping suggests that the Irish keep an 'open door' to Europe.

Relating the average euro-attitudes to the Hofstede dimensions, it has been shown that country attitudes in the EU correlate positively and significantly with *Power Distance* and *Uncertainty Avoidance*. Hence, European countries viewing EMU as a supranational institution moulding economic and financial policies, and accepting (new) control and legislative measures, are more in favour of the euro. This can be interpreted as if those countries that are relatively more positive towards EMU expect (economic) life to become more predictable and structured.

On the other hand, it is not so clear that countries in favour of the euro also expect to become part of a new collective entity, i.e. Europe. Yet, the major dimension that explains attitude differences between countries, i.e. *National Economic Pride and Satisfaction*, is positively and significantly related to *Individualism*, indicating that collective thinking in a country is counterproductive for national economic pride and satisfaction, which – in turn – is negatively related to a favourable euro-attitude.

This chapter clearly underlines the fact that elements of national cultures, represented by national features and their perception by citizens, have an impact on the average attitudes countries display towards the euro. The regression analysis shows a high percentage of the variance in the country attitudes to be explained by three dimensions: *National Economic Pride and Satisfaction*, *Progressive Non-nationalism* and Hofstede's *Uncertainty Avoidance*. This means that the less a country is proud and satisfied about its economic situation, the more it considers itself non-conservative and non-nationalistic and prefers a structured and ordered society, the more a country adheres to the euro. In fact, at country level, EMU seems to be favoured by somewhat progressive countries that expect – at the same time – order as well as national economic benefits, making them more proud then they are now. Whether that is what EMU is going to deliver, is of course a different question.

Our results indicate that people have a particular view of the euro that is, in an important way, influenced by how they subjectively assess their personal situation and the situation of their country. This again proves the point that Katona (1951) (see also Katona *et al.*, 1971) made several years ago about the relationship between psychological variables and economic phenomena.

In a separate analysis it was even shown that the psychological constructs used in this study have a significant region-specific impact on euro-attitudes, and ought in this respect to be considered more important than socio-demographic variables (Pepermans and Verleye, 1998). Furthermore, this chapter highlights the appropriateness of the Hofstede dimensions for analysing international issues beyond the more traditional applications in organisational policy making. The present analyses also endorse Hofstede (1991) stating that people from different countries operate according to different mental programmes, making the core of national cultures. Citizens from the United Kingdom are taking a unique and distant position towards the euro and Italian and Spanish citizens are very much in favour of European matters, expecting a lot of change for the better for the situation of their country. As a consequence, it will be clear that efforts towards European integration in such an environment will require more than just economic or political initiatives. Rather, country specific communication strategies are required, which take account of the psychological, social and cultural particularities of each country (Pepermans and Müller-Peters, 1998).

NOTES

1. The author acknowledges the financial support from the European Commission (DG X), as well as the scientific and logistic support from a number of researchers from various European universities (cf. Müller-Peters *et al.*, 1998).
2. COUNTRY and CURRENCY were replaced by a nation's specific name and currency in each of the national (translated) versions of the questionnaire.
3. Not including the measure for attitudes towards the euro.
4. Since the data for the different variables were not all based on similar scale ranges, z-transformations have been applied.
5. This analysis did not include Luxembourg since no Hofstede scores were available for this country.
6. Due to space limitations, statistical details cannot be given here. They can be obtained from the author.
7. Regional averages are taken from the countries' averages.
8. Multicollinearity was tested through regressing all independent variables in the equation on all other independent variables and proved not to be problematic.
9. Averages are on a 5-point scale (from 1 to 5), except for the value-indices – *Self-transcendence*, *Conservatism* and *Wealth* – (7-point scale, from 1 to 7), and can be compared with the averages across countries in Table 6.1.

REFERENCES

Barnum, C. (1997), 'A Reformulated Social Identity Theory', in B. Markovsky, M.J. Lovaglia and L. Troyer (eds), *Advances in Group Processes*, Greenwich, CO: Jai Press, pp. 29-57.

Burgoyne, C.B. and D. Routh (1998), 'The Psychology of the European Monetary Union in the UK: 'No S.E.C. please, we're British'', in A. Müller-Peters, R. Pepermans and G. Kiell (eds), *The Psychology of the European Monetary Union: A Cross-national Study of Attitudes towards the Euro*, Cologne/Brussels: Universität zu Köln/Vrije Universiteit Brussel, 6/325-6/348.

Cinnirella, M. (1997), 'Towards a European Identity? Interactions between the National and European Social Identities Manifested by University Students in Britain and Italy', *British Journal of Social Psychology*, **36**, 19-31.

Cliff, N. (1972), 'Consistencies among Judgements of Adjective Combinations', in A.K. Romney, R.N. Shepard and S.B. Nerlove (eds), *Multidimensional Scaling: Theory and Applications in the Behavioral Sciences, Vol. II*, New York: Seminar Press, pp. 163-182.

Crawford, M. (1993), *One Money for Europe? The Economics and Politics of Maastricht*, London: Macmillan Press.

Currie, D. (1997), *The Pros and Cons of EMU*, London: The Economist Intelligence Unit.

Hewstone, M. (1986), *Understanding Attitudes to the European Community: A Social-psychological Study in Four Member States*, Cambridge, UK: Cambridge University Press.

Hoecklin, L. (1995), *Managing Cultural Differences: Strategies for Competitive Advantage*, New York: Addison-Wesley.

Hofstede, G. (1980), *Culture's Consequences: International Differences in Work-related Values*, Beverly Hills: Sage.

Hofstede, G. (1984), 'The cultural relativity of the quality of life concept', *Academy of Management Review*, **9**, 389-398.

Hofstede, G. (1991), *Cultures and Organizations: Software of the Mind*, New York: McGraw-Hill.

Katona, G. (1951), *Psychological Analysis of Economic Behavior*, New York: McGraw-Hill.

Katona, G., B. Strumpel and E. Zahn (1971), *Aspirations and Affluence*, New York: McGraw-Hill.

Laurent, A. (1983), 'The Cultural Diversity of Western Conceptions of Management', *International Studies of Management and Organization*, **13**, 5-96.

Levin, I. P., S.V. Faraone and J.A. McGraw (1981), 'The Effects of Income and Inflation on Personal Satisfaction Measurement in Economic Psychology', *Journal of Economic Psychology*, **1**, 303-318.

Müller-Peters, A., R. Pepermans and G. Kiell (eds) (1998), *The Psychology of the European Monetary Union: A Cross-national Study of Attitudes Towards the Euro*, Cologne/Brussels: Universität zu Köln/Vrije Universiteit Brussel.

Müller-Peters, A. *et al.* (1998), 'Explaining Attitudes towards the Euro. Design of a Cross-national Study', *Journal of Economic Psychology*, **19**, 663-680.

Pepermans, R., C.B. Burgoyne and A. Müller-Peters (1998), 'European Integration, Psychology and the Euro', *Journal of Economic Psychology*, **19**, 657-661.

Pepermans, R. and A. Müller-Peters (1998), 'Differential Information Requirements among European Citizens: more Psychology than Socio-demographics', *Journal of Consumer Policy*, **21**, in press.

Pepermans, R. and G. Verleye (1998), 'A Unified Europe? How Euro-attitudes Relate to Psychological Differences between Countries', *Journal of Economic Psychology*, **19**, 681-699.

Pitchford, R. and A. Cox (eds) (1997), *EMU Explained: Markets and Monetary Union*, London: Kogan Page.

Reif, K. and R. Inglehart (1991), *Eurobarometer: the Dynamics of European Public Opinion*, London: Macmillan.

Ronen, S. and O. Shenkar (1985), 'Clustering Countries on Attitudinal Dimensions: a Review and Synthesis', *Academy of Management Journal*, **10**, 445-454.

Schwartz, S.H. (1997), 'Values and Culture', in D. Munro, J.F. Schumaker and S.C. Carr (eds), *Motivation and Culture*. New York: Routledge, pp. 69-84.

Shepard, R. N. (1962), 'The analysis of proximities: multidimensional scaling with an unknown distance function – I', *Psychometrika*, **27**, 125-139.

Spence, I. and J.C. Ogilvie (1973), 'A Table of Expected Stress Values for Random Rankings in Nonmetric Multidimensional Scaling', *Multivariate Behavior Research*, **8**, 511-517.

Tajfel, H. and J.C. Turner (1986), 'An Integrative Theory of Intergroup Conflict', in S. Worchel and W.G. Austin (eds), *Psychology of Intergroup Relations*, 2nd ed., Chicago: Nelson-Hall, pp. 33-47.

Trompenaars, F. (1993), *Riding the Waves of Culture*, London: Economist Books.

Young, F.W. and R.M. Hamer (1987), *Multidimensional Scaling: History, Theory and Applications*, Hillsdale, NJ: Erlbaum.

7. Towards a Monetary Model for the Euro/USD Exchange Rate

Sonja Hellemann and Luc Hens[1]

1. INTRODUCTION

Despite the vast literature on EMU and the euro, little work has focused on the determination of its external exchange rate. Most research addresses the question whether the euro will be a stable currency, but offers little insight into the levels at which the euro is likely to trade. Exchange rate modelling in itself is an area where little consensus exists. Modelling an exchange rate with little or no history is even more difficult. We start from a monetary model of the Deutsche mark (DEM) exchange rate as a first indicator of the likely behaviour of the euro, under the premise that the EMS has in fact been a Deutsche mark-zone, and that euroland will behave in a way similar to the EMS. The monetary model focuses on the interaction between monetary variables (money supply, interest rates and inflation rates), income, and the exchange rate. This model is theoretically appealing, but initial empirical testing for the floating period showed little support for it. Furthermore, it has proven to be very fickle in its in-sample behaviour when presented with different sample periods and data sets. However, empirical tests based on the Johansen cointegration technique indicate that the monetary model performs rather well if treated as a long-run equilibrium relationship (MacDonald and Taylor, 1994).

We test two versions of the model: a more traditional sticky-price monetary model, and an extended version that includes real variables to allow for deviations from purchasing power parity. The results are rather supportive of the extended version of the latter model.

2. THE MONETARY MODEL OF EXCHANGE RATE DETERMINATION

The first building block of the monetary model is purchasing power parity (PPP):

$$e_t = p_t - p_t^* , \qquad (7.1)$$

which is simply a statement of the law of one price, where e_t is the domestic price of foreign currency and the asterix denotes foreign variables. The second equation is uncovered interest rate parity (UIP):

$$e_{t+1} - e_t + \phi_t = i_t - i_t^* , \qquad (7.2)$$

where ϕ_t is the risk premium on foreign assets, reflecting the difference between the riskiness of domestic and foreign bonds. Individuals will only be willing to hold more domestic bonds if their rate of return rises relative to the domestic currency return on foreign bonds. Thus net or aggregate demand for domestic bonds is an increasing function of their expected excess rate of return over foreign bonds. Supply of domestic bonds is equal to the value of domestic currency government bonds held by the public, less the value of domestic currency assets held by the central bank. If the central bank sells domestic assets, then the amount of bonds held by the public increases and so does the risk premium. If we assume that foreign and domestic assets are perfect substitutes, the risk premium equals zero. The uncovered interest rate parity relationship then simplifies to:

$$e_{t+1} - e_t = i_t - i_t^* . \qquad (7.3)$$

Money market equilibrium, assuming iso-elastic money demand, requires:

$$M_t / P_t = Y_t^{\alpha} (1 + i_t)^{-\beta} \qquad (7.4)$$

for both countries, where M_t is the nominal money supply, P_t is the price level, Y_t is income, and i_t is the interest rate. Taking logs and using the approximation $ln(1+x) \cong x$ for small values of x, we obtain:

$$m_t - p_t = \alpha y_t - \beta i_t \qquad (7.5)$$

$$m_t^* - p_t^* = \alpha y_t^* - \beta i_t^* . \qquad (7.6)$$

We assume that the elasticity with respect to output α and the semi-elasticity with respect to interest rates β are equal across the two countries. We can now combine the equations presented above to derive the flexible-price monetary model. Combining equations 7.5 and 7.6, we obtain:

$$p_t - p_t^* = m_t - m_t^* - \alpha(y_t - y_t^*) + \beta(i_t - i_t^*) \quad . \tag{7.7}$$

Substituting out $p_t - p_t^*$ from the PPP relations, we get:

$$e_t = (m_t - m_t^*) - \alpha(y_t - y_t^*) + \beta(i_t - i_t^*) \quad , \tag{7.8}$$

which is the flexible price monetary model in restricted form. Equation 7.8 states that an increase in the domestic money supply, relative to foreign money supply, will lead to a depreciation of the domestic currency. An increase in domestic output appreciates the currency, while an increase in the domestic interest rate causes a depreciation of the currency. This last point is one of the distinguishing factors of the monetary model. In the Mundell-Fleming framework an increase in the interest rate leads to capital inflows and thus to an appreciation of the currency. In the monetary model as presented above, the emphasis is however on the relative money supplies, and the exchange rate is mainly influenced by the demand for money in the two countries. An increase in the interest rate causes a drop in the demand for real money balances, which causes a drop in output and thus a depreciation of the currency. In the unrestricted form the model would be written as:

$$e_t = \beta_1 m_t + \beta_2 m_t^* + \beta_3 y_t + \beta_4 y_t^* + \beta_5 i_t + \beta_6 i_t^* + \phi_t \quad . \tag{7.9}$$

The flexible price model relies on the assumption of UIP. We can therefore replace the interest rate differential in (7.8) with the expected depreciation of the exchange rate:

$$e_t = m_t - m_t^* - \alpha(y_t - y_t^*) + \beta \Delta e_{t+1}^E \quad , \tag{7.10}$$

where the superscript 'E' indicates expectations. Relaxing the constraint on the coefficient of the income variable and rearranging we can express this equation equivalently as:

$$e_t = (1+\beta)^{-1}(m_t - m_t^*) - \alpha(1+\beta)^{-1}(y_t - y_t^*) + \beta(1+\beta)^{-1}e_{t+1}^E \quad . \tag{7.11}$$

If we now assume rational expectations (based on information at time t), it can be easily shown that the exchange rate is effectively equal to the present value of the expected future forcing variables (money supply and income), discounted at the rate $1/\beta$.

One major flaw of the flexible price model is the assumption that PPP holds continuously, implying constant real exchange rates (see Rogoff, 1996 for a survey of the evidence on PPP). The relationship between interest rates and the exchange rate in the flex-price model is unrealistic especially in the short-term. The second generation of monetary models (Frankel, 1979; Boothe and Glassman, 1987) includes a *real* interest differential to capture the liquidity effects of monetary policy. These sticky-price models have typically been tested either in static form or with very limited dynamics, either reflecting an implicit belief that agents are able to achieve their desired position very quickly, or because the researcher was testing a long-run relationship between the exchange rate and the monetary variables (MacDonald and Taylor, 1991).

Early empirical studies of the floating exchange rate period give little support to the monetary model: coefficients are unstable, predictive power is low, restrictions are usually rejected, and the model does not seem to offer a long-run explanation for the behaviour of the exchange rate (Moosa, 1994). MacDonald and Taylor (1994) argue that one of the main reasons why there was so little support for the monetary model over the floating period is the use of inappropriate econometric methods. The advent of the Johansen co-integration technique fundamentally changed this. The Johansen technique allows for endogeneity of all variables in the system and fully captures the underlying time series properties of the data. The results in MacDonald and Taylor (1991, 1994) and Moosa (1996) – all using the Johansen technique – are quite supportive of the (unrestricted) monetary model.

A different approach to testing the validity of the monetary model was taken by MacDonald and La Cour (1997) and Baillie and Pecchenino (1991). They not only estimated the monetary model (in an unrestricted version), but also separately estimated some of the underlying equilibrium relationships. MacDonald and la Cour (1997) test the money demand equations and an exchange rate block. Their study gives support to the monetary model as it shows that there is some validity to the underlying equations (which has been a point of debate) as well as the entire model. Other studies (Cushman *et al.*, 1996; Sarantis and Pu, 1997) have extended the monetary model by allowing for real exchange rate variations by including real factor variables, as is explained in the next section.

3. AN EXTENDED MONETARY MODEL

The extended monetary model by Sarantis and Pu (1997) allows for a time-varying equilibrium real exchange rate, sticky prices, and imperfect asset substitutability. They argue that although there is a long-run equilibrium real exchange rate, it is determined not only by relative prices but also by real factors. Thus PPP is assumed to hold in the long-run but the model makes some accommodations to the evidence that PPP does not appear to hold continuously. The PPP relationship then becomes:

$$e_t = k_t + (p_t - p_t^*) \ , \tag{7.12}$$

where e is the nominal USD/ECU exchange rate, k is the real exchange rate and p and p^* are the price-level in the US (home country) and Europe (foreign country). This equation suggests that relative prices (and hence monetary factors) are not the sole determinants of the long-run movements in the nominal exchange rate. Deviations from long-run PPP can be accounted for by demand and supply factors.

Supply factors are normally accounted for by productivity gains in the traded goods sector relative to the non-traded goods sector. This is the Samuelson-Balassa effect, which is stated as:

$$k = \alpha_1(A_N - A_N^*) - \alpha_2(A_T - A_T^*) \ , \tag{7.13}$$

where A_N is the productivity in the non-traded sector, and A_T is the productivity in the traded sector (as before the asterix denotes foreign variables). According to equation 7.13 an increase in the relative productivity in the domestic non-tradable sector will lead to a depreciation, while an increase in the relative productivity in the domestic tradable sector will lead to an appreciation of the currency. A major problem with the empirical application of this equation is that we are usually not able to collect sufficient data on the productivity in the non-tradable sector. De Grauwe (1996) has shown that if we assume that (a) the relative share of non-tradables and tradables is the same in both countries, and (b) the productivity in the non-tradable sector is the same in both countries, we can ignore the non-tradable sector and the real exchange rate then becomes a function of the productivity differential in the tradable sector. Demand factors are accounted for by government spending. We can thus write:

$$k = \alpha_0 - \alpha_1(q_T - q_t^*) - \alpha_2(g_T - g_T^*) \ , \tag{7.14}$$

where the real exchange rate k is an increasing function of the productivity in the traded sector in the home and foreign country (q_T and q_T^* respectively) and a decreasing function of government spending on tradables in both countries (g_T and g_T^*). Consequently a relative drop in the government spending on non-tradables leads to an appreciation of the domestic currency. Relative prices are determined by the money demand functions of the two countries. Sarantis and Pu (1997) use the typical Cagan money demand function, adding the expected inflation rate π: excluding this variable would lead to structural breaks. The money demand function is therefor written as:

$$m_t - p_t = \alpha_1 y_t - \alpha_2 i_t - \alpha_3 \pi_t \ . \tag{7.15}$$

The last equation of the model is the interest rate parity condition:

$$i_t - i_t^* = \Delta e_{t,t+1} + \gamma \phi_t \ , \tag{7.16}$$

where ϕ again stands for the risk premium. The risk premium is assumed to be determined by the differential of the relative current account positions $ca_t - ca_t^*$, where ca_t stands for the current account balance divided my nominal GDP). A current account surplus in the US will lead to an increased supply of European bonds, which leads to an increase in the risk premium on European bonds, which lowers the relative premium on US bonds and thus causes an appreciation of the USD. Based on the assumption of static expectations the expected depreciation of the currency is assumed to be zero.
We finally arrive at the following model:

$$e_t = \alpha_0 + \alpha_1(m_t - m_t^*) - \alpha_2(y_t - y_t^*) + \alpha_3\gamma\phi_t - \alpha_4(q_t - q_t^*) - \alpha_5(g_t - g_t^*) \tag{7.17}$$

This model suggests that the long-run equilibrium nominal exchange rate will be affected by both monetary and real factors. If $\alpha_4 = \alpha_5 = 0$ and if the risk premium is set to zero we obtain the flexible price monetary model.

4. A TEST OF THE MONETARY MODEL

4.1. Data and time series used

We use industrial production as a proxy for quarterly income (*GY* for Germany, *UY* for the US) and M1 for money supply (*GM* and *UM*). Interest rates are the bond yield on public bonds (maturity 3 to 7 years) for Germany

(*GI*), and the one-year yield on treasury bills for the USA (*UI*). The exchange rate is the DEM/USD exchange rate (*LNE*). Productivity is measured by industrial productivity per man-hour, and the current account variable is computed as the ratio of the current account balance to industrial production. The price level is the wholesale price index (as it contains more traded goods than the consumer price index); *GR* and *UR* are the corresponding inflation rates. Government spending is government consumption for Germany and government purchases of goods and services for the USA. All variables are quarterly and seasonally unadjusted. Data are obtained from Datastream and all variables with the exception of the inflation rate, the interest rate, and the current account variable are in logarithms. The estimation period is 1979Q1-1998Q1.

4.2. Estimation of the traditional monetary model

We test the following version of the sticky-price monetary model:

$$ e_t = \alpha_0 + \alpha_1(m_t - m_t^*) - \alpha_2(y_t - y_t^*) + \alpha_3(i_t - i_t^*) - \alpha_4(\pi_t - \pi_t^*) , $$

(7.18)

where e_t is the home price of foreign (USA) currency, π is inflation and the asterix indicates a foreign variable (in this case the US variables).

4.2.1. Specification of the dynamic model

In order to determine the dynamic specification of the VAR the model was estimated using different lag-lengths and dummies. Each time a series of tests was performed to check for the significance of the lags included ($F_{k=..}$), autocorrelation (F_{AR}), heteroskedasticity (LM test for autocorrelated squared residuals, F_{ARCH}), and residual normality (χ^2 test, 2 degrees of freedom).[2]

The system was first estimated with 2 lags and centered seasonal dummies. The test statistics (not shown here) indicated that there was serial correlation for the German interest and inflation rate, that the US interest rate was heteroskedastic and that four variables (the German and US interest rate, the US inflation rate and US industrial production) were non-normal. There was a problem of non-normal residuals which can be solved by accounting for outliers in the data by introducing dummy variables. These dummies are not necessarily related to events, but are simply chosen to achieve residual normality. The result of the regression including the dummies (for all four variables) are shown in Table 7.1.

Table 7.1.　　Traditional monetary model: specification tests

Statistics	LNE	GM	UM	GI	USI	GR	UR	GY	UY
$F_{k=1}(9,51)$	6.97**	5.14**	23.00**	4.00**	9.92*	1.21	0.62	4.40**	14.00**
$F_{k=2}(9,51)$	1.44	0.62	3.29**	1.26	3.35*	1.20	1.50	1.88	2.61
$F_{AR}(5,54)$	0.31	1.44	3.27*	1.67	4.05*	1.10	1.17	0.95	1.35
$F_{ARCH}(5,51)$	0.29	0.26	0.15	1.15	0.51	0.50	1.24	0.28	0.25
$\chi^2(2)$	4.13	1.03	1.78	0.93	0.71	1.14	7.83*	8.28*	0.65

Multivariate
Statistics
$F_{AR}(405,76)$　　　1.33
$\chi^2(18)$　　　28.90*

Note:　　** rejects the null hypothesis at the 1% significance level; * rejects the null at the 5% significance level.

This result is still far from ideal. There does not seem to be a common lag-length, there is some autocorrelation, and two of the equations have non-normal residuals. Different specifications in terms of the lag-length and the dummy variables did not yield a better specification. We will therefore proceed with the above-described model with two lags and four seasonal centered dummies.

4.2.2. Determination of the number of cointegration vectors

Before we can set the number of cointegration vectors r in the model we have to consider whether to include an intercept and trend in the system. There are four possible models to be considered:
- model 1: no deterministic trends in the data or the cointegration space;
- model 2: no linear trends in the levels of the data, the intercept is restricted to the long-run model (i.e. the cointegration space);
- model 3: there are linear trends in the data;
- model 4: there is a linear trend in the cointegration space as well.

Using the so-called Pantula principle all four models are estimated and the results are presented from the most restrictive to the most unrestricted model (i.e. $r = 0$ and model 1, to $r = 6$ and model 4). The test procedure is to start from the most restrictive model and at each stage compare the trace statistic with the critical value until we reach a specification for which we do not reject the null (the null for example being $r = 1$ against $r > 1$).

Applying the Pantula-principle to the monetary model (results not shown) indicates that we should proceed with a model that allows for linear trends in the data (model 3), and that there are four cointegration vectors.

4.2.3. Testing the cointegration relationships

The test for weak exogeneity (Table 7.2) seems to indicate that the exchange rate is weakly exogenous (as well as *UM*, *USI* and *GY*). Weak exogeneity of a variable indicates that it does not appear on the left-hand side of any of the long-run relationships. This defeats the 'purpose' of the monetary model as we are effectively looking for an equation (or equations) which have the exchange rate on the left hand side as a function of other explanatory variables.

Table 7.2. Traditional monetary model: tests for exclusion, weak exogeneity, and stationarity

	LNE	GM	UM	GI	USI	GR	UR	GY	UY	Critical Value
Exclusion	20.71	10.05	5.51*	21.6	17.88	10.95	21.07	26.05	29.78	9.49
Weak exogen.	2.39*	14.76	6.54*	12.8	7.88*	12.42	23.60	5.84*	26.94	9.49
Stationarity	18.90	22.14	22.91	15.5	23.57	7.02*	24.80	24.12	21.63	11.00

Note: * means a significance level of 5%.

However, the result of the test for weak exogeneity might seem worse than it really is. We should keep in mind that the tests are performed for all four vectors simultaneously. Hence this result does not exclude the possibility that there is one vector for which the exchange rate is endogenous. The next step is to re-estimate the system based on exogeneity of the variables (Table 7.3). We did not condition the new estimation on weak exogeneity of the exchange rate and still assume that there are four cointegration vectors.

Table 7.3. Traditional monetary model: re-estimated system based on exogeneity of variables

vector no	LNE	GM	GI	GR	UR	UM	UY	USI	GY	# of correct signs
1	1.00	9.35	-1.81	-26.58	-87.01	2.07	-58.09	0.25	32.23	6
2	1.00	1.05	-0.10	-8.65	17.54	0.08	-4.12	0.05	4.12	7
3	1.00	1.90	0.57	-102.10	31.18	-2.51	8.56	-0.26	-10.45	4
4	1.00	0.45	0.02	20.23	5.09	0.35	-0.75	-0.09	-1.36	3

For the first and second vectors most of the coefficients have the correct sign, while for the last two vectors, most of the coefficients have the wrong sign. This seems like a good result, but we should keep in mind that we cannot be sure whether the exchange rate is not really weakly exogenous in all relationships. Economically it seems plausible that there must be at least one such relationship. The coefficients of the first vector are economically less appealing than those of the second vector. Particularly damaging is the finding that for all four vectors the coefficient of the Germany money supply has the wrong sign, while the coefficient on the US money supply variable is wrongly signed for the first two vectors. This would suggest – implausibly – that an increase in the money supply in Germany leads to an appreciation of the Deutsche mark (the problem of the 'multiplying marks', Frankel (1982)). Equally implausible is the result that the US money supply does not seem to enter the equation (test for exclusion). Economically this is very much contrary to the fundamental idea of the model. Positive is that the coefficients on the German and US interest rate variables are correctly signed for the first two vectors. This is evidence of the positive relationship between interest rates and the exchange rate proposed in the monetary model. The coefficients on the first vector seem unreasonably large which makes the second vector more attractive.

Overall, the result of the above investigation is not very supportive of the monetary model for our sample. The exchange rate does not seem to appear on the left hand side of any of the relationships found, the money supply variables have the wrong sign, two of the vectors found have most of the coefficients with the wrong sign, while one of the two vectors with quite a large proportion of correct signs does not seem to have economically reasonably sized coefficients. We will now proceed to look at an alternative specification of the monetary model.

4.3. Estimation of the extended monetary model

We now consider the monetary model as proposed by Sarantis and Pu (1997), which includes productivity and government spending to account for real factors (see section 3):

$$e_t = \alpha_0 + \alpha_1(m_t - m_t^*) - \alpha_2(y_t - y_t^*) + \alpha_3\gamma\phi_t - \alpha_4(q_t - q_t^*) - \alpha_5(g_t - g_t^*)$$
$$(7.19)$$

Before we can start the determination of the cointegration rank it is necessary to find the correct dynamic specification of the VAR. The variables are: the exchange rate (LNE), the money supply differential (M), the inflation rate differential (R), the output differential (Y), the current account differential as proxy for the risk premium (CA), the productivity and government spending differential (PY and GOV respectively), and the inflation rate differential (the latter is included to prevent structural breaks – see section 3). We have chosen a restricted model which assumes that the coefficients on the variables are the same across countries. Although this assumption is questionable,

Cushman *et al.* (1996) argue that adding on more variables to the model (i.e. the real factor variables) sometimes necessitates the restriction in order to avoid an excessive number of coefficients. There is a trade-off between imposing restrictions, which might not be appropriate, and keeping the number of coefficients manageable.

4.3.1. Determination of the dynamic specification

Again, we need to find the correct dynamic specification of the model first. The first estimation included three lags, a constant and trend, and centered seasonal dummies (results not shown here). Although there seemed to be a common lag-length, the residuals of the equations for *CA* and *GOV* were not normal. Adding dummies and deleting one of the lags we obtain the result reported in Table 7.4. This seems like a much better specification. All equations seem to have normal residuals. The multivariate tests on the vectors also indicate that the vector is normal and there is no autocorrelation.

Table 7.4. *Extended monetary model: Specification tests (intercept, seasonal dummies, trend, 2 lags, and dummies to account for outliers)*

Statistics	LNE	M	R	CA	PY	GOV	Y
$F_{k=1}(7,58)$	9.86**	15.70**	1.12	4.57**	8.43**	6.88**	9.96**
$F_{k=2}(7,58)$	1.30	1.22	0.42	1.94	0.36	2.78*	0.30
$F_{AR}(5,59)$	0.33	0.29	1.04	0.08	1.83	0.17	1.20
$F_{ARCH}(4,56)$	0.61	0.65	1.98	0.49	0.13	2.24	0.57
$\chi^2(2)$	0.33	0.21	0.05	3.05	1.85	2.00	5.40

Multivariate
Tests
$F_{AR}(245,170)$ 1.15
$\chi^2(14)$ 17.00

Note: ** Rejects null hypothesis at the 1% significance level; * rejects the null at the 5% significance level.

4.3.2. Determination of the number of cointegration vectors

The next step is to determine the number of cointegrating vectors in each system. Using the Pantula method we can simultaneously test for the parameterisation of the VAR. The results (not shown) indicate that we should use a model which allows for linear trends in the data, and that there are three cointegration vectors. As discussed above, there has been very mixed evidence for the monetary model (especially for Germany) and it has been argued that the model is not appropriate as it fails to represent a long-run relationship of the exchange rate. The result that there appear to be three cointegration vectors for this model specification suggests that a long-run relationship of the exchange rate does exist.

4.3.3. Testing the cointegration relationships

We can now set the number of cointegration vectors to three and perform tests of weak exogeneity, stationarity and exclusion on the variables considered (Table 7.5).[3]

All of the variables seem to be significant in the model (we reject the null for all the LR tests), all variables are non-stationary, and only M and GOV are weakly exogenous. We can now re-estimate the system conditional on the weak exogeneity of these two variables. The resulting vectors are displayed in Table 7.6.

Table 7.5. *Monetary model: tests for exclusion, weak exogeneity, and stationarity*

	LNE	M	R	CA	PY	GOV	Y	Critical Value
Exclusion	8.76	10.49	24.64	25.32	23.78	22.76	32.42	7.81
Stationarity	11.91	23.63	14.09	22.25	20.34	19.85	15.13	9.49
Weak exogeneity	10.64	4.80	25.69	12.40	20.46	3.81	10.90	7.81

Note: * rejects the null at the 5% significance level.

Table 7.6. *Extended monetary model: re-estimated system based on exogeneity of variables*

vector no.	LNE	R	CA	PY	Y	M	GOV
1	1.00	-37.26	-0.003	-7.00	-10.61	2.69	-4.16
2	1.00	-28.87	0.001	3.09	4.78	0.07	0.28
3	1.00	-7.32	-0.001	1.96	-0.49	-1.24	0.57

Whereas the first vector only has 3 coefficients with the anticipated sign, the second and third vectors have 5 and 6 respectively. The third vector thus has only one incorrect sign (the income variable) out of 7.

We have found three vectors and now face the problem of identifying the single long-run relationship of interest. One logical way to do this would be to pick the vector which makes most economic sense. Given the coefficient values, there does not seem to be a vector which is completely consistent with the model as proposed theoretically. The second and third vector have most signs correct, but there is no way to tell which one of the two (if any of them) represents the relationship we seek: '[an] arbitrary selection of one statistically significant cointegration vector involves making the implicit assumption that the conditional model which is isolated is valid. This problem cannot be tackled by the Johansen procedure because it does not partition the variables into endogenous and (weakly) exogenous, which his central to estimating a single behavioural equation' (Moosa, 1994, p. 285). An additional problem is that the Johansen approach only allows us to test restrictions on all vectors simultaneously, so we cannot rule out the possibility that there may exist a cointegrating vector that satisfies all the restrictions.

The coefficient on the inflation rate differential in the second vector is very large, while the coefficient on the money supply variable is negative. This is again the problem of the 'multiplying marks' as, according to this economically implausible result, an increase in the money supply at home leads to an appreciation of the home currency. The third vector has only one wrongly signed coefficient (that of income). According to the coefficients of this vector, a 1% increase in the inflation differential (i.e. a 1% increase in German inflation or a 1% decrease in the US inflation rate) leads to a depreciation of the DEM by 7.31%. The coefficient on the current account differential (which proxies the risk premium) indicates that an increase in the current account differential by 1% leads to a depreciation by 0.02% while an increase in the productivity differential by 1% leads to an appreciation by 1.96%. The coefficient on output (as measured by industrial production) is wrongly signed, as according to the theoretical model there should be a negative relationship between output and the exchange rate. The relationship above indicates that an increase in output leads to a depreciation (by 0.49% for a 1% increase), thus the income elasticity is positive. Previous studies of the monetary model have experienced problems of very large income elasticities, but while in the above equation the size of the coefficient is reasonable, the sign is wrong. The coefficient on the money supply has the correct sign and is close to unity, which is supportive of our choice of this vector as representation of the monetary model (both of the other vectors have a negatively signed coefficient for the money supply). The government spending coefficient indicates that a 1% increase in Germany's government spending leads to an appreciation by 0.57%. All of the coefficients seem economically reasonable, although the coefficient of the inflation rate differential appears large in comparison to the others. It seems that the DEM/USD exchange rate is very responsive to the inflation rate in Germany and the US, possibly as a consequence of the inflation target policy of the German Bundesbank.

Now we can also look at the α-matrix of adjustment coefficients (Table 7.7). The value of α estimates the proportional change in the given variable in response to a 100% deviation of the exchange rate from equilibrium. The adjustment is stabilising if the sign of α is equal to the sign of the corresponding value of in the β-vector (Cushman et al., 1996).

Table 7.7.   Extended monetary model: matrix of adjustment
              coefficients (t-values between parentheses)

	Vector 1	Vector 2	Vector 3
DLNE	-0.03	0.04	0.04
	(-2.97)	(1.60)	(1.17)
DR	-0.01	-0.02	-0.00
	(-5.32)	(-5.01)	(-1.08)
DCA	31.82	105.47	-193.59
	(2.16)	(3.26)	(-4.36)
DPY	-0.01	-0.01	0.01
	(-4.82)	(-2.22)	(0.83)
DY	-0.02	0.01	0.01
	(-3.81)	(1.28)	(0.66)

The inflation rate adjusts correctly in all three cases, while the exchange rate, current account, productivity and output adjust correctly in two cases each. The size of the adjustment factors is between 0.01 and 0.04 (in absolute terms) with the exception of the adjustment for the current account variable. Recall that this variable replaces the interest rate differential, based on the UIP equation with the added assumption that the expected depreciation of the currency is equal to zero. A quick adjustment here seems to indicate that the interest rate and hence the risk premium adjusts quickly to a change in the exchange rate. This is consistent with our view that asset prices are quickest to adjust. For the second and third vectors the signs of all but one of the α values match the signs of the β coefficients; however, the t-values indicate that several coefficients are not statistically significant, especially in the third vector. The t-values are only indicative of statistical significance for the first vector which we earlier discarded as not seeming to represent the exchange rate relationship we seek.

Cushman et al. (1996) point out that although the values of the α matrix give us an idea of the size of the adjustment, it does not tell us how successful this adjustment is. They argue that the adjustment of a given variable is faster if it has a large coefficient in the cointegration vector. To measure the success of adjustment to disequilibrium they multiply the α values with the corresponding values of the vector. The resulting values (Table 7.8) give the proportion of the deviation from equilibrium that will be removed by the adjustment of that variable.

Table 7.8. *Extended monetary model: proportion of deviation from equilibrium that will be removed by adjustment of the variable*

	Vector 1	Vector 2	Vector 3
DLNE	-0.03	0.04	0.04
DR	0.37	0.61	0.04
DCA	-0.10	0.11	0.00
DPY	0.10	-0.05	0.02
DY	0.18	0.06	-0.00

Noticeable is the apparent importance of the adjustment of the inflation rate in vectors 1 and 2, the current account variable in the second vector, and the productivity and output variable in the first vector. The fact that the productivity variable seems to be significant in the adjustment of the exchange rate from disequilibrium is yet another factor in support of the extended monetary model.

Overall there is more support for the extended model as proposed by Sarantis and Pu (1997) than for the more traditional monetary model investigated before. Coefficients for the real factor variables *PY* and *GOV* are statistically significant, which show that fiscal policy is of considerable importance.

5. CONCLUSION

The aim of this paper was to find an exchange rate determination model which fits the DEM/USD exchange rate and use the results to draw some conclusions on the likely behaviour of the euro/USD exchange rate. The traditional monetary model does not seem to fit the data well, and despite finding several cointegration relationships, we were unable to find long-run relationships with the exchange rate as the dependent variable. The extended monetary model proposed by Sarantis and Pu (1997) allows for real exchange rate variations by introducing real factor variables. For this model we found three cointegration relationships, one of which closely resembles the model as predicted theoretically. The real factor variables (government spending and productivity) were statistically and economically significant. This suggests that more attention needs to be paid to those real factors as determinants of the external euro exchange rate, the current discussion surrounding the euro exchange rate focusing almost exclusively on monetary policy.

A number of important issues remain unresolved. First, the DEM/USD exchange rate was used here to avoid problems of aggregation across countries; further research should extend the approach to euroland aggregates. Second, the introduction of EMU may lead to structural parameter changes. Third, the fundamental critique remains that nominal exchange rates are more variable than the macroeconomic fundamentals (both nominal and real) that typically enter the regression equations, suggesting that the models miss the speculative elements that account for this variability (Taylor, 1995).

NOTES

1. Sonja Hellemann is at the Banque Paribas in London and Luc Hens is at the Free University of Brussels (VUB) and the University of Antwerp (RUCA).
2. PcFiml 8.0 was used for these tests. PcFiml also performs multivariate tests for vector auto-correlation (F-test) and vector normality (χ^2).
3. Johansen's CATS procedures for the RATS econometrics software contain the required batch tests.

REFERENCES

Baillie, T. R. and R.A. Pecchenino (1991), 'The Search for Equilibrium Relationships in International Finance: the case of the monetary model', *Journal of International Money and Finance*, **10**, 582-93.

Boothe, P. and D. Glassman (1987), 'Off the Mark: Lessons for Exchange Rate Modelling', *Oxford Economic Papers*, **39**, 443-57.

Cushman, D.O., S.S. Lee and T. Thorgeirsson (1996), 'Maximum Likelihood Estimation of Cointegration in Exchange Rate Models for Seven Inflationary OECD Countries', *Journal of International Money and Finance*, **15**, 337-68.

De Grauwe, P. (1996), *International Money* (2nd edition), Oxford: Oxford University Press.

Frankel, A.J. (1979), 'On the Mark: A Theory of Floating Exchange Rates Based on Real Interest Differentials', *American Economic Review*, **69**, 610-22.

Frankel, A.J. (1982), 'The Mystery of the Multiplying Marks: A Modification of the Monetary Model', *Review of Economics and Statistics*, **64**, 515-19.

MacDonald, R. and L. la Cour (1997), 'Modelling the ECU Against the US Dollar: A structural monetary interpretation', Centre for Financial Markets Research University of Strathclyde, Discussion Paper No.2.

MacDonald, R. and M.P. Taylor (1991), 'The Monetary Approach to the Exchange Rate: Long-run Relationships and Coefficient Restrictions', *Economics Letters*, **37**, 179-85.

MacDonald, R. and M.P. Taylor (1994), 'The Monetary Model of the Exchange Rate: Long-Run Relationships, Short-Run Dynamics, and How to Beat a Random Walk', *Journal of International Money and Finance*, **13**, 276-87.

Moosa, A.I. (1994), 'The Monetary Model of Exchange Rates Revisited', *Applied Financial Economics*, **4**, 279-87.

Rogoff, K. (1996), 'The Purchasing Power Parity Puzzle*', Journal of Economic Literature*, **34**, 647-68.

Sarantis, N. and Y. Pu (1997), 'Determination of ECU Exchange Rates, and Lessons for the Euro', London Guildhall Centre for International Capital Markets Discussion Paper, No. 97-05.

Taylor, M.P. (1995), 'The Economics of Exchange Rates', *Journal of Economic Literature*, **33**, 13-47.

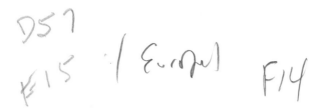

8. Historical Lessons from Trade Flows During the Benelux and EEC periods: Comparative Advantage, Bilateralism and Intra-Industry Trade

Herbert Glejser[1]

1. INTRODUCTION

Although I have been working for a quarter of a century on customs unions and the trade shifts that accompany them, this paper is not a case of pouring old wine in new goatskins. Admittedly the data series end twenty years ago. But it is also true that it is in the Benelux, EEC-6 and EEC-9 that the biggest shocks of successive enlargements were felt: the transition to EEC-12 and ultimately EEC-15 were of a much smaller amplitude (except of course for the new members themselves), and NAFTA and Mercosur are a little bit too close to call.

The historic lessons that can be drawn may give additional insight into the kind and magnitude of the turmoil on the international goods markets that is before us, now that the EU is on the verge of another major enlargement.

I will basically follow the same procedure as in my 1976 contribution (Glejser, 1976) and use a spline version of the share and shift method (see also Balassa, 1976; Hufbauer and Adler, 1968; Prewo, 1974). For the share of exports from country i, to country j, a regression of the following type was estimated:

$$S_{ij} = \sigma_{ij} + \theta_{ij}T + \theta'_{ij}T' + u_{ij} , \qquad (8.1)$$

where S_{ij} is country i's share in the import of country j and where σ_{ij}, θ_{ij}, θ_{ij} are the constant share term and trend parameters respectively. The last but one pertains to the whole period $(T=1,...,n,...,N)$ and the last to the final period $(T'=0,...,0,n+1,...,N)$. We thus surmise a general trend, with co-efficient θ_{ij}, and a break in the trend after the first n years.

In a similar way, S_{ij}^* is country j's share in the export to i (as a percentage of j's total export). We have now:

$$S_{ij}^* = \sigma_{ij}^* + \theta_{ij}^* T + \theta_{ij}^{*'} T' + u_{ij}^* .$$ (8.2)

Both S_{ij} and S_{ij}^* are expressed in percentage points.

Using this approach, the new wine in the old goatskins amounts to the following questions:

- Which theory of international trade – comparative advantage, bilateralism or intra-sector trade – is supported by our analysis?
- What happens – in terms of trade flows – when small customs unions (e.g. the Benelux) are absorbed by a larger one (the EEC)?

We analyse the following periods:

- 1950 to 1958: the pre-EEC period, i.e. the Benelux period;
- the period from 1959 to 1972: the first phase EEC (with 6 members);
- the period from 1973 to 1977: the second phase EEC with 9 countries (essentially plus the UK).

In section 2 we discuss the trade flow effects outside the EEC following the creation of the latter. We focus first on the external effects of European integration on US trade specifically, and continue after that, more in general, with the induced integration effects on the trade among excluded countries. We conclude the section with a discussion of correlation results obtained from the parameter estimates. This will allow us to evaluate the relevance of different trade models. Section 3 deals with the trade effects of the absorption of a small custom union, the Benelux, by a larger one, EEC-6 first and, after that, EEC-9.

2. SOME IMPORTANT EXTERNAL TRADE FLOW EFFECTS OF THE CREATION OF THE EEC: 1950-1972

2.1.

The calculated share of the six founders of the EEC in US import in 1949 ($\hat{\sigma}_{6,US}$) was extremely low (see also Glejser and Moro (1996)): between 6.8 and 7.5% – i.e. less than a quarter of Canada's share (23.5%). Italy and France were lowest: 0.9% and 1%, about two thirds of Australia or Japan (see Table 8.1).

From 1950 to 1958 $\hat{\theta}_{i,US}$ was positive for Japan and Europe, particularly for Japan, W. Germany and the UK. The coefficients were however low or negative for Belgium and the Netherlands (diversion by the Benelux), and also negative for Australia and Canada from which war deliveries had been switched to continental Europe. We can surmise that either US import did not rise much from Latin America, Asia (outside Japan) and Africa and from Eastern Europe or went down for most of these areas, as the trend is mostly positive for Europe and part of the Pacific.

The change that came about around 1958 was more dramatic, especially outside the EEC: for Japan, $\theta + \theta'$ was estimated at 0.75 percentage points a year and for Canada at 0.52 pp. This is considerably higher in absolute value than the highest figures for the EEC: 0.22 pp. for Germany, 0.10 for Italy, -0.05 for Belgium and France, and close to zero for the Netherlands. Thus import shares from Germany to the US rose after the advent of the EEC and the decline in the trade with some other EEC members was very small. For the US induced trade was huge (see below). The same was true for Australia, Canada and Japan, the percentage-point increase of the latter three together being 0.04 + 0.52 + 0.75 = 1.31 !

Summarising, the US import share of the countries considered increased after 1950 with an estimated yearly trend-value (i.e. $\hat{\theta} + \hat{\theta}'$) of 1.31 pp. because of induced trade with the five non-EEC nations, by 0.32 pp. because of an increasing trend with Germany and Italy, and by -0.12 because of diversion in Belgium, France, the Netherlands and the remaining EFTA countries.

There must thus be an enormous yearly loss of 1.51 pp. (= 1.31 + 0.32 - 0.12) in trade with other areas of the world as EEC diversion was practically inexistent and even replaced by an astonishing creation (for Germany and Italy).

The conclusions in Table 8.2 are very similar to those that we obtained for US imports (Table 8.1): after 1950, the US export share yearly grew by 0.54 pp. (0.41+0.13) in the case of Japan, by 0.40 in the case of Canada and by 0.11 in the case of Australia. The only considerable increase inside Europe (0.16) was for the group of non-UK EFTA countries.

For the UK and the rest of the EEC, the coefficients are also all positive but very small: 0.05 for France, 0.04 for Germany, the UK and the Netherlands and 0.03 for Italy. It is again clear that induced integration took place (especially with Japan and Canada) without any clear diversion from EEC and EFTA countries. Diversion must then have occurred in the four geographic-political areas mentioned before (Latin America, Africa, Eastern Europe and Asia). One sector where imports and exports to Europe and Canada went up in relative terms was agriculture, especially with France, Germany, and Canada (see Table 8.3).[2] It must be that this rise again happened at the expense of agricultural trade with the rest of the world.

Table 8.1. Parameter estimates of the US import shares as in equation 8.1 in 1949, from 1950 to 1958 and from 1959 to 1972 (t-values between brackets)

	$\hat{\sigma}$	$\hat{\theta}$	$\hat{\theta}'$	$\hat{\theta}+\hat{\theta}'$	$\bar{R}^2$	D.W.
Belgium	1.7	0.12	-0.17	-0.05	0.55	2.06
		(4.70)	(-5.02)			
W. Germany	1.7	0.49	-0.27	0.22	0.96	2.02
		(11.25)	(-4.53)			
France	1.0	0.23	-0.28	-0.05	0.73	1.38
		(7.05)	(-6.10)			
Italy	0.9	0.17	-0.07	0.10	0.94	1.37
		(7.24)	(-2.07)			
The Netherlands	1.5	-0.03	0.02	-0.01	0.31	1.68
		(-2.23)	(1.38)			
EEC	(7.5)	(1.00)	(-0.77)	(0.23)	0.73	1.86
		(8.28)	(-4.85)			
UK	3.5	0.32	-0.32	0.00	0.73	1.43
		(5.93)	(-4.27)			
Other EFTA countries	3.9	0.10	-0.11	-0.01	0.60	2.01
		(3.31)	(-0.27)			
Australia	1.5	-0.07	0.11	0.04	0.32	0.88
		(-1.70)	(2.32)			
Canada	23.5	-0.39	0.91	0.52	0.61	1.41
		(-2.19)	(3.70)			
Japan	1.4	0.58	0.17	0.75	0.98	2.42
		(5.59)	(1.43)			
Rest of the world	–	-1.52	0.01	-1.51	–	–
		(-)	(-)			

For all countries, the sign of $\hat{\theta}^* + \hat{\theta}'^*$ is positive which indicates no diversion of US exports. For imports there were four (small) negative coefficients out of ten, but the sum of the six positive coefficients was larger than that of the ten in Table 8.2 (1.51 as against 1.43), indicating an equal yearly decline both ways. The similarity between 1.43 and 1.39 (1.51 - 0.12) is also remarkable. Note that the sum of the $\hat{\sigma}$'s is larger for exports than for imports (48.7 as against 40.6), meaning that at the start of the period considered the penetration of US exports into these ten countries was larger than the share of their imports from the US.

Table 8.2. *Parameter estimates of the US export shares as in equation 8.2 in 1949, from 1950 to 1958 and from 1959 to 1972 (t-values between brackets)*

	$\hat{\sigma}^*$	$\hat{\theta}^*$	$\hat{\theta}^{**}$	$\hat{\theta}^* + \hat{\theta}^{**}$	$\bar{R}^2$	D.W.
Belgium	2.0	-0.02	0.04	0.02	0.01	2.05
		(-0.66)	(0.92)			
W. Germany	2.0	0.66	-0.62	0.04	0.83	1.33
		(7.33)	(-4.48)			
France	2.3	0.21	-0.16	0.05	0.63	1.84
		(3.16)	(-2.04)			
Italy	2.2	0.15	-0.12	0.03	0.29	1.20
		(2.07)	(-1.22)			
The Netherlands	1.7	0.16	-0.12	0.04	0.72	1.81
		(3.89)	(-2.54)			
EEC	(8.3)	(1.63)	(-1.65)	(-0.02)	0.83	1.51
		(7.97)	(-6.14)			
UK	5.1	0.22	-0.18	0.04	0.21	2.13
		(1.60)	(1.11)			
Other EFTA countries	6.6	0.45	-0.29	0.16	0.66	2.33
		(2.32)	(-1.30)			
Australia	1.4	0.00	0.11	0.11	0.73	0.95
		(0.00)	(2.57)			
Canada	21.2	-0.24	0.64	0.40	0.64	1.00
		(-0.99)	(1.95)			
Japan	4.2	0.41	0.13	0.54	0.79	1.93
		(3.39)	(0.74)			
Rest of the world	–	-2.00	0.57	-1.43	–	–
		(-)	(-)			

2.2.
To investigate induced integration, i.e. the large increase in mutual trade between a small number of countries excluded from a customs union, we shall consider the values of $\hat{\theta}^* + \hat{\theta}^{**}$ for the trade with each other (see Table 8.3). As can be verified this induced integration phenomenon can be very important.

The highest figures are shown for the imports of the smallest country considered here, Australia, from the US (1.06) and Japan (1.03). These values turn out to be the largest in this exercise. Then follow: the US from Japan (0.75), Canada from the US (0.52), the US from Canada (0.52), Canada from the US (0.37), Canada from Japan (0.24), etc., the lowest ones being Canada from Australia (0.03), Australia from Japan (0.01) and, strangely enough, Japan from the US (-0.91).

Table 8.3. *Shares in the imports of Australia, Canada, Japan and the US (induced integration)*

	t^s	$\hat{\sigma}$	$\hat{\theta}$	$\hat{\theta}'$	$\hat{\theta}+\hat{\theta}'$	$\overline{R}^2$	D.W.
Australia from:							
Canada	1958	4.28	-0.19	0.32	0.13	0.30	2.12
			(-1.47)	(2.03)			
Japan	1959	1.65	0.16	0.87	1.03	0.94	1.54
			(0.83)	(3.61)**			
US	1958	11.70	0.31	0.75	1.06	0.89	1.51
			(0.87)	(1.78)			
Canada from:							
Australia	1960	0.48	0.02	0.01	0.03	0.28	1.45
			(1.17)	(0.20)			
Japan	1960	0.17	0.17	0.07	0.24	0.88	0.69
			(2.95)**	(0.87)			
US	1960	76.30	-1.04	1.41	0.37	0.65	0.68
			(-6.09)**	(5.94)**			
Japan from:							
Australia	1958	5.85	0.29	-0.28	0.01	0.24	1.62
			(2.16)	(-1.72)			
Canada	1958	5.76	-0.27	0.34	0.07	0.66	1.85
			(-5.87)**	(6.17)**			
US	1960	34.50	0.03	-0.94	-0.97	0.74	2.11
			(0.09)	(-2.45)*			
US from:							
Australia	1958	1.50	-0.07	0.11	0.04	0.32	0.88
			(-1.76)	(2.32)*			
Canada	1960	23.50	-0.39	0.91	0.52	0.61	1.41
			(-2.19)**	(3.70)**			
Japan	1958	1.40	0.58	0.17	0.75	0.98	2.42
			(5.59)**	(1.43)			

Note: Figures in parentheses are *t*-values, * means significant at the 5 % level, and ** significant at the 1 % level. $\overline{R}^2$ is the determination coefficient corrected for the loss of degrees of freedom. t^s is the start of the second period.

The increase is largest for large exporters (US and Japan) but tends to be also considerable for small importers - cf. Australia from the US and Japan and Canada from the US. Note that the 10 sums of the estimated $\hat{\theta}^* + \hat{\theta}^{*}$ are positive. Yet five in twelve of the $\hat{\theta}^*$'s (i.e. the trend before the advent of the EEC) are negative (by far the lowest is -1.04). A further 'détricotage' could probably have prevented the birth of NAFTA thirty years later.

Table 8.3 shows a clear increase of the parameters, i.e. of induced integration after the start of EEC: ten coefficients out of 12 are positive, five of which are significant. This is very different from $\hat{\theta}$, before the European customs unions, for which only 7 coefficients are positive and only two significantly so (3 are negatively significant).[3] There has been a general acceleration after the EEC started, especially with respect to imports of Canada from the US (1.41 as against -1.04 before) and US from Canada (0.91 as against -0.39).

2.3.

Before discussing the correlation present in the tables, let us first clarify the interpretation of the possible results (all our correlations are Spearman rank correlations in view of our ignorance of the form of the underlying function). We distinguish the following cases:

1. $\rho_{\sigma_{ij}\sigma_{ji}} > 0$ over all couples $i \neq j$ or, in short, $\rho_{\sigma,\sigma^*} > 0$. This means bilateralism and/or intra-specialisation in the past. The two are however hard to distinguish. Since bilateralism seems more connected with the results, we will henceforward use the term bilateralism only.

2. $\rho_{\sigma,\sigma^*} \leq 0$. There is not a positive link between the intercepts, which means, in other words, the occurrence in the past of 'free' flows in both directions. This is interpreted as comparative advantage.

3. $\rho_{\sigma,\theta}$ or $\rho_{\sigma^*,\theta^*} > 0$: perpetuation of the large and small flows, meaning dynamic bilateralism.

4. $\rho_{\sigma,\theta}$ or $\rho_{\sigma^*,\theta^*} \leq 0$ which indicates a tendency to equality, i.e. small σ accompanying large θ or vice versa: dynamic comparative advantage.

5. $\rho_{\theta,\theta^*} > 0$: trends go in the same direction, meaning dynamic bilateralism.

6. $\rho_{\theta,\theta^*} \leq 0$: a tendency towards a larger spread of flows between trade partners. There is probably comparative advantage at play.

7. $\rho_{\theta,\theta}$ or $\rho_{\theta^*,\theta^*} > 0$: dynamic comparative advantage, i.e. the evolution of the flows goes on during the two periods.

8. $\rho_{\theta,\theta}$ or $\rho_{\theta^*,\theta^*} \leq 0$: slowdown of rises or declines of trade flows between partners: dynamic bilateralism.

The rank correlation (Spearman) between $\hat{\sigma}$ and $\hat{\sigma}^*$ in Table 8.3 is negative (-0.01). This would indicate comparative advantage (case 2 above), but the correlation is of course not statistically significant. The only similarities in ranking are for Canada (ranks 1 and 1) and the US (ranks 2 and 3). Those relate to trade flows which were relatively little affected by the war operations. There is also no significant correlation between $\hat{\sigma}$ and $\hat{\theta}$, which indicates a trend towards equality of shares, viz. case 4.

For Tables 8.1 and 8.2 the rank correlation between $\hat{\theta}$ and $\hat{\theta}^*$ is 0.72 with standard error of 0.31.[4] The rank correlation between $\hat{\theta}'$ and $\hat{\theta}'^*$ is 0.84 with a standard error of 0.28. The rank correlation between $\hat{\theta}+\hat{\theta}'$ and $\hat{\theta}^*+\hat{\theta}'^*$ is 0.71 with again the same standard error 0.31. All three correlations are statistically significant at the 5 % confidence level. They indicate dynamic bilateralism (case 5). The exceptions are small liberal European countries like some EFTA countries, Belgium and the Netherlands. This contrasts with nations like Japan, Canada, Germany, the UK and Australia where positivity dominates.

If we now look for evidence on dynamic comparative advantage or, on the contrary, either intra-industry trade or bilateralism, on the basis of rank correlation between the $\hat{\theta}$'s in the two directions in Table 8.3, we obtain $\rho = -0.15$ which does not significantly differ from zero. This probably points at comparative advantage (case 7). The only pairs showing a significant positive correlation in the set are: Canada and the US, Australia and the US, and, with some reservation, Australia and Canada. Japan stands outside this short list of positive trends after the war, contrary to the three allies which, as we saw, showed some dynamic bilateralism (case 5).

We also looked at differences in $\hat{\theta}+\hat{\theta}'$ in exports and imports of the four Pacific countries (six flows in each direction). We obtain a negative rank correlation of -0.49, which is non-significant, but which is essentially due to the negative correlation between the US and Japan (-0.94 and 0.17). There is however also a positive link for the US and Canada (0.37 and 0.07) and Australia and Canada (0.13 and 0.03): again small countries, especially Canada, dominate this grouping of positive links between additional exports and imports, whereas the two large nations exhibit strong negative links.

But all in all, negativity dominates, suggesting comparative advantage.

3. FROM THE BENELUX TO THE EEC WITHOUT AND WITH THE UK

The first sections were devoted to the EEC and EFTA members and to the main outsiders. We thought however that some lessons could be learned for a previous customs union: the Benelux, which started a decade before the EEC (six members, including the three Benelux countries), which would become nine as of 1973 when the UK, Denmark and Ireland joined.

Table 8.4 presents the main results from our regressions: $\hat{\sigma}$ is as before, $\hat{\theta}$ now pertains to the pure Benelux period (not the global trend as in equations 1 and 2), $\hat{\theta}'$ to the EEC-6 period (1959-1972) and $\hat{\theta}''$ to EEC-9 from 1973 to 1977.

Belgium and the Netherlands differ greatly in their $\hat{\sigma}$: Belgium is the main origin of imported goods in the Netherlands in 1950 but the US comes first for Belgium. As to exports, Germany comes first for the Netherlands whereas the Netherlands lead the way for Belgian sales.

The rank correlation of the $\hat{\sigma}$'s (with respect to imports and exports) amounts to 0.71 for the Netherlands and 0.66 for Belgium. In view of the small number of observations (six for the Netherlands and five for Belgium) these results are not significant and therefore only weakly point to past bilateralism.

The $\hat{\theta}$ and $\hat{\theta}'$ correlations for the Netherlands and Belgium are generally high (0.54 and 0.59). Yet all the results are overshadowed by the portentous come-back of Germany after the war[5] (e.g. on the Belgian market) and to a much lesser extent of Italy and France. The brunt of trade diversion in the West is borne by the UK and by the US: the Belgian export share to the UK declines yearly with 0.49 pp. while its import share from the US falls yearly with 0.66 pp.

When EEC-6 soars, there is trade diversion between the Benelux-members. $\hat{\theta}'$ is particularly low for the import of Belgium from The Netherlands (-0.59), whereas the fresh members usually benefit from the new customs union. The US and the UK go on losing.

As from 1973, the UK gains enormously whereas the others lose. The losses of Germany are most impressive. Notice that the sum of the three coefficients $\hat{\theta}+\hat{\theta}'+\hat{\theta}''$ for the UK is always positive (e.g. 0.25 in the imports-equation for Belgium). As said before, this contrasts with Germany and also the US and Italy where this sum is negative (with at least two of the three terms) in all cases (e.g. -0.93 for Germany in the imports-equation of the Netherlands). The last three countries, France, the Netherlands and Belgium, show a mixed picture with a dominance of positive coefficients.

For the US this is, of course, a case of blatant trade diversion. But what about Germany and Italy?[6] Could it be that the former became more oriented towards Central (Switzerland and Austria) and Northern and Eastern Europe, and Italy towards the Mediterranean world? The integrated Benelux, the UK and France would represent the Northwest economic hub of Europe where economic integration would be at its highest in 1973. Of course this should be checked, among other things, by the study of the trade flows between France and the UK. Let us in this context not forget the effects of the soaring oil price.

Table 8.4. *Results for the trade shares of Benelux for the periods 1950-1959, 1960-1972 and 1973-1977*

	$\hat{\sigma}$	$\hat{\theta}$	$\hat{\theta}'$	$\hat{\theta}''$	$\overline{R}^2$	D.W.
Imports of the Netherlands from						
Belgium	18.4	0.00	-0.05	-1.10	0.99	1.92
Germany	12.0	1.00	-0.47	-1.46	0.99	1.96
France	4.1	-0.13	0.50	-0.64	0.99	1.79
Italy	1.2	0.21	-0.01	-0.39	0.99	1.82
UK	9.9	-0.27	0.10	0.42	0.99	1.70
US	11.5	0.10	-0.32	0.17	0.99	2.01
Rest of the World	42.9	-0.91	0.25	2.90		
Imports of Belgium from						
the Netherlands	10.4	0.54	-0.59	–	0.84	2.20
Germany	7.5	1.02	0.52	–	0.98	1.94
France	8.6	0.26	0.12	–	0.88	1.07
UK	9.1	-0.11	-0.03	0.39	0.76	1.89
US	15.9	-0.66	0.46	–	0.27	2.38
Rest of the World	48.5	-0.21	-.48	–		
Exports of the Netherlands to						
Belgium	13.8	0.21	-0.32	0.20	0.99	2.02
Germany	15.0	0.48	0.52	-1.70	0.90	1.74
France	4.4	0.09	0.34	-0.58	0.93	1.79
Italy	1.2	0.23	-0.05	-0.35	0.99	1.79
UK	14.0	-0.42	0.17	0.53	0.99	1.86
US	6.2	-0.09	-0.04	0.02	0.75	1.74
Rest of the World	46.4	-0.50	-0.62	1.88		
Exports of Belgium to						
the Netherlands	18.5	0.35	-0.26	–	0.41	1.59
Germany	6.1	0.71	0.37	–	0.95	1.68
France	8.6	0.12	0.69	–	0.91	1.60
UK	10.0	-0.49	0.38	0.69	0.82	1.57
US	7.6	0.28	-0.49	–	0.27	2.38
Rest of the World	49.2	-0.97	-0.69	–		

We rank-correlated the $\hat{\sigma}$'s for both trade flows with six countries (in the case of the Netherlands) and five countries (in the case of Belgium). We obtained $\rho = 0.71$ and $\rho = 0.40$. With such small numbers of observations, none is significantly different from zero. The same exercise for $\hat{\theta}$ and $\hat{\theta}^*$ yields values of 0.88 and 0.60. The former is significantly different from zero. This points to plain or dynamic bilateralism.

For $\hat{\theta}$ and $\hat{\theta}'$ we obtain -0.10 and -0.03 respectively, and finally for $\hat{\theta}'$ and $\hat{\theta}''$ (in the case of the Netherlands) 0.66 which suggests dynamic comparative advantage.

At last in Table 8.4: do the $\bar{R}^2$ and D.W. values correlate between exports and imports? The answer seems to be mostly positive. E.g. for Belgium we obtain the value of 0.90 for the adjusted coefficient of determination (significant), whereas for the Netherlands the result is negative, but not significant (-0.55). With respect to the D.W. coefficients we get respectively 0.70 and 0.37: this could suggest the use of the S.U.R.E. method of estimation instead, handling the two regressions simultaneously (between Tables 8.1 and 8.3 we found for the DW-statistic a rank correlation of 0.51).

4. CONCLUSION

There is plenty of evidence in our results, yet they are sometimes contradictory as far as choosing one particular theory of trade is concerned: comparative advantage however comes out most frequently, sometimes in its dynamic form.

Induced integration effects on trade flows are a real and important phenomenon. So much has taken place, e.g. between Canada and the US, that we may find in a couple of years that the effects of NAFTA are rather weak.

As to newcomers in the EU in the next century, we may expect that one of the results will be, like was in the past the case of other relatively less wealthy countries entering the EEC, an increased trade with each other. This is first of all because the abolition of barriers to trade among them will be relatively more important than the removal of obstacles by the original 15; secondly, because those markets are for the time being still less exacting than the Western ones; thirdly because of proximity.

One might however deplore that the EU is going perhaps to include six new members at one stroke. Such a high number of new members has never before been tried. Three was the maximum so far, and they were easier cases. Welcoming first one or two countries (but faster) would have taught useful lessons for the rest.

NOTES

1. The author is grateful for the assistance of S. Charlier, J. Desmidts, O. De Marchant, X. Gérard, T. Kalonji and M. Schöller.
2. It seems that the CAP which favoured the production of meat and dairy products necessitated more cereal imports from the US.
3. θ and $\hat{\theta}$ are both positive in 5 cases out of 12. The highest values are for Australia from Japan and the US, and for Japan from the US The latter shows the reconstruction of the Japanese economy from the start onwards oriented towards the Pacific (except Canada). Note also the negative value of $\hat{\theta}$ for Japan from the US
4. According to the formula $se_\rho = 1/(n-1)^{1/2}$.
5. Germany is first in all four rankings of Table 8.4. It probably accounts for the value zero of θ in the first line of Table 8.4 (the Netherlands from Belgium).
6. Italy is the only European country examined here that borders only on one EEC country (with some generosity two). With some generosity again, the Netherlands, the UK and France border three and Belgium and Germany four. This is without counting Luxembourg which would add one unit to France, Belgium and Germany (now five). This consideration may shed some light on the Italian case, but of course not on the German.

REFERENCES

Balassa, B. (1976), 'Trade Creation and Trade Diversion in the European Common Market: an Approach of the Evidence', in H. Glejser (ed.), *Quantitative Studies of International Economic Relations,* op. cit., pp. 91-132.

Glejser, H. (1976), 'The Respective Impacts of Relative Income, Price and Technology Changes, US Foreign Investment, the EEC and EFTA on the American Balance of Payments', in H. Glejser (ed.), *Quantitative Studies of International Economic Relations*, op. cit., pp. 133-171.

Glejser, H. (ed.) (1976), *Quantitative Studies of International Economic Relations,* Amsterdam: North Holland.

Glejser, H. and S. Moro (1996), 'Estimates of Trade Effects of Portugal's and Spain's Entry to the European Union', *De Economist,* **144**, 285-304.

Hufbauer, G.C. and F.M. Adler (1968), 'Overseas Manufacturing Investment and the Balance of Payments', Institute for International Economics, Washington D.C.

Prewo, W.F. (1974), 'Integration Effects in the EEC: an Attempt at Quantification in a General Equilibrium Framework', *European Economic Review,* **5**, 482-505.

PART II

Public Policy Issues

033 F14 L96 L98 (handwritten)

9. The Impact of the RTD Policy of the EU on Technological Collaboration: A Case Study of the European Telecommunications Industry

Michel Dumont and Wim Meeusen[1]

1. INTRODUCTION

In this chapter we will evaluate – by means of a case study – the impact, if any, that the S&T policy of the EU may have had on the creation of specific new patterns of private trans-European collaboration, or if, to some extent, it merely reinforced an already existing network of private collaboration, adding only to existing determinants like globalisation forces and technological progress.

The methodological approach which will be followed is that of social network analysis. We shall concentrate on the virtual network formed by R&D-active firms in the telecommunications sector linked among each other by partnerships in EU RTD and EUREKA projects and by non-subsidised technological alliances, and examine the degree of *coincidence* of different types of lines, and the possible *sequentiality* which is involved.

With regard to the 'pre-competitive' RTD-lines it is – particularly because of the relatively recent character of the phenomenon of joint European R&D projects – indeed of some interest to analyse the extent to which these lines coincide in the global graph with EUREKA- and alliance-lines and how often they precede these lines in time. The 'linear' causal model of innovation would lead us to expect that near-market co-operation between firms would follow an earlier phase where this co-operation runs along the more loose and informal channels of pre-competitive research, and not the other way round. From the evaluation of EUREKA, quoted in the *European Report on*

S&T Indicators 1994 (European Commission, 1994), we learn however that 'The original policy conception of a "pipeline model", whereby pre-competitive EC projects are followed by nearer-market EUREKA projects has not materialised to date. Rather there has emerged a complex picture in which involvement in EC programmes could either precede or follow a EUREKA project'.

What is involved in this is not so much the effectiveness and the efficiency of the S&T policy which is pursued by the EU, which anyway should not only be evaluated in terms of the possible direct effects in the sphere of private business. The often cited beneficiary effect of the creation of an environment where technological expectations stabilise and converge springs to the mind as one of the most convincing arguments in favour (see e.g. Håkansson, 1989). What is at stake is instead the paradigmatic validity of the above mentioned linear causal model, as opposed to that of the 'systemic' approach implied by the analysis of 'national innovation systems' (see e.g. Edquist, 1997).

After a general description of the emerging European S&T policy in section 2 we will focus in section 3 on the European telecommunications industry as a key industry of the information society and as a good example of what some have called 'alliance capitalism' (Dunning, 1995, 1997).

In section 4 we will present our results of some empirical research on the coincidence of private and subsidised trans-European collaboration in the field of telecommunications. We conclude in section 5.

2. THE DEVELOPMENT OF A EUROPEAN RTD POLICY

Although a 'European Technological Community' was from the outset envisaged by the founding fathers of the EU it was only during the 1980s that R&D collaboration on a European level emerged.

The deterioration of European competitiveness in emerging technologies like IT, the relative failure of policies to promote 'national champions', the skyrocketing costs and risks of R&D and the general view that at least part of the Japanese success was the result of (state-supported) inter-firm collaboration, led to a shift from national R&D support to subsidised trans-European collaborative programmes (Peterson, 1991; Sandholtz, 1992; Sharp and Pavitt, 1993). The same motivation was among one of the reasons for the creation of the Single Market (see Emerson, 1988, part B1).

This shift was partly due to the strengthening of the position of the European Commission and some emerging 'Euro-groups' at the expense of the sovereignty of national governments.

The then Commissioner of Industry, Etienne Davignon, got support of the 12 largest European IT companies to launch a large scale programme of R&D co-operation in information technologies in 1982.[2] The programme, which was called ESPRIT, was integrated in the Framework Programmes (FWP) that started in 1984 and aimed to co-ordinate all RTD actions of the European Union.

The dominance of the 'Big 12' was overwhelming. They got 80 per cent of all contracts and 70 per cent of all funds in the 1983 ESPRIT pilot phase, and by 1986 still more than half of the ESPRIT budget was granted to them (Peterson, 1991; Sandholtz, 1992).

ICT was to remain the major technological domain in financial terms in the successive FWP, but due to a relative shift towards other emerging technologies like biotechnology, environmental technology and new materials its relative share in the EU RTD budget gradually decreased.

2.1. Competition and collaboration

The EU has imposed, ever since the Treaty of Rome, the rather strict competition rules put down in the articles 85 up to 94 of the Treaty, which deal with anti-competitive behaviour, alliances, dominant market practices, dumping and state aids.

The theoretical underpinning of the competition policy enforced by the European Commission (EC) however gradually shifted from strict neo-classical to more 'Schumpeterian'. By doing so they accepted the dynamic aspects of innovation-based competition. It resulted in 1971 in block exemptions to allow for the application of standards and the possibility of joint initiatives in the field of R&D up to the stage of industrial exploitation, and in 1985 in block exemptions to cover the joint exploitation of common R&D initiatives (Young and Metcalfe, 1997).

At the same time however the Commission reinforced the more traditional aspects of its competition policy during the 1980s. In 1989 a regulation was adopted to tackle the problem of increasing concentration through mergers and acquisitions which could not be satisfactorily coped with within the existing legal framework. This new regulation signified a further transfer of decision power from the national to the supranational level (Sachwald, 1994).[3]

Sachwald (1994) therefore argues that EC competition policy in the strict sense is somewhat contradictory with one of the main rationales for the Single Market, namely economies of scale. As pointed out by some other authors, concentration through mergers and acquisitions can be regarded as a likely (and intended) result of European integration and might, according to Schumpeterian reasoning, even lead to better innovative performance (Gregersen *et al.*, 1994; Foray, Rutsaert and Soete, 1995; Caracostas and Soete, 1997; Moore, 1994). The EC seems therefore to be in some kind of quandary. On the one hand the EU industrial policy – following a 'Schumpeterian' lead – regards inter-firm agreements as beneficial to the European position in the high-tech sector and favours alliances and mergers, and encourages the growth of large European firms (Foray, Rutsaert and Soete, 1995; Moore, 1994). On the other hand – following a neo-classical lead – the competition policy of the EC puts a brake on the emergence of large European corporations.

The apparent contradiction between the industrial and the competition policy might even be more important than would appear at first sight, since the consensus for trans-European collaborative research in the IT field only came about after EC-induced talks to create large joint European IT companies, along the lines of the Airbus consortium, had failed (Stubbs, 1997). Moreover the EU not only finances so-called 'pre-competitive' R&D projects, but more and more also supports 'near-market' EUREKA projects,[4] and promotes the follow-up of its own RTD projects by these EUREKA projects. EUREKA from its inception was indeed viewed as a forum to push precompetitive R&D in ESPRIT closer to the market (Peterson, 1991).

Although the higher mentioned quandary may perhaps only exist in the head of some academic economists, and does not necessarily imply that the actual consistency of EU economic policy is under threat, researchers seem in this field to have found new alleys along which the intricate relationships between market form, efficiency, economic policy and innovativeness can be explored.

So far indeed economic theorising does not seem to have come up with a coherent and generally accepted view on this dualism, which seems to be a feature of economic development after having entered what has been called the era of the higher mentioned 'alliance capitalism'. In this alliance capitalism competition, sharpened by globalisation, deregulation and liberalisation, coexists with an increasing number of co-operative arrangements (Dunning, 1995, 1997), and 'networking effects' (especially for SMEs) may have become an alternative for scale effects.

It is for instance, on the one hand, generally contended that the EU 'Framework Programmes', and ESPRIT more specifically, have established a European IT community and a mechanism for co-operation in R&D, as well as to have created an awareness of the technological know-how that is available in Europe (Sandholtz, 1992; Hobday, 1994; Kastrinos, 1995; Koutrakou, 1995; Stubbs, 1997). Equally in a positive vein, but with respect to concentration in the strict sense, rather than to co-operation, Jacquemin, Buigues and Ilzkovitz (1989) have argued that in high-tech sectors like telecommunications, electronics, advanced materials and pharmaceuticals, characterised by high economies of scale and high R&D expenditures and risks, as well as being open to strong non-EU competition, the harmfulness of concentration should not be overrated.

On the other hand Sharp and Pavitt (1993) observe that the EU RTD policy reveals a lasting 'fixation with scale' (the policy of picking 'national champions' shifting to a policy of picking 'European champions'), which means that governments fail to recognise that size cannot compensate for poor management. Particularly in relation to R&D alliances and co-operation, Porter (1990, p. 635) has the view that: 'firms will usually try to bring their own proprietary technologies on the market and will only divert a modest part of their R&D facilities to joint projects'. Also Geroski (1994) remains reluctant to the idea of horizontal relationships.

Two main research questions – leaving the tricky question of the effects of concentration sensu stricto aside – have to be addressed in this context. First, does the present EU S&T policy contribute to the establishment of more technological alliances between European firms? Second, do technological alliances lead to a higher degree of innovativeness?

We will limit our attention to the first question, and focus on the telecommunication industry.

2.2. The impact of EU S&T policy on alliances

As the harmonisation of regulations lowers co-ordination and monitoring costs of cross-border co-operative agreements, it might at first sight have been expected that during the late 80s the number of firms undertaking alliances within the EU would have increased more in preparation to market integration, than the number of alliances between EU and non-EU firms. The 1985 White Paper on the Completion of the Internal Market expected indeed that market completion would foster trans-European collaboration, and that firms would respond to increased competition by forming alliances (Jacquemin and Wright, 1993).

An opposite view was proposed by Kay (1991) and Kay, Ramsay and Hennart (1996) who argued that European integration would favour mergers and acquisitions to alliances, and that non-EU firms would be more inclined than EU firms to undertake collaborative agreements with EU firms, as potential EU partners for EU firms were also likely to be potential competitors, and non-European firms would try to consolidate their global position (Narula, 1998). The direct effects of EU integration would according to these authors rather be to diminish than to increase cross-border co-operative agreements, such as joint ventures, within the EU.

Empirical research on the impact of the Single Market on trans-European collaboration is not very conclusive and to a great extent depends on the data sources that are used. Narula (1998) analyses the tendency of European firms to undertake strategic technology partnering and finds that the start of the EU FWP and the EUREKA initiative occurred around the same time as the surge in alliance activity by which European firms sought to improve their technological advantages.

Duysters and Hagedoorn (1996) confirm this and show evidence that the share of 'intraregional' (Europe, US, Japan) technology alliances increased between the 1980-84 and the 1985-89 periods, at the expense of interregional alliances. They distinguish moreover R&D-oriented from market- or production-oriented technology alliances. For all technological disciplines combined the share of intra-European R&D alliances only slightly increased from 18.0% in the period 1980-84 to 18.2% in the period 1985-89, and market-oriented alliances from 12.3% to 13.1%. On the contrary, specifically for IT alliances the intra-European share of R&D oriented strategic technology alliances increased from 13.9% to 19.7%. A further specification reveals that although for computers the intra-European share of R&D-oriented alliances decreased from 10.0% to 3.8%, it increased from 11.5% to 18.9% in microelectronics, and for telecommunications it even more than doubled from 10.2% to 24.0%.

The period of the first FWP (1984-88) coincides with a disproportional growth of private intra-European R&D alliances in two of the major technological domains of the FWP, namely microelectronics and telecommunications.

But the apparently important influence of the framework-programmes on the propensity of European firms to conclude trans-European R&D alliances indeed only holds for the eighties. When compared with EU-US and EU-Japan alliances the development of intra-EU alliances did not seem to confirm that the FWP objective has been achieved in the somewhat longer run. Apparently EU firms from 1990 onwards were continuously and increasingly inclined to participate in EU-US and EU-Japan collaboration, whereas intra-EU co-operation declined.

Narula proposes some explanations of which the most important probably is that globalisation is a more powerful force than economic integration within one region (Narula, 1998; see also Sachwald, 1994). Narula points at the findings of Veugelers (1996) that EU firms are actively looking for allies in those industries in which they lack comparative advantage, and as EU firms still tend to lag behind in IT and biotechnology, the preference for US and Japanese firms should therefore not come as a surprise.

Figure 9.1 gives a concise summing-up of the evidence. It shows – on the basis of the MERIT-CATI dataset of private R&D alliances – the evolution of the numbers and of the share of intra-EU technological alliances in telecommunications for four consecutive periods between 1980 and 1995. In the figure we distinguish between the sets of alliances 'Intra-EU', 'Nat-EU' (alliances between firms of the same EU country), 'EU-US', 'EU-JP', 'EU-OTH' and 'non-EU'. There is a sharp increase in the share of intra-EU alliances in the period 1984-87 compared with 1980-83. The share almost doubled and further increased slightly in the 1988-91 period. This increase of the intra-EU *share* coincides with an increase in the number of international alliances in which EU firms participate. The second and the third period are the periods of the 1st and the 2nd FWP, as well as of the pre-1992 preparation for the Single Market, instigated by the publication of the 1985 White Paper.

Figure 9.1.   Evolution of the number and share of intra- and interregional alliances in telecommunications

Total number of alliances

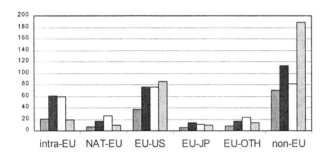

Shares

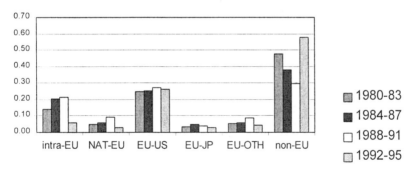

Source: Own calculations from MERIT-CATI data

For the period 1992-95 there is a dramatic decrease in the share of intra-EU alliances. As this decrease coincides with a sharp increase (from 29.5% in 1988-91 to 58.2% in 1992-95) of alliances in which no EU firm participates, it cannot merely be explained by the internationalisation process: the share of EU-US, EU-Japan and EU-Others decreased as well, or at best stagnated. The evolution of the pattern of alliances in the telecommunication sector in the early nineties is therefore somewhat divergent from the overall pattern documented by Narula, which showed a shift from intra-EU towards EU-US alliances

While the emergence of some Asian countries in the telecommunications industry and the alliances resulting from liberalisation of non-triad markets in recent years could account for part of the increased share of non-EU alliances, the sharpness of the decline of the intra-EU share can only fail to reflect a declining competitiveness of European telecommunications firms and thus a declining attractiveness for alliances with these firms if it would mean that EU firms rely more on alliances that were established in previous periods. Further research is needed to decide this issue.

3. THE EU TELECOMMUNICATIONS INDUSTRY

Before 1980 competition in the international telecommunications industry (especially as regards services) was close to non-existent, and most national markets were monopolised by state-owned telecom operators who bought their equipment from affiliated domestic suppliers. This changed quickly in the course of the 1980s. We can quote Curwen (1995, p. 331) literally :

> By the end of this century, the telecommunications market in the European Union will have been transformed from a collection of national monopolies providing little apart from basic voice telephony and Value-Added Network Services (VANS) into a unified, competitive market for multimedia services – or at least that is the intention behind a series of directives issued by the European Commission.

The situation of the European telecommunications industry since the middle of the eighties is a good example of the dualism of EU policy and the emergence of 'alliance capitalism'.

On the one hand the EU promotes inter-firm collaboration in this field, whereas on the other hand the Commission has played a crucial role in the deregulation and liberalisation of the telecommunications market whilst, on the other hand, at the same time enforcing protectionist high tariffs and anti-dumping measures (Sharp and Pavitt, 1993). All measures taken to increase competition in the telecommunications industry have therefore coincided with an increasing number of alliances, mergers and acquisitions.

The same situation emerged in the US where the US Telecommunications Act of 1996, intended to increase competition by allowing all companies to compete in each others areas, so far mainly seems to have encouraged large-scale mergers. Of the 7 'Baby Bells' created with the forced dismantlement of AT&T in 1983, in 1998 only four independent firms remain.

Just as the shift from nation-wide analogue systems to digital systems and multimedia services reduced the need for single national telecom operators, the required investments and the uncertainty in the present telecommunications industry are so large that they cannot be met by any single firm. This brought about the creation of worldwide alliances (Curwen, 1995). This might, in the longer run, lead to higher levels of concentration on a world-wide scale, again introducing monopolism on the market. In a strong plea for deregulation Porter (1992) however has argued that regulators often have a wrong perspective on competition by overly focusing on seller concentration and barriers to trade. In his view deregulation is likely to sharpen competi-tion, also in the longer run, as buyers become more powerful, more price sensitive and more sophisticated. Furthermore he believes that deregulation will intensify strategic heterogeneity and innovativeness.

Already by the end of the 1970s communication policy had been regarded as an important factor determining European industrial competitiveness. Through the ESPRIT programme this led to relative large-scale support to trans-European R&D co-operation in the successive Framework pro-grammes. Before, there had already been international co-operation in tele-communications through the European Conference for Post and Telecom-munication (CEPT), which, apart from tariff matters, sought to implement technical standards for interconnecting telecommunications networks. The CEPT gathered representatives of European PTT administrations, thereby reflecting the 'market' at the time, of mostly state-owned telecom operator monopolists (see Schneider, Dang-Nguyen and Werle, 1994).

Triggered by the deregulation and liberalisation of the US and UK tele-communications market and the entrance of US telecom multinationals (in the broad sense) on some European national markets the Commission, through the publication of the 1987 Green Paper on the development of the common market for telecommunications services and equipment, and subse-quent directives, sought to liberalise the market. The legislative process cul-minated in the liberalisation of basic voice telephony services in January 1998.

Yet, telecommunications is apparently however the sector lagging behind most others as regards the implementation of EU rules. Still 64% of all telecommunications-related directives are waiting to be implemented in at least one EU country (EC Monthly Newsletter, June/July 1998, p. 3).

In 1997 telecommunications services alone accounted for 42% of the Western European ICT market, and telecommunications equipment for another 9% (EITO, 1998).

Services play an increasingly important role in the ICT market with average annual growth exceeding the growth rates of software and even more growth rates of equipment.

The customer premises equipment (CPE) and services markets are very competitive, with new small firms being able to achieve strong niche positions, whereas the switching and transmission markets are increasingly evolving towards oligopolistic markets dominated by a small number of large global firms. On the latter markets, characterised by high R&D thresholds and economies of scale, traditional telecommunications companies retained their dominant positions due to their integrated networks and technological competencies (Duysters, 1996).

One of the key issues in the telecommunications industry is compatibility and interconnectivity and the ensuing need for international standards. The implications for the propensity to conclude alliances in the field of technology, although probably important and unambiguous, have however a somewhat complicated character.

On the one hand there is the EU-sponsored European Telecommunications Standards Institute (ETSI) which tries to establish trans-European standards ensuring that the number of potential customers is not constrained by the number of customers within national boundaries. ETSI is active in an environment in which single firms find it increasingly difficult to impose standards. This thwarts the anti-competitive use of standards, as well as avoids the adverse effects of single-firm standards on the rate of technological progress.

On the other hand, the absence of univocal standards procedures that can be enforced, the pace of technological progress, and the growing importance of the software-aspects of R&D in telecommunications may, despite obvious advantages of economies of scale and scope, lead to the decreased importance of standards in ICT, resulting in a 'post-standards' market of open systems in which customers cannot be locked-in by any suppliers' technology and in which the development of new software will bridge the gaps between the different co-existing technologies (Bradley *et al.*, 1993).

Alliances between telecommunication firms may in these circumstances serve both the (offensive) aim of joining forces to permit more efficient lobbying in standards institutes like ETSI, and the (defensive) aim of protecting oneself in a 'post-standards' market environment.

4. TRANS-EUROPEAN R&D COLLABORATION IN TELECOMMUNICATIONS

4.1. Introduction

ICT is the main field in the EU technology policy although its share in the RTD budget fell from 42.2% in the second FWP (1987-91) to 27.7% in the fourth FWP (1994-98) (EC, 1994, pp. 213-16).

In Table 9.1 the EU RTD programmes in the field of communications technologies are listed.

Table 9.1.   EU RTD Programmes in the field of telecommunications

Acronym	Period	Budget (MEcu)	Objectives
COST	1971-		COST was the first programme for trans-European pre-competitive research in different technological fields (e.g. telecommunications) and as such a precursor of EU programmes that were to be co-ordinated under the FWP from 1984 onwards.
RACE	1985-94	1126	Contribution to the introduction of Integrated Broadband Communications (IBC) and to support the use of integrated services like ISDN.
TELEMATICS	1991-98	1327	Umbrella Programme covering distinct subprogrammes aiming at supporting the development and interoperability of telematics systems and services and the establishment of trans-European networks between administrations with applications in transport services, health care, distance learning, libraries, linguistic research and the use of telematics in rural areas.
ACTS	1994-98	671	In succession to the RACE programmes this programme aims to develop advanced communication systems (optical networks, high-speed networks) and services (digital multimedia broadband services).

Source: EC, 1997.

In addition to the EU programmes in the above table, the ESPRIT programme should be mentioned. ESPRIT mainly focuses on R&D in the fields of microelectronics and information processing, which obviously to a great extent concerns developments in telecommunications.

EUREKA is not a EU initiative, but the EU participates financially in some of its important programmes. In EUREKA some 29 finished projects with a total value of 1391 Mecu and some 29 ongoing projects with a total value of 824 Mecu relate to telecommunications.

The largest EUREKA-project in this field, and one which is exemplary for the possible hazards of publicly supported technological alliances, is executed by the so-called EU95 HDTV Consortium. It started in 1986 and finished in 1995, and aimed to promote co-operation in HDTV-technology and to develop a European Standard for High Definition Television. Because of its strategic importance the EC supported the HDTV-initiative financially as well as politically. The official total budget of the HDTV-project amounted to 730 Mecu but already by 1992 the project was reported to have cost over 2 billion Ecu, more than half of it coming from the European taxpayer. It is more and more accepted that the project has failed to a large extent, partly because it relied on analogue instead of digital technology (Dai, Cawson and Holmes, 1996).

4.2. Coincidence and sequentiality of collaborative links in EU RTD-projects, EUREKA and private technological alliances

The main conclusion of Hagedoorn and Schakenraad (1993), in their often cited paper, is that the EU-subsidised IT network seems to be a reflection of an already existing private network. Results of a questionnaire survey with FWP participants indeed seem to corroborate this, suggesting that the Framework programmes were building upon and expanding an existing network of scientific co-operation (EC, 1994).

Hagedoorn and Schakenraad do not analyse the chronology nor the identity of the partners involved in the networks studied. With the construction of our graph it is however possible to analyse the coincidence and the sequence of links in EU projects, EUREKA and private alliances as they appear in the MERIT-CATI database, while explicitly taking the identity of the partners into account.

The analysis which follows takes place with the 'pipeline model' of innovation as background. For an analysis of the coincidence and sequentiality of subsidised links with private collaborative links in telecommunications we retrieved all alliances that were established between 1980 and 1995 in the field of telecommunications from the MERIT-CATI database, which contains information on some 13000 inter-firm co-operative agreements, including strategic alliances, which contain some arrangements for joint research or transferring technology. This resulted in some 1000 alliances between 591 firms. We also gathered information on the partnerships in all EUREKA-projects in telecommunications until 1995. This resulted in 155 firms (and 2048 lines). For all firms (720) that participated in at least one EUREKA-project or alliance, we retrieved from the CORDIS-database partnership and other data on their participation in EU projects in the field of telecommunications or information processing. RTD-partnerships in tele-communications which at some period did not correspond with the same partnerships, in a EUREKA or an alliance context were neglected.

In this way we constructed a multi-graph in which the nodes (firms) were linked by a line or lines whenever the two corresponding firms were allied, and/or partners in a same EUREKA and/or EU RTD-project.

A more detailed description of the methodological aspects of the graph-theoretical approach to describe technological collaboration can be found in Meeusen and Dumont (1997a,b).

Table 9.2 summarises the characteristics of the graph which was obtained, and Table 9.3 gives the result with respect to the coincidence of different types of lines in this graph.

Table 9.2. *Description of the complete graph and its three subsets*

	FWP (1984-95)	EUREKA (1986-95)	private alliances (1980-95)	complete graph
number of firms (nodes)	136	155	591	720
number of lines	5543	2048	1964	9555

Table 9.3. *Coincidence and sequentiality of projectlines and alliance-lines*

set A/set B	# of coinciding lines in A/B (% /%)	# of dyads	# of dyads with 'right' se-quence (%)
FWP/ EUREKA	1690 / 255 (– / 12%)	197	46 (23%)
FWP/ private alli-ances	2235 / 405 (– / 21%)	255	87 (42%)
EUREKA/ private alli-ances	60 / 80 (3% / 4%)	38	10 (26%)

As co-operation in EU projects between two partners of which one does not appear in a single EUREKA-project or private alliance is neglected in the exercise, the reported share-value of coinciding FWP-lines would be highly biased. It is therefore not reported. On the contrary, the low coincidence between EUREKA and private alliances reflects real coincidence as all EUREKA-projects and all private alliances in the field of telecommunications (1980-95) were considered. It should also be mentioned that the share-values of EUREKA in the first column should be interpreted with some care. Some EUREKA projects have a very high number of partners (up to 60 for the HDTV project) and generate therefore a very high number of, often non-significant, lines in the network. This gives a downward bias to the reported share-value.

For each pair of two partners that co-operate in both given sets it was verified in which set co-operation took place the first time. This resulted in the computation of the share of the total number of coinciding pairs for which the earliest link was established according to the logic of the linear causal model, meaning that FWP links would have to precede EUREKA links and alliances, and EUREKA links in turn would have to precede alliances. This 'right' proportion is given in the last column of Table 9.3.

The said proportion may have a sizeable downward bias because of two restrictions that were applied while computing them. First, we did not consider a set of links for a dyad to have the 'right' sequence if there were two or more contemporaneous links which were 'earliest' and belonged to different families (FWP, EUREKA and the set of alliances). In other words, we required the time sequence to be 'right' in the strict sense. Second, by concentrating on the earliest link, and expecting it to be of the 'right' family, we are perhaps unduly severe for the linear causal model, because, as an example, we would then consider the sequence of 10 links in a dyad to be 'wrong' if the earliest link is in the 'wrong' family, even if in the nine others early 'pre-competitive' links outnumber later 'near-market' links or alliances. We shall cope with the latter complication in the regression exercises that will follow later in this section.

In all fairness it should also be mentioned that there may be a conceptual problem with sequence analyses of this kind. A sequence analysis indeed loses meaning as the period in which joint projects and alliances have been set up grows longer. The reason is a 'demographic' one: older R&D initiatives set up between two partners which are in a mature stage of co-operation will, as time goes by, be more often coexistent with new 'pre-competitive' initiatives between the same partners. The result is that simple comparisons of the starting date of the project or alliance, without verifying the content of the co-operation, will then often be misleading. This aspect is set aside for later research. We expect however the reliability of the results to be only slightly affected by the adverse influence of this 'overlapping generations effect' because of the relatively recent start of massive EU financing of the telecommunications industry (the beginning of the nineties), and the equally recent phenomenon of technological alliances, mergers and acquisitions going on in that sector.

The relatively low coincidence of FWP with EUREKA (only 12% of all EUREKA lines in the graph), and also the high number of pairs for which cooperation took place in a near-market EUREKA-project (EUREKA started in 1986) before it took place in a pre-competitive EU project (the FWP started in 1984) would seem, within the limits of the analysis mentioned above, to corroborate previous findings about relatively weak relations between EUREKA and FWP (Peterson, 1993; EC, 1994).

The greater part of coinciding links result from a small group of mostly large telecom operators and equipment and services suppliers, which comes as no surprise as these major firms actively steered the FWP as well as EUREKA into a direction that matched with their individual as well as their common interests.

For a more detailed analysis of the sequentiality of the links between the different subgraphs we now turn to regression analysis focused on the set of the 20 firms who had highest degree-centrality in the global graph described above.[5]

The centrality-variable which was chosen to make the selection is of course a criterion which is 'internal' to the network which is examined, and this might in principle raise a methodological problem. It should however be realised that what is under discussion is not coincidence as such, but sequentiality. In other words, we are looking for an answer to the question if there is evidence for the 'right' sequence of subsidised 'pre-competitive' projects to subsidised 'near-market' projects to private alliances.

Incidentally, the selected set of 20 actors nearly coincides with the set consisting of the 15 largest European telecommunications firms (according to sales in 1993), as reported in EC (1994, table II.5), plus the five largest national telecom operators in Europe. The 'internal' centrality-criterion in other words yields nearly the same result as the 'external' size-criterion. By choosing the 'internal' criterion we however maximalise the opportunities for investigating the 'rightness' of the sequence.

The links between these 20 firms account for 39% of EU lines in our larger telecommunications graph, 13% of 'MERIT-CATI'-lines and 4% of EUREKA-lines.

Of the 197 coinciding combinations between EUREKA and EU projects 45 are between two of the selected firms, for EU projects and private alliances this is 94 out of 208 coinciding combinations, and for EUREKA and private alliances 27 out of 38 coinciding tail-head combinations.

For each possible combination in the set of 20 actors we computed the number of links $NL_{ij}^{S}(p)$ between the actors i and j ($i,j = 1,...,20$) in the subgraph S ($S = F, E, a$) during the period p ($p = 1980\text{-}83, 1984\text{-}87, 1988\text{-}91, 1992\text{-}95$); F, E and a are shorthand for 'FWP', 'EUREKA' and 'private alliances', respectively. The vector $NL_{ij}^{a}(p)$ was computed for all four 4-year periods. The FWP- and EUREKA-equivalents were only computed for the last three 4-year periods. This resulted in 10 NL-vectors, each vector containing of course 190 elements.

For each of the NL-vectors a regression equation was estimated in order to ascertain the impact of the Framework programmes (in the case of the EUREKA and private alliances regressions), and to assess the validity of the Hagedoorn-Schakenraad thesis (in the case of the FWP regressions). The list of explanatory variables in the right-hand side of each equation therefore initially included the NL-vectors relating to the previous 4-year period for each of the three sets (FWP, EUREKA and private alliances).

Since the chosen 4-year intervals in the case of the EU RTD programmes coincide with the periods of the successive framework-programmes, the 'lagged' FWP-vector in the FWP-equations will capture the possible tendency of partners to continue co-operation in the next phase. The same inertia effect may apply in the case of technological alliances. We did however not try to control for the inertia effect in the case of EUREKA because many important EUREKA projects typically extend over a longer period of time. Statistical significance of the 'lagged' EUREKA NL-variable will then only express a trivial truth, namely that the same project continues over different 4-year periods.

We also gathered company data in order to augment the right-hand-side of the equation with additional explanatory variables. We used annual sales to compute the relative size-differential between two partners. Some authors have indeed suggested that, although they will consider themselves often as direct competitors, larger firms have a tendency to collaborate with firms of roughly the same size, especially when the size is big (Geringer, 1988).

The geographical distance between the headquarters of the 20 firms was also considered. In this way we tried to correct for proximity effects.

As absolute values for the number of links in different subgraphs might possibly introduce a bias in the relationships, we also computed Revealed Comparative Preference (RCP_{ij}) indicators. These indicators reveal to which extent there is a preference between two firms to collaborate with each other, compared to the average collaborative pattern of those firms with other firms (for a definition see Meeusen, Capron *et al.*, 1998). Working with RCPs did however not yield better quality regression results. Therefore the multiple regression was carried out with absolute numbers.

The regression equation finally estimated had the following general form:

$$NL_{ij}^S(p) = constant + \sum_{k \in \{F,E,a\}} \beta_k^S NL_{ij}^k(p-1) + \gamma^S \log(dist)_{ij} + \qquad (9.1)$$

$$\delta^S relSIZdiff_{ij} + u_{ij}^S \ .$$

$i, j = 1,...,20$, $i \neq j$ and $S \in \{F, E, a\}$, where F, E and a are shorthand for 'FWP', 'EUREKA' and 'private alliances'. The final regression results, obtained after stepwise elimination of the regressors with a t-value larger than one in absolute value, are in Table 9.4.

The overall quality of the regression results is certainly not overwhelming, but the contrary would of course have come as a surprise, considering the kind of variables that are used and the subtle causal mechanisms that are examined. Nevertheless, notwithstanding the often very low adjusted R^2 values, all the retained regressors reported in Table 9.4 are jointly significant in each of the regression equations.

The evidence in our telecommunications sample for the Hagedoorn-Schakenraad thesis that the EU-subsidised IT network seems to be a reflection of an already existing private network is relatively scarce. Only for the first Framework Programme do we obtain a statistically significant coefficient with respect to the private alliances in the previous 4-year period. There is however some indirect support for this thesis since ties created by FWP projects seem to correlate with ties which came about through EUREKA projects in the previous 4-year period.

Some evidence for the 'pipeline-model' of public R&D funding is present in the regression equations for EUREKA in the periods 1988-91 and 1992-95 in which there is a statistically significant coefficient for the links created during the preceding Framework Programme, and also a statistically significant coefficient for the FWP link-variable in the private alliances equation for the period 1988-91.

On balance it is however fair to say that the statistical significance of the regression coefficients is lower in the equations which illustrate the 'right' causal sequence, than in the equations where a 'wrong' causality is suggested. In this particular sense we might say – in accordance for that matter with the bulk of the recent literature on technology and innovation – that it would be more natural, on the basis of the regression results, to chose for a 'systemic' approach to the subject, than to stick to the older idea of the linear causal chain between R&D and innovation.The results in Table 9.4 give little consistent support to the thesis that with increasing distance the propensity to collaborate would decline, except for the EUREKA projects where this phenomenon indeed seems to play a role.

The conjecture of Geringer about the importance of differences in size among potential partners is more or less verified.

Table 9.4. Regression results for equation 9.1

Dependent	Intercept	FWP (1984-87)	FWP (1988-91)	EUREKA (1984-87)	EUREKA (1988-91)	private alliances (1980-83)	private alliances (1984-87)	private alliances (1988-91)	log(dist)	diffsize	R^2 adj.	$F_{n-k,k-1}$ (p)
FWP (1984-87)	1.99** (4.41)	–	–	–	–	1.34** (5.79)	–	–	-0.13* (-2.23)	-0.03 (-1.74)	.19	15.38 (.000)
FWP (1988-91)	2.47** (6.64)	1.34** (11.77)	–	1.22** (3.33)	–	–	0.52 (1.79)	–	–	-0.12** (-3.38)	.51	49.71 (.000)
FWP (1992-95)	0.28 (0.70)	–	0.97** (14.74)	–	3.08** (6.98)	–	–	0.54 (1.48)	–	–	.68	134.73 (.000)
EUREKA (1984-87)	0.66** (4.37)	–	–	–	–	0.14 (1.82)	–	–	-0.05** (-2.65)	-0.01 (-1.51)	.06	4.95 (.002)
EUREKA (1988-91)	0.65** (4.07)	0.06* (2.48)	–	–	–	–	–	–	-0.06** (-2.84)	–	.08	9.06 (.000)
EUREKA (1992-95)	0.06** (3.36)	–	0.03** (2.80)	–	–	–	–	–	-0.06* (-2.54)	–	.07	8.39 (.000)
private alliances (1988-91)	0.22** (3.01)	0.66* (2.46)	–	–	–	–	0.08 (1.27)	–	–	–	.03	4.29 (.015)
private alliances (1992-95)	0.40* (2.19)	–	–	–	–	–	–	0.17* (2.29)	-0.35 (-1.40)	–	.03	3.71 (.026)

Note: t-values in brackets below the coefficients; ** means 99% statistical significance; * means 95% statistical significance.

5. CONCLUSIONS

In this chapter we proposed a method to analyse, on the one hand, the impact cost-sharing EU projects may have had on 'near-market' EUREKA-collaboration and on the establishment of private technological agreements, and to find out, on the other hand, to which extent possibly EU collaboration (merely) reflected existing private collaboration.

After describing the gradual development of the EU policy of trans-European 'pre-competitive' R&D co-operation we focused on the complex trade-off between competition and collaboration that characterises the position of the EC in the emerging era of 'alliance capitalism'.

The cost-sharing Framework Programmes and the development of a single market seem to have favoured, at least implicitly, trans-European collaboration in telecommunications, and concentration through mergers and acquisitions in this technological discipline. This position seems also to have been prompted by a shift from a strict neo-classical policy approach towards a more Schumpeterian focus on the dynamic aspects of innovation-based competition and the policy implications of the lagging of European firms in emerging technologies.

The share of intra-EU alliances in telecommunications increased significantly during the first and the second FWP, which coincided with the pre-1992 period. The share of alliances in which at least one EU firm was involved fell however dramatically from 1992 onwards. This might suggest a weakened position of EU firms or might indicate that EU firms in the telecommunications sector rely on the considerable number of already existing agreements.

As to the coincidence between and the sequence of subsidised and private collaborative links in the field of telecommunications, there seems to be some evidence that the R&D network that was created through the consecutive FWP was a reflection of an already existing network of private collaboration, as well as for the traditional pipeline-model in which 'precompetitive' research is considered logically to precede.

On balance however the regression results on the number of links generated by the EU RTD projects, EUREKA projects, and private alliances respectively, suggested that it would be more natural to chose for a 'systemic' approach to the influence of subsidised 'pre-competitive' R&D on near-market R&D initiatives and private alliances, than to stick to the older idea of the linear causal chain between R&D and innovation.

NOTES

1. The authors benefited from research grants from the Belgian Federal Office for Scientific, Technological and Cultural Affairs, and from IWT, the Flemish Institute for Science and Technology.
2. Bull (FR), CGE (FR), Thomson (FR), AEG (DE), Nixdorf (DE), Siemens (DE), Olivetti (IT), STET (IT), Philips (NL), GEC (UK), ICL (UK) and Plessey (UK).
3. See also Wilks and McGowan, 1995, and Armstrong and Bulmer, 1998.
4. EUREKA is an intergovernmental initiative which was proposed by the French government in 1985 as an alternative to the American Star Wars programme. EUREKA aims at fostering co-operation between firms. It is not an EU mechanism although as a member the EU finances some large EUREKA projects mainly in the field of ICT like Jessi (microelectronics) and HDTV (high definition television).
5. CGE-Alcatel (FR), France Telecom (FR), Matra (FR), Thomson (FR), Daimler Benz (DE), Deutsche Telekom (DE), Siemens (DE), Fiat (IT), Olivetti (IT), IRI-STET-Telecom Italia (IT), Telefonica (ES), GEC (UK), Plessey (UK), BT (UK), Philips (NL), Nokia (FI), Ericsson (SE), AT&T (US), HP (US), IBM (US).

REFERENCES

Armstrong, K.A. and S.J. Bulmer (1998), *The Governance of the Single European Market*, Manchester: Manchester University Press.
Bradley, S.P., J.A. Hausman and R.L. Nolan (eds) (1993), *Globalization, Technology and Competition: The fusion of Computers and Telecommunications in the 1990s*, Boston (MA): Harvard Business School Press.
Caracostas, P. and L. Soete (1997), 'The building of cross-border institutions in Europe: towards a European system of innovation?', in C. Edquist (ed.), *Systems of Innovation*, London: Pinter, pp. 359-419.
Curwen, P. (1995), 'Telecommunications policy in the European Union: developing the information superhighway', *Journal of Common Market Studies*, **33**(3), 331-360.
Dai, X., A. Cawson and P. Holmes (1996), 'The rise and fall of High Definition Television: the impact of European technology policy', *Journal of Common Market Studies*, **34**(2), 149-166.
Dunning, J.H. (1995), 'Reappraising the eclectic paradigm in an age of alliance capitalism', *Journal of International Business Studies*, **26**(3), 461-491.
Dunning, J.H. (1997), *Alliance Capitalism and Global Business*, London: Routledge.
Duysters, G. (1996), *The Dynamics of Technical Innovation: the Evolution and development of Information Technology*, Cheltenham (UK): Edward Elgar.
Duysters, G. and J. Hagedoorn (1996), 'Internationalization of corporate technology through strategic partnering: an empirical investigation', *Research Policy*, **25**(1), 1-12.
Edquist, C. (1997), 'Systems of Innovation Approaches – their emergence and characteristics', in C. Edquist (ed.), *Systems of Innovation. Technologies, Institutions and Organizations*, London and Washington: Pinter, pp. 1-35.
EITO (1998), *European Information Technology Observatory*, Frankfurt.
Emerson, M. *et al.* (1988), *The Economics of 1992*, Oxford: Oxford University Press.

European Commission (1985), *Completing the Internal Market. White Paper from the Commission to the European Council*, CEC, Luxembourg.

European Commission (1994), *The European Report on S&T Indicators 1994*, Report EUR 15897 EN, Luxembourg.

European Commission (1997), *CORDIS - Community R&D Information Service*, Brussels/Luxembourg.

Foray, D., P. Rutsaert and L. Soete (1995), 'The coherence of EU Trade, competition, and industry policies in the high tech sector: the case of the telecommunications services sector', paper presented at the International Conference on EC Policies on Competition, Industry and Trade: Complementarities and Conflicts, Louvain-la-Neuve, 27-28 October 1994.

Geringer, J.M. (1988), *Joint Venture Partner Selection. Strategies for Developed Countries*, New York: Quorum Books.

Geroski, P.A. (1992), 'Vertical Relations between Firms and Industrial Policy', *Economic Journal*, **102**(1), 138-147.

Gregersen, B., B. Johnson and A. Kristensen (1994), 'National systems of innovation and European integration', paper presented at the EUNETIC Conference on Evolutionary Economics of Technical Change: Assessment of results and new frontiers, Strasbourg, 6-8 October.

Hagedoorn, J. and J. Schakenraad (1993), 'A comparison of private and subsidized inter-firm linkages in the European information technology industry', *Journal of Common Market Studies*, **31**(3), 373-390.

Håkansson, H. (1989), *Corporate Technological Behaviour: Cooperation and Networks*, London: Routledge.

Hobday, M. (1994), 'The Semiconductor Industry', in F. Sachwald (ed.), *European Integration and Competitiveness: Acquisitions and Alliances in Industry*, Aldershot: Edward Elgar, pp. 145-193.

Jacquemin, A., P. Buigues and F. Ilzkovitz (1989), 'Concentration horizontale, fusions et politique de la concurrence dans la Communauté Européenne', *Economie Européenne*, May.

Jacquemin, A. and D. Wright (1993), 'Corporate Strategies and European Challenges Post-1992', *Journal of Common Market Studies*, **31**(4), 525-537.

Kastrinos, N. (1995), 'The impact of EC R&D programmes on corporate R&D practice in Europe: a knowledge approach', *R&D Management*, **25**(3), 269-279.

Kay, N. (1991), 'Industrial Collaborative Activity and the Completion of the Internal Market', *Journal of Common Market Studies*, **29**(4), 347-362.

Kay, N.M., H. Ramsay and J.-F. Hennart (1996), 'Industrial Collaboration and the European Internal Market', *Journal of Common Market Studies*, **34**(3), 465-475.

Koutrakou, V.N. (1995), *Technological Collaboration for Europe's Survival*, Aldershot (UK): Avebury.

Meeusen, W., H. Capron *et al.* (1998), 'National Innovation Systems – Pilot Study of the Belgian Innovation System', report prepared for SSTC (Belgium) in the Framework of OECD-DSTI activities on National Innovation Systems.

Meeusen, W. and M. Dumont (1997a), 'Some results on the graph-theoretical identification of micro-clusters in the Belgian Innovation System', presented at the OECD/DSTI-workshop on 'Cluster-analysis and Cluster-based Policies', Amsterdam, October 1997.

Meeusen, W. and M. Dumont (1997b), 'The network of subsidised and spontaneous R&D co-operation between Belgian and foreign firms, research institutes and universities: a graph-theoretical approach', presented at the Conference 'Uncertainty, Knowledge and Skill', Hasselt, 6-8 November 1997.

MERIT (1998), MERIT-CATI database, Rijksuniversiteit Limburg, Maastricht.

Moore, L. (1994), 'Developments in Trade and Trade Policy', in M. Artis and N. Lee (eds), *The Economics of the European Union: Policy and Analysis*, N.Y.: Oxford University Press, pp. 292-327.

Narula, R. (1998), 'Strategic technology alliances by European firms since 1980: questioning integration?', MERIT Research Memorandum 98-009.

Peterson, J. (1991), 'Technology Policy in Europe: Explaining the Framework Programme and Eureka in Theory and Practice', *Journal of Common Market Studies*, **29**(3), 269-290.

Peterson, J. (1993), 'Assessing the performance of European collaborative R&D policy: The case of EUREKA', *Research Policy*, **22**(3), 243-264.

Porter, M.E. (1990), *The Competitive Advantage of Nations*, London: Macmillan.

Porter, M.E. (1992), 'On thinking about deregulation and competition', in H.M. Sapolsky *et al.* (eds), *The Telecommunications Revolution: Past, Present and Future*, London/NY: Routledge, pp. 39-44.

Sachwald, F. (1994), 'The Single Market', in F. Sachwald (ed.), *European Integration and Competitiveness: Acquisitions and Alliances in Industry*, Aldershot: Edward Elgar, pp. 5-29.

Sandholtz, W. (1992), 'ESPRIT and the Politics of International Collective Action', *Journal of Common Market Studies*, **30**(1), 1-21.

Schneider, V., G. Dang-Nguyen and R. Werle (1994), 'Corporate Actor Networks in European Policy-Making: Harmonizing Telecommunications Policy, *Journal of Common Market Studies*, **32**(4), 473-498.

Sharp, M. and K. Pavitt (1993), 'Technology Policy in the 1990s: Old Trends and New Realities', *Journal of Common Market Studies*, **31**(2), 129-151.

Stubbs, P. (1994), 'Science and Technology Policy', in M. Artis and N. Lee (eds), *The Economics of the European Union: Policy and Analysis*, N.Y.: Oxford University Press, pp. 139-169.

Veugelers, R. (1997), 'Alliances and the pattern of comparative advantages: a sectoral analysis', *International Business Review*, **4**, 213-231.

Wilks, S. and L. McGowan (1995), 'Disarming the Commission: The Debate over a European Cartel Office', *Journal of Common Market Studies*, **33**(2), 259-273.

Young, D. and S. Metcalfe (1994), 'Competition Policy', in M. Artis and N. Lee (eds), *The Economics of the European Union: Policy and Analysis*, N.Y.: Oxford University Press, pp. 118-138.

10. European Works Councils: a New Approach for Information and Consultation of Employees in Multinational Enterprises[1]

Daniel Van Den Bulcke

---

1. INTRODUCTION

On September 22, 1994 the Council of Ministers of the European Union (EU) finally agreed to the establishment of a European Works Council (EWC) or a procedure to provide information and consultation of employees in Multinational Enterprises (MNEs). Almost 25 years had passed since the Commission of the European Community (or Union), in the framework of its European Company proposal of 1970, for the first time included the right of employees to participate in the decision-making of MNEs. Ten years later the European Commission got entangled in a ferocious controversy with the European employers' associations (e.g. UNICE and the American Chambers of Commerce in Europe) about the so-called proposed directive Vredeling (named after the Dutch Commissioner for Social Affairs during those years) which would have obliged MNEs to inform and consult the employees of their subsidiaries about their worldwide activities and a number of intended decisions with important repercussions for the workforce.

According to Padraig Flynn, the Commissioner for Social Affairs in the European Commission, the employees and their representatives 'have fought hard to establish at European level the ways and means to exercise what is generally accepted fundamental right of workers to be informed and consulted on a transnational basis where appropriate' (European Commission, 1994a, p. 1). 'That the EWC and information and consultation of employees at plant and enterprise level (again) resulted in heated debate between the representative organisations of employers and employees is because it affects the power structure in the enterprises [and the] managerial prerogative and consequently goes to the essence of the free enterprise system and the market economy' (Blanpain and Windey, 1994, p. 15). Even before the finalisation of the EU's draft directive on this sensitive issue, the World Investment Report of 1994 claimed that 'it would merge the practical and legislative strands of industrial relations in Western Europe and create a new form of international industrial relations mechanisms with, perhaps implications beyond the European Union' (UNCTAD, 1994, p. 358).

Several reasons account for the success of the renewed attempt of the European Commission to introduce information and consultation for employees of MNEs after so many years. First, the Treaty of Maastricht, signed in February 1992, more particularly the European Social Charter (December 1989) and the Agreement on Social Policy, annexed to the Treaty, allowed the European Commission to avoid an important institutional hurdle, i.e. the veto of the United Kingdom which was linked to the need to come to an unanimous decision on the basis of the Treaty of Rome. Although measures regarding representation and collective defence of workers and employees – including co-determination – need an unanimous vote in the Social Charter, the information and consultation procedure could now be approved by qualified majority voting by its eleven signatories, i.e. without the United Kingdom that had refused to join this agreement (the so-called 'social opt-out'). However, the new British socialist government at the end of 1997 asked to be included in the EWC-directive, which meant that an extension directive and a special procedure was needed to allow the UK to 'opt-in' after all. Figure 10.1 illustrates the different steps that lead to the agreement by the EU Council of the EWC.

Secondly, the European Commission followed a much more flexible approach during the beginning of the 1990s as compared with previous initiatives such as the Vredeling proposal of October 1980. The integrationist principles that were pursued by the European Commission during the 1970s showed the limits of the strategy of 'harmonising' employment practices across the Community (Teague, 1989). Under the terms of the agreement on social policy the European Commission is obliged to involve the social partners at the European level and enter into a consultation procedure with them before submitting a proposal in the social affairs area (Bellace, 1997). Thirdly, the so-called Hoover incident in January 1993 provided a new impetus when the public opinion was confronted with possibilities of social dumping within the EU itself. Hoover's American parent company Maytag decided to relocate its French plant to Scotland when the French workers did not accept the new and less favourable social conditions laid down by the company. Consequently, European trade union leaders argued that EWCs

Figure 10.1. *The European decision-making process with respect to the establishment of the European Works Council Directive (1990-1994)*

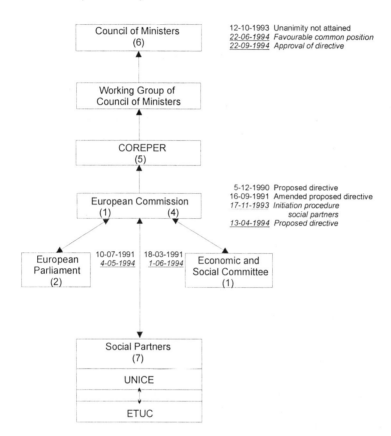

would have prevented Hoover from playing off the workers in two different countries against each other (D. Goodhart, in Dowling, Schuler and Welch, 1994). Fourthly, the practice by a limited number of influential MNEs to introduce so-called prototype EWCs – of which the Thomson agreement of 1985 is generally considered as the first one – paved the way for a changed attitude by other multinationals and certain employers' federations. The united opposition of the employers' associations could not be maintained particularly after the European Roundtable of Industrialists – a select group of some forty European industrial managers – stated that EWCs with a limited role were acceptable. Fifthly, the existing impact of the national regulations of certain individual EU countries, especially of France and Germany increased the pressure for MNEs to accept that the existing mechanisms and procedures for the information and consultation of employees at the national level were no longer compatible with the decision-making structures of companies which operated across national borders (European Commission, 1994b). As a result, especially German and French state-owned firms signed up voluntary agreements in the second half of the 1980s and beginning 1990s (Veersma, 1994). Sixthly, the European Commission in the pursuit of its longstanding policy to help the trade unions to develop into valuable countervailing forces to MNEs, contributed financially to the European trade union movement. In 1992 the Commission granted financial support for about 50 million ECU to facilitate meetings of workers of MNEs at the European level (Carley, 1993). Finally, the wave of corporate restructuring which followed the establishment of the Single European Market and the ensuing closures, disinvestments and mergers, convinced a number of MNEs that a vehicle to inform and consult with employees might be a useful prerequisite to successfully carry out their restructuring plans (Marginson, 1992).

2. KEY FEATURES OF THE EUROPEAN WORKS COUNCIL DIRECTIVE

2.1. General characteristics

The EWC established by the Directive of September 22, 1994 consists of a works council in the narrow sense. The EWC is actually limited to information and consultation of employees. At one stage in the negotiations the term EWC was even dropped from the proposal, while the final version of the directive leaves the option of either establishing a EWC or introducing a procedure for information and consultation of employees. Article 6(3) actually states that the social partners may decide to establish information and consultation procedures 'instead of a EWC' (Bellace, 1997). Blanpain and Windey (1994, p. 81) argue that it is not very clear where the procedure ends and the EWC begins, but that 'it seems logical that a EWC is a more institutionalised form of communication and dialogue, while the procedure is a much looser one'. Certain authors (Cuthbert and Johannissen, 1997) even advocate three different types of procedures or arrangements that differ from EWCs, i.e. so-called localised arrangements, European Information Forums, and Business Improvement Groups and claim that they are better suited to the business concerned while still complying with the directive. In the case of Ireland's implementation of the directive the consultation body is called European Employees' Forum (EEF) because of its marked preference for a consultation procedure rather than an institutionalised mechanism, as detailed prescriptive rules were deemed to be incompatible with the voluntarist traditions of the country. Yet, apart from these semantics, Ireland embraced the principle of information and consultation of employees completely (Scorey, 1997).

While the distinction between information and consultation is fairly evident, there might be more confusion about the respective meaning of consultation and negotiation. While consultation is more passive or neutral, negotiation intends to resolve a conflict and consists of a search for a compromise. Consultation in the context of the EWC means that the decision-making authority of the employer is left intact. 'It implies that the employer retains the power to make decisions, after having listened to the views of the employee representatives' (Blanpain and Windey, 1994, p. 71). Another issue about the concept of consultation concerned the attempt by Digital Equipment Company (DEC) to replace the periodic meetings of employees by the computer intranet network for the purpose of disclosing information to employee representatives and for the purpose of permitting electronic discussion among them and members of management. This proposal was rejected by the representatives of the employees, however (Bellace, 1997; EIRR, 1995). Yet, it is generally recognized that e-mail has enormously facilitated the exchange of information among employees of different subsidiaries.

An important feature of the 1994 directive is its voluntary nature. As a matter of fact, the directive explicitly encourages voluntary agreements to be concluded before it enters into force on September 22, 1996, i.e. after the national governments have been given two years to incorporate it into their national laws. This means that fully autonomous agreements can be concluded that are less far-reaching than the provisions of the directive itself and can be extended even after the directive has become European law.[2]

2.2. Business scope

The EU directive about the EWC or procedure for information and consultation of employees is not aimed at all MNEs that operate in the European Union, but at so-called 'Community-scale undertakings' (CSU) and 'Community-scale groups of undertakings'. A CSU is defined as an undertaking with at least 1,000 employees in the member states and minimum 150 employees in each of at least two member countries that signed the Agreement on Social Policy. The directive also applies to two CSUs with each 150 employees when they form, or are part of, a Community-scale group of undertakings.

In a certain sense the directive uses the traditional definition of a MNE as an enterprise with subsidiaries in at least two countries. Yet, the application of this conventional and broad definition is limited both in terms of size, dispersion and geographical scope. If, on the basis of this definition, the directive becomes applicable to a particular MNE, the EWC or procedure is relevant to all its subsidiaries in the European Union, even those that employ less than 150 people.

A 'controlling undertaking' is defined as an undertaking which can exercise a dominant influence over another (the so-called 'controlled') undertaking by virtue of e.g. ownership, financial participation or the rules which govern it. This dominant influence is assumed to exist when the former company in relation to the latter one: a) holds a majority of the subscribed capital; b) controls a majority of the votes with respect to the issued share capital or c) can appoint more than half the members of the undertakings' administrative, managerial or supervising body. Other criteria that may indicate a controlling influence – even in the absence of an equity capital participation – might be management contracts or situations of dependency or of exclusive subcontracting or distribution arrangements. Especially in shared management joint ventures it may be difficult to identify the parent company which has a controlling influence (Decrem, 1997). Because of the complexity of enterprise structures encompassing several countries it will be inevitable that legal conflicts between governments will occur, e.g. when different companies located in different countries influence decision-making of a particular firm and different national criteria apply.

2.3. Territorial scope

That the UK originally did not sign the Agreement on Social Policy of the Treaty of Maastricht complicated the geographical scope of the directive on EWCs enormously. While UK employers in principle did not need to implement the directive's provisions for their employees in the UK, the overall picture was more complicated. As a matter of fact, British firms which employed more people in the EU (not including the UK) than the thresholds of, on the one hand 1,000 in total and on the other hand two subsidiaries of at least 150 in two other member states, were obliged from the beginning to set up a EWC for their non-UK undertakings in the EU. Employees in subsidiaries in the UK which depended on non-UK multinationals which reached the aforementioned double thresholds in the continental countries of the EU had to be covered by EWCs.

This meant that even before 'opting-in' a number of British MNEs and foreign subsidiaries located in the UK had to take the EWC-directive into account. Actually many British MNE that set up an EWC for their continental subsidiaries included their UK subsidiaries, even though there was no real obligation to do so. According to Taylor (1995), the British TUC identified 109 UK based companies that had to comply with the directive, at least as far as their mainland European workforce was concerned. UK firms did not follow a two-track approach in their human resource policies, in which they excluded British workers from their EWC. Indeed, the European Commissioner for Social Policy, Mr Flynn, claimed that MNEs include their UK subsidiaries to establish the lower limit of 1,000 employees even though they do not have to. Besides many of the voluntary agreements (see further) are also applied to the British subsidiaries of these groups. British enterprises apparently established voluntary EWCs even when there was no obligation to do so (Flynn, 1995; Cressey, 1998).

The number of countries to which the EWC directive applied at the beginning increased to fourteen after three new members (Austria, Finland and Sweden) joined the eleven countries which signed the Agreement on Social Policy (i.e. Belgium, Denmark, France, Germany, Greece, Ireland, Italy, Luxembourg, the Netherlands, Portugal and Spain). Moreover because of the EEA (European Economic Area) agreement the EFTA countries, Iceland, Liechtenstein and Norway also accepted the EWC directive. With the adherence of the UK, the total number of countries will go up to 18. Yet in July 1998 only 13 of the 17 signatories had transposed the directive into their national legislation. Two EU members (Luxembourg and Portugal) and two EFTA members (Iceland and Liechtenstein) have not yet completed the transposition process, which has been called 'one of the most complex exercises in the history of Community social policy' (EIRR, 1997, p. 18). The EU directive on the EWC or a procedure on information and consultation of employees even extends beyond the territory of the EU and the EEA. MNEs which have a headquarter in e.g. the United States or Japan also fall under the directive if they reach the previously mentioned thresholds of a total of 1,000 employees in the EU and two times at least 150 employees in two subsidiaries in two member countries.

3. SCENARIOS FOR THE ESTABLISHMENT OF A EUROPEAN WORKS COUNCIL

The second version of the Vredeling proposed directive was put on the agenda of the Council of Ministers for the first time on December 8, 1983. While its possible acceptance was discussed in a number of other Council meetings, the opposition – mainly from the UK – succeeded in blocking the proposal. Even though the Vredeling directive was not formally withdrawn the employers' associations seemed to have won the battle and had fended off the dreaded interference from employees with their decision-making authority at the level of the parent company. And yet certain MNEs recognised the usefulness of transnational agreements and set up their own structures to inform their employees about worldwide developments and certain decisions of great importance to them. Also, since the EWC directive was accepted in 1994, a number of companies have opted for the establishment of a voluntary agreement. The multinational firms which do not enter into voluntary agreements before that date, have to set up a special committee to negotiate with the employees or their representatives about a EWC. When these deliberations are not engaged into or remain unsuccessful, the EWC – as defined and described in the directive – will be applied obligatory. These different stages and their major characteristics are explained in the next paragraphs and briefly summarised in Figure 10.2.

Figure 10.2. Establishment of the EWC, or procedure for information and consultation of employees in MNEs: stages and options

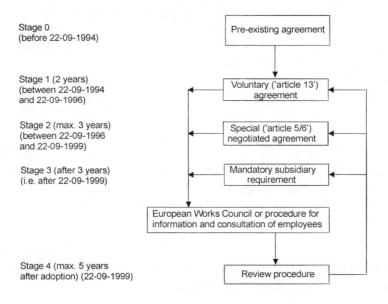

3.1. Pre-existing agreements

Agreements that existed before the EWC directive was signed, have been called pre-existing agreements (Blanpain and Windey, 1994), prototype EWCs (Gold and Hall, 1994) or pre-directive agreements (Scorey, 1997). The first one was established by the French MNE Thomson Consumer Electronics in 1985 (and reviewed in 1992), while 30 more were set up before the directive was approved. An analysis of these agreements shows not only that there is a great diversity but also that the competencies of the councils are often limited to information and that consultation is not always included (Blanpain and Windey, 1984).[3] The liaison committee set up by Thomson, has to be informed, prior to implementation, of major structural, industrial and commercial changes and of adaptations in the economic and legal organisation of the company. The agreement signed by Volkswagen in 1992 between management and trade unions is generally regarded as an important step, as it was the first formal agreement to provide employee representatives with information and also consultation rights about e.g. international transfers of production and investments (Marginson, 1992; Gold and Hall, 1993; Vitols, 1993). In other companies informal initiatives were taken either by the central management (e.g. Rhône-Poulenc and Saint-Gobain) or by employee representatives (e.g. Allianz, Mercedes Benz and Volkswagen up to 1992). BSN (food and drinks division), Nestlé and Pechiney made such arrangements into 'agreed practice' in their relations with the employees. BSN set up a more ambitious agreement in May 1994 and commits both labour and the management to monitor the observance of basic trade union rights as defined in certain ILO-conventions.

Although only a limited number of companies have stepped into pre-existing arrangements there are some common characteristics that can be identified (Marginson, 1992; UNCTAD, 1994; Gold and Hall, 1993). Such arrangements have mainly been concluded in companies that are engaged in similar types of activities in different countries, i.e. the so-called 'multi-domestic' multinationals. The agreements are often concluded with the relevant trade union organisation at the European level e.g. the European Metalworkers Federation (EMF) or Euro-FIET (International Federation of Commercial, Clerical, Professional and Technical Employees). Initiatives were taken by trade unions as well as management. Especially at the beginning most of the companies were French, underlining the influence of national legislation (the Aurouxe laws of 1982) and social climate. The companies that entered into pre-existing arrangements follow European production strategies, supported by unified management structures at that level and a number of firms carried out restructuring activities in view of the completion of the Single European Market.

3.2. Voluntary agreements

The EWC directive which was voted in the European Council, on the one hand stipulates that pre-existing arrangements can be maintained and on the other hand invites companies to enter into voluntary or 'article 13' agreements during a two-period timespan during which national governments have to introduce the directive into their legal system.

Blanpain and Windey (1994) mentioned the following advantages of a voluntary EWC or procedure to inform and consult the workforce. There were no mandatory conditions for voluntary agreements, which meant that there was considerable flexibility as to with whom to negotiate and about the contents of the agreement. The scope of the agreement could also be better adapted to the particular needs of the company or group. Certain firms considered it to be an advantage to be able to take proactive measures instead of having to wait until one was pressured into a negotiated agreement or forced into a mandatory EWC. Especially in cases of major restructuring the establishment of a proactive EWC might have fostered a better climate for industrial relations and human resource management. A social dialogue at the international level with its many cultural and possible adversarial aspects takes time to develop and suggests a gradual and step by step approach.

The most serious disadvantage of the voluntary agreement was the lack of legal certainty. Companies that started early might find out later that they do not completely respect all the rules. Because the directive does not indicate the negotiating parties, there is indeed a risk that certain employees or trade unions might legally challenge such an agreement, e.g. because the employees of their country of location have not been involved. It is not excluded that companies might be forced to reopen the negotiations and because of the delays get into the stage where a stricter EWC will be imposed (Storm, 1995).[4]

Table 10.1 presents some major characteristics of seven voluntary agreements. According to a study by the European Foundation for the Improvement of Living Conditions (1998) about 386 so-called 'article 13' agreements, the dominating home countries of the MNE were Germany with 23% of the total, the UK and USA with 15%, France with 11% and Sweden, the Netherlands and Switzerland with 6 to 5%. If the number of agreements that have been concluded are compared with the MNEs that come under the EWC directive, i.e. the so-called 'strike rate', Belgium and Ireland which have relatively few home based multinationals scored highest (respectively 80 and 60%) for the voluntary agreements, as compared to about 40% for Finland, Norway, Japan, Sweden and the UK and about 20% or less for the Netherlands, Spain and Denmark. The voluntary agreements were strongly concen-

Table 10.1. *Comparison of some recent voluntary agreements to form a European Works Council or procedure to inform and consult employees (1994-1996)*

	Beiersdorf	Schering	Crédit Lyonnais	Norsk Hydro	SKF	Honda	Marks and Spencer
Sector	Pharmaceuticals	Rubber Plastics	Banking	Chemicals and Gas, Aluminum	Machine construction	Automotive	Retailing
Country of origin	Germany	Germany	France	Norway	Sweden	Japan	UK
Total number of employees	18,000	26,000	53,000	14,000	45,000	5,000 (in Europe)	50,000
Negotiating parties	German central works council	–	National trade unions and European union FIET	National trade union and EMF (aluminium)	EMF and existing world council	–	Opposition of Euro-FIET
Geographic scope	EU	EU	EU	EEA	Worldwide	EU	EU
Composition of EWC	External members allowed if all parties agree		–	–	External members allowed	–	–
Management and workers representation	Parity	–	Parity	Parity	–	–	–
Number of meetings	Only if written information insufficient	At least once a year and additional meetings if necessary				Annually	Annually

Source: based on Storm (1995) and EIRR (1995)

Note: a dash means 'unknown'.

trated in manufacturing (80%) and only 12% in services. Within manufacturing the following subsectors dominate: 35% in metalworking, 17% in chemicals and 12% in the food sector. The highest sectoral 'strike rates' are in the food sector (40%), chemicals and mining and oil, while textiles, commerce and transport reach the lowest scores (EIRR, 1998).

3.3. Special negotiated agreements

Enterprises which have not concluded a voluntary agreement during the two year period which started on September 22, 1996 have to establish, on the basis of the articles 5 and 6, a 'Special Negotiating Body' (SNB) at the written request of at least 100 employees or their representatives in at least two member countries. The negotiations have to be started by the central management of the MNE within six months after the request and have to result in the establishment of a Special Negotiating Body (SNB). This SNB should be composed of minimum 3 and maximum 17 members with at least one representative per country of location of the subsidiaries. The other seats should be distributed in proportion to the number of the employees in the subsidiaries. The SNB may either accept the negotiated agreement by majority voting or decide not to negotiate or terminate the negotiations with a two thirds majority.

3.4. Mandatory subsidiary requirements

A EWC will be automatically installed during stage 3 when after six months the central management of the MNE has not reacted to the written request to set up a SNB. When no agreement has been reached after a negotiating period of three years, i.e. in September 1999, the application of the EWC directive will also become mandatory. The purpose of these provisions is on the one hand to push MNEs into negotiations about an agreement and on the other hand to avoid that the discussions drag on too long. In this case the EWC which will be set up must satisfy the subsidiary requirements as stipulated in the directive.

The mandatory EWC of stage 3 of the directive lays down a number of specific requirements which have to be followed by the companies which have not taken up the options of a voluntary or a negotiated agreement. The minimum and maximum membership of the EWC is from 3 to 30 members, with possibility for the formation of a 'select committee' of 3 persons for the large MNEs. While each subsidiary has to be represented by at least one representative, the additional ones can be attributed on the basis of their total number of employees. The EWC is allowed to meet with the central management at least once a year and if there are special circumstances affecting the interests of the employees, on an ad hoc basis (see further).[5]

As to the frequency and the type of information and consultation, a distinction is made between annual general information and *ad hoc* information. For the yearly overview the central management has to provide a written report on the structure, economic and financial situation, the probable trends in terms of production, sales, employment and investments, and substantial changes with regard to the organisational set-up, the introduction of new working methods or production processes, transfer of production, mergers, closure of certain departments or undertakings as a whole, collective redundancies, etc. With regard to the *ad hoc* information it is stipulated that when there are exceptional circumstances affecting the employees' interests to a considerable extent, i.e. particularly in the event of relocations, the closure of establishments or undertakings or collective redundancies, the EWC has the right to be informed and, at its request, meet the central management in order to be informed and consulted about these issues. It should be added that the management side can invoke confidentiality if this would seem necessary.

Maximum five years after the adoption of the EWC-directive, i.e. in September 1999, its operation (especially the thresholds) has to be reviewed by the European Commission. If necessary, amendments to the Council should be proposed.

4. THE EUROPEAN WORKS COUNCIL DIRECTIVE: AN APPRAISAL

4.1. The assumptions of the Vredeling proposed directive

Employers' associations were vehemently opposed to the first version of the Vredeling proposal of October 1980 and claimed that it 'misinterprets the responsibility of company directors, will undermine the authority of local management and will disrupt existing industrial relations' (UNICE, 1981, p. 4). One of the central objections of the employers' representatives was directed at the so-called 'bypass' which authorised the employees' representatives to open consultations with managers of the parent company when the management of the subsidiaries failed to communicate the information it was required to pass on to the employees or did not arrange the necessary consultations as specified in the proposed directive. Yet, when the Vredeling proposal was made public in 1980 the outcry by the MNEs against the bypass was such that the European Commission in its second version of the Vredeling directive of 1983 much toned down the original formulation and replaced it by a one-way written direct request for information to the parent company, to be answered by the management of the local subsidiary. The Vredeling proposal implicitly started from the assumption that the subsidiary is largely dependent upon the decision-making authority of the parent company. Trade union officials considered the 'bypass' provision as formulated in 1980 as essential, as it would allow the employees in the local subsidiary to have the necessary access to the 'real decision makers' in the parent company (Van Den Bulcke, 1984). Therefore, the watered down version of the Vredeling proposal of 1983 did no longer appeal to them.

Table 10.2.   Comparison between the second version of the Vredeling proposed directive (1983) and the European Works Council or procedure (1994) on information and consultation of employees in multinational enterprises

Characteristics	Vredeling proposed directive (1983)	European Works Council directive (1994)
Legal basis	Treaty of Rome (1957)	Treaty of Maastricht, Agreement on Social Policy (1989)
Voting procedure	Unanimity	Qualified majority
Influence of social partners	Lobbying	Negotiations, dialogue Quasi legislative power
Size of parent company	1,000 employees	1,000 employees
Size of subsidiary	No restriction	Threshold of 150 employees in 2 subsidiaries in at least 2 countries. No restriction if thresholds apply
Territorial scope	All member countries	Member countries except UK (in principle)
Access to decision-makers in parent company	Only via 'by-pass' (written contact only)	Direct contact during meetings
Contacts with other subsidiaries	Not applicable	Automatically applicable
Form and contents	Mandatory	Voluntary or mandatory according to the different stages and options
Freq. of information and consultation	Annual and *ad hoc*	Annual and *ad hoc*

Table 10.2 highlights a number of differences and similarities between the new EWC directive and the second version of the directive as proposed by Vredeling. Although some of these have already been referred to, e.g. the legal basis, the voting procedure, the territorial scope, etc., it is important to stress that while the Vredeling proposed directive was limited to vertical contacts between the employees of one particular subsidiary and the parent company, the new directive also extends the contacts in a horizontal way as the representatives of different subsidiaries belong to the same EWC. It is in this sense that the EWC may be considered as being more influential than the Vredeling proposal.

Both the Vredeling and the EWC proposal assume that the information and consultation rights for employees are most relevant for large MNEs employing at least 1,000 employees in the EU. There certainly is no convincing evidence that the size of the multinational group as a whole, and the size of the European operations, in terms of employment increases the centralisation of decision-making in MNEs (Van Den Bulcke, 1984). The first version of the Vredeling directive was directed towards all MNEs operating within the EC and did not specify any size limitations.[6]

While the Vredeling proposal was to be applicable to all subsidiaries of the MNEs with more than 1,000 employees, the EWC directive introduced a second threshold and as such limits even further the number of companies that have to establish a EWC. Although there is no clear relationship between the absolute and relative size of the subsidiary and the centralisation of decision-making, it has been admitted that subsidiary autonomy, after having increased with growing size, decreases again for subsidiaries that were very large in relation to the parent company (Van Den Bulcke, 1984).

4.2. Centralisation versus decentralisation

Since the Vredeling proposal was first put forward there have been such important changes in the international business environment, in the internal management strategies, and in industrial relations that one may wonder if the establishment of EWCs on the basis of a EU directive is not an exercise in futility.

The centralisation-decentralisation debate between representatives of employers and employees that occurred during the 1970s and beginning 1980s was rather simplistic. A number of studies of the decision-making role of the local managers covering a period of almost twenty years between 1960 and 1980, had shown that at least in one of four subsidiaries, sometimes in one of two, decision-making was quite autonomous (cf. Van Den Bulcke, 1984 and 1986).[7] Although these studies focus on the relationship between headquarters and subsidiary management and neglect the participation of employees as such, they are still relevant because it is a major preoccupation of employee representatives to have access to the decision-makers, wherever they are located.

One of the few determining factors of centralisation in MNEs that clearly was significant in a number of the early studies was the degree of intersubsidiary production integration as measured by intra-group trade. Centralisation of management decisions in general and employment decisions in particular were typically higher in multinational groups with a high degree of integration (Van Den Bulcke and Halsberghe, 1984 and Dowling, Schuler and Welch, 1994).

4.3. New developments in international strategic management and environment and human resource trends

It has been claimed that the EWC directive is already outdated because it tries to deal with a situation of an earlier interaction and confrontation between trade unions and employers' federations and does not take into account new corporate strategies and management methods.

One of the most important developments in the world economy is the so-called globalisation of competition and corporate strategies. As the intensity of global competition increased and the environment became more turbulent, MNEs reacted either by establishing complex internal integration strategies or by entering into strategic alliances via external networks or by both of these strategies together. The increased volatility of the international environment increases the interfirm and intrafirm rivalries with regard to the different locations and product lines. To achieve rapid responses, decision-making has to be devolved and internal entrepreneurship must be encouraged (Casson *et al.*, 1995). According to *The Economist* (1995, p. 8): 'In complex integration, companies locate all their activities according to the logic of the market, and disperse decision-making throughout the organisation. Their hallmark is the endless flow of information in all directions instead of a command-and-control system'. A recent empirical study of major US, Japanese and European MNEs provides strong support for these differentiated knowledge flows and the suggestion that innovation by foreign subsidiaries is more typically the result of an autonomous initiative by these subsidiaries rather than strategic directives issued from corporate headquarters (Gupta and Govindarajan, 1994). Many MNEs evolved from a hierarchical system to a network. 'In fact, to the extent that the individual units of the transnational system assume responsibilities that are clearly defined as part of an intra-firm international division of labour, the distinction between parent firm and affiliates becomes less meaningful' (UNCTAD, 1994, p. 139). Also, these networks are not closed systems but are often linked to other corporate systems through strategic alliances, i.e. subcontracting, licensing, consortia, etc. thereby extending the boundary of the individual MNE. Strategic alliances 'used to be seen as a way of filling well defined competence gaps through learning and restructuring. Not anymore. They are becoming a basic, permanent building block of 'global network' companies. Such a network corporation comes about only through an imaginative reconceptualisation of businesses, and in more and more industries such entrepreneurial globalisation is becoming the norm' (Yoshino and Rangan, 1995).

All these developments (see Table 10.3) have a profound effect as they result in international restructuring in which new roles and responsibilities for certain subsidiaries will be attributed, disinvestment and mergers and acquisitions may be carried out. As managing a MNE more and more requires a global mindset, the shift to informal controls obliges management to trust their staff members and employees more than before and to use social knowledge as a control system (Sohn, 1994) as well as to exercise 'procedural justice' (Kim and Mauborgne, 1993). That more trusted employees are allowed to make a wider range of decisions is the result of de-layering and necessitates the so-called empowerment of employees. Smaller head-offices improve communications and consequently accelerate decision-making (Casson *et al.*, 1994). As a result more and more MNEs recognised that industrial relations and human resource management could no longer be considered as marginal issues and have to be integrated in the overall strategic objectives. There are indications that firms with close matches between business strategy and human resource strategy actually perform better than firms with mismatches (Bird and Beechler, 1995). Yet, Brewster (1995) has criticised the assumption that resource management is in some sense 'strategic' when it follows closely the corporate strategy of the corporation.

Information technology also plays an important role in facilitating strategic human resource management. The improvement of the performance of managers is helped by giving them access on demand to a centralised relational data base (Casson, *et al.*, 1995). ABB for instance is known to have a management system that is based on a uniform reporting system called ABACUS with timely, detailed and accurate information about all activities vital to decision making (Yoshino and Rangan, 1995). In order to exchange information on a more structural basis so that trade union and worker representatives are provided with relevant information on the Unilever group, the so-called Unilever Company Information System, set up by two International Trade Secretariats with the support of the EU, relies on the computer. 'It appears that in this case the promise of the information society has come true as real possibilities have been created for getting information to people who are usually not in a position to acquire such information' (Veersma, 1994, p. 223).[8] On the other hand there is likely to be a need for more research on the

effects of electronic communications before profound practical recommen-
dations can be made about their most effective use (Janssens and Brett,
1993). MNEs whose networks are information or knowledge intensive may
well develop – or require – a better understanding of cross-cultural differences than those who are not (Kobrin, 1994).

*Table 10.3.   Some relevant new developments with respect to the issues of
information and consultation of employees in multinational enterprises*

General areas	Trends	Effects
International management strategies	Globalisation of competition and corporate strategies Complex interaction strate-gies: internal strategies Strategic alliances: external strategies	International restructuring Mergers and acquisitions Intrapreneurship Outsourcing Benchmarking Networking
Technological developments	Information technology: improved communications Flexible production methods and custom made production	Centralised relational data base Organisational changes in work system
Industrial relations developments	Strategic orientation of hu-man resource management Increased involvement of employees Changing power relationship between MNEs and trade unions	De-layering Empowerment Decentralisation of bargaining
Socio-cultural and political developments	Democratic deficit of the European Union Recognition of multicultural-ism Declining role of national governments in socio-economic affairs	Principle of subsidiarity Importance of social skills Deregulation

It is generally accepted that the powerbasis of trade unions has shrunk
(Nagelkerke, 1994). This is clearly illustrated by the declining unionisation
rates since the early 1980s. An indirect result of the weakening position of
trade unions is their diminishing bargaining power versus national governments. Consequently they have been less successful in placing their objec-

tives towards MNEs high on the agenda of lobbying governments. Also national governments have continued to deregulate their foreign investment activities. Confronted with a 'democratic deficit' the European Union became less insistent on integrationist policies and wrote the principle of subsidiarity into the Treaty of Maastricht, meaning that decisions should be taken at the lowest appropriate level, i.e. as close as possible to the people who are affected by them (European Commission, 1994b). The more constructive attitude of the European Commission towards MNEs, not only with regard to industrial policy and research and development but also in the area of social policy was thereby strengthened (Van Den Bulcke, 1993).

5. CONCLUDING REMARKS

It took the European Community or Union 15 years, after it was launched in 1958, before a fully fledged programme towards MNEs was developed in 1973. On the one hand it tried to bolster European firms in their competitive position with regard to American and Japanese companies on the basis of a new industrial policy and on the other hand it attempted to foster the social responsibility of MNEs by insisting on information, notification, transparency and industrial democracy and took measures to support the trade unions as a countervailing force. However, this action programme towards MNEs was withdrawn in 1976, when the European Commission realised that in the total package it had introduced, there were a number of proposals that were unacceptable to the Council. As a result of this, about 30 different proposed measures were blocked. Later initiatives like the Vredeling proposed directive indicate that the decision to abandon the 1973 package was inspired by tactical considerations even though the general attitude towards MNEs during this period was becoming more favourable and governments increased the deregulation of foreign direct investment (Van Den Bulcke, 1993).

It would seem that after a long period of an apparent disinterest the European Commission has again taken up its double track approach towards MNEs. While on the one hand, the European Commission has opted for the model of a worldwide level playing field for foreign direct investment on the basis of multilaterally agreed investment rules (EC Commission, 1995 and Brittan, 1995), on the other hand the EWC directive was approved as its first legally binding instrument on MNEs. This means that information and consultation of employees in multinational subsidiaries will have to be provided and arranged by MNEs. Although the agreement has been heralded as a linchpin in the realisation of the Single European Market, there is no single EWC or procedure that has to be followed. This voluntarism was necessary to appease the fears of the employers' federations and MNEs which had been strongly opposed to information and consultation of employees since the European Commission first introduced co-determination in the proposal for a European Company Statute in 1970 and even more so after the ferociously contested Vredeling proposed directive in 1980.

The obligation of MNEs to inform and consult can hopefully reassure the employees and placate their fears that the global changes in the world economy will occur completely unexpectedly and leave them little or no time to react. When on February 27, 1997 the French automobile company Renault, announced its decision to close down its factory in Vilvoorde, Belgium and to collectively dismiss its more than 3,000 employees during the coming summer, the EWC arrangement received a serious blow as to its potential effects. It was quite ironic that the French Renault Group after having been one of the pioneering firms to set up a pre-directive agreement in 1993 and an 'article 13' voluntary agreement in 1995, choose to disregard its previous engagements and to proceed with the closure without the necessary information and consultation procedure. Renault argued that it had not breached the EWC agreement because its sole obligation was to provide the information, and implied that this information did not have to be given prior to the decision. The judgement of the Nanterre Tribunal and its confirmation by the Court of Appeal of Versailles as well as the judgements of the Brussels Court, clearly state that the information should have been given prior to the disinvestment decision and that penalisation should be possible (Lorber, 1997 and Moreau, 1997).

Employee representatives have the feeling that when the intra-competitive pressures within MNEs increase, there is a danger of being presented with misleading information on e.g. the level of wages and salaries, the flexibility of the labour regulations and productivity in the subsidiaries of the multinational group in other countries. With the EWC they hope to have acquired an instrument to exchange information and check out the relevant data.

An increasing number of MNEs, and certainly those that have already set up pre-existing or voluntary agreements, expect that the involvement of employees in decision-making will improve the quality of the decisions, the motivations of the management and the workers and even productivity as a whole. The European Commission has stressed from the beginning that the implementation of the directive should be regarded as 'part of good management practice' (EC Commission, 1994a, p. 6) and that it will facilitate the success of business and is beneficial to both companies and workforce.

It has been estimated that about 1,200 MNEs in Europe will have to introduce a EWC or a procedure for information and consultation of employees and that about 4.5 million employees would be covered by these arrangements. (Jeffers, 1997). As was indirectly mentioned before 416 firms already did so either through concluding a pre-existing agreement (30) before September 1994 or through a voluntary agreement (386) before September 1996. Until June 1998 only 45 so-called 'Article 6' or negotiated EWCs had been concluded, 29 of which have their parent companies in continental EU countries and 6 in the UK. Of the non-member countries the US firms negotiated 7 such arrangements as compared to only 1 for Japan. As was the case for the 'article 13' agreements, the number is likely to increase with the approach of the deadline in September 1999.

The European Commissioner for Social Affairs has stressed 'that there will not be a competitive Europe without a vibrant social policy' (Flynn, 1994, p. 2) and that information and consultation of employees 'are a major precondition of economic and social progress in Europe and are vital to the development of European industry' (Flynn, 1995, p. 3). The so-called 'European model' in industrial relations and human resource management (Brewster, 1995) has undoubtedly received an additional dimension by the EWC directive. Although it is generally agreed that there are differences amongst the European countries themselves, Western Europe as a whole has a clearly distinct human resource management as compared with e.g. the US or Japan (Sparrow and Hiltrop, 1994, Bellace, 1997). Even if the EWC directive leaves a lot of autonomy to the MNEs as to how to achieve the necessary information and consultation of employees, there is an obligation as to the final outcome.

The extent to which the European social model can be extended to the rest of the world is certainly limited. Nevertheless there will be pressure for MNEs which come from home countries outside the EU and have operations within the European Union, to emulate the European policies in this particular area. Certain US and Japanese MNEs in Europe (e.g. CPC and Honda) have already entered into a voluntary EWC or procedure to inform and consult employees, while others (e.g. General Motors, IBM, Citybank, Toyota) seem to be inclined to do so (Flynn, 1995). This latter group of MNEs will then have to decide to limit the EWC either to their European operations or to extend them to their worldwide activities as did e.g. SKF, Ericsson and Natwest (Cressey, 1998). It was indicative that UK MNEs which were not obliged to include their UK subsidiaries in the EWC they had set up in Continental Europe, have done so all the same. Decrem (1997) states that in 20% of the voluntary agreements Central and East European countries are included, especially Hungary. With regard to the Japanese firms the European Commission is confident that most of them – with their very particular human resources management practices – will take a positive approach to the directive's objectives (Flynn, 1995).

NOTES

1. This chapter is an updated version of a paper originally presented at the Annual Conference of the European International Business Academy (EIBA) at the University of Urbino, Italy, December 10-12, 1995.
2. The trade unions are not formally mentioned in the directive, even though they played an important part in the establishment of a number of voluntary councils. As employee representation in the EWCs is determined in accordance with national legislation and practice and the directive does not as such rule out trade union officials as members, they have been actively involved in many voluntary agreements.
3. Europipe, which has accepted equal representation of German and French workers in its Supervisory Board, is considered an exception, especially because this board has to give its consent before a number of important economic and financial decisions can be taken.
4. Taylor (1995) points out that it is not unlikely that recent consultation agreements reached at non-union companies in the UK e.g. Marks and Spencer and Honda, would be 'tested in the courts if it is unclear whether the employees have genuinely agreed to what has been decided through authentic employee representatives' (See also EIRR, 1995 and Bellace, 1997).
5. It is stated in the directive that the prerogatives of central management cannot be encroached upon. The EWC may be assisted by experts of its own choice, who can also be outsiders, i.e. non-employees and therefore also trade union officials. The EU has intervened financially to stimulate the social dialogue on a European level between employers and employees and for the establishment of the EWCs mainly through training sessions (Decrem, 1997). Also the EWC directive decided that the expenses (e.g. costs of organising the meeting, interpreters, travelling, accommodation) have to be paid for by the parent company, unless otherwise agreed.
6. This restriction of size in the second version of the proposal was the result of extensive discussions in the European Parliament and was basically a way to limit the impact of the Vredeling directive. During the deliberations in the European Parliament of the EWC directive it was proposed to lower the overall threshold to 500 employees. The European Commission did however not take up this suggestion in the final version it submitted to the Council of Ministers.
7. Although the so-called centralisation indices used in these studies present a number of methodological shortcomings, they show that autonomous subsidiaries are a reality, even if one takes into account that local management tends to overestimate its degree of independence.
8. *The Economist* (1995, p. 21) states that videoconferencing technology, once cumbersome, is developing rapidly and becoming increasingly popular. Mercedes' new factory in the US holds a two-hour teleconference with the parent company in Germany every day. Again an extension to employees in different subsidiaries of MNEs around the world may be coming nearer.

REFERENCES

Anon. (1995), 'Richtlijn Europese ondernemingsraden leidt tot vrijwillige akkoorden', *Financieel Economische Tijd*, July 12.
Anon. (1995), 'Big is back. A Survey of multinationals', *The Economist,* June 24.
Anon. (1995), 'European Works Councils: Social Partners Anticipate a Directive', *International Labour Review*, No 1, 91-104.

Bellace, J. (1997), 'The European Works Council Directive: Transnational Information and Consultation in the European Union', *Comparative Labor Law Journal*, **18**, 325-361.

Bird, A. and S. Beechler (1995), 'Links between Business Strategy and Human Resource Management Strategy in US based Japanese Subsidiaries: an Empirical Investigation', *Journal of International Business Studies*, 1st Quarter, 23-46.

Blanpain, R. and P. Windey (1994), *European Works Councils. Information and Consultation of Employees in Multinational Enterprises in Europe*, Leuven: Uitgeverij Peeters.

Brewster, C. (1995), 'Towards a "European" Model of Human Resource Management', *Journal of International Business Studies*, 1st Quarter, 2-21.

Brittan, L. (1995), 'Investment Liberalization: the Next-great Boost to the World Economy', *Transnational Corporations*, April, No 1, 1-10.

Carley, M. (1993), 'Initiatives Volontaires – une mise à jour', *Moniteur Européen de la Participation*, No 6, 16-23.

Casson, M., R. Loveridge and S. Singh (1995), 'Economics of Human Resource Management in Large Multinational Enterprises: A Summary of New Evidence', Discussion Papers in International Investment and Business Studies, University of Reading, No. 195.

Colaianni, T. (1996), *European Works Councils*, London: Sweet and Maxwell.

Cressey, P. (1998), 'European Works Councils in Process', *Human Resource Management Journal*, **8**, 67-79.

Cuthbert, D. and H. Johannissen (1997), 'European Works Councils: the Value Added Approach', *Benefits and Compensation International*, June, 2-6.

Decrem, W. (1997), *De Europese ondernemingsraad en haar omzetting in de nationale wetgevingen*, Diegem: CED-Samsom.

Dowling, P., R. Schuler and D. Welch (1994), *International Dimensions of Human Resource Management*, 2nd edition, Belmont: Wadsworth Publishing.

European Commission (1994a), 'Information and Consultation of Employees in Multinational Enterprises', IP/94/572, Brussels.

European Commission (1994b), 'Report to the European Council on the Application of the Subsidiarity Principle 1994', Com (94) 533, Brussels.

European Commission (1995), 'A Level Playing Field for Direct Investment Worldwide', Com (95) 42, Luxembourg.

EIRR (1995), 'European Works Councils – Trends and Issues', *European Industrial Relations Review*, May, 14-22.

EIRR (1997), 'European Works Councils Update', *European Industrial Relations Review*, December, 18-20.

EIRR (1998), 'European Works Councils Update', *European Industrial Relations Review*, July, 34-36.

Flynn, P. (1994), 'The Social Policy of the European Union', European Commission, Key points, Lecture at the University of Ulster, IP 94/1015, Brussels.

Flynn, P. (1995), 'European Works Councils', European Commission, Lecture at the College of Europe, IP/95/150, Brussels.

Gold, M. and M. Hall (1994), 'Statutory European Works Councils: the final Countdown?', *Industrial Relations Journal*, **25**, 177-186.

Gupta, A. and V. Govindarajan (1994), 'Organizing for Knowledge Flows within MNEs', *International Business Review*, No 4, 443-457.

Janssens, M. and J. Brett (1993), 'Coordinating Global Companies. The Effects of Electronic Communication, Organizational Commitment, and a Multi-Cultural Managerial Workforce', Working Paper No 9334, Katholieke Universiteit Leuven.

Jeffers, R. (1997), 'European Works Councils Directive; Where Are We Today?', *International Business Lawyer*, June, 246-252.

Kim, W.C. and R. Mauborgne (1993), 'Effectively Conceiving and Executing Multi-nationals' Worldwide Strategies', *Journal of International Business Studies*, 3rd Quarter, p. 419-448.

Kobrin, S. (1994), 'Is there a Relationship between a Geocentric mind-set and Multi-national Strategy? *Journal of International Business Studies*, 3rd Quarter, 493-511.

Lorber, P. (1997), 'The Renault Case: The European Works Council Put to the Test', *International Journal of Comparative Labour Law and Industrial Relations*, **13**, 135-142.

Marginson, P. (1992), 'European Integration and Transnational Management – Union Relations in the Enterprise', *British Journal of Industrial Relations*, **30**, 529-545.

Moreau, M.A. (1997), 'A Propos de l'Affaire Renault', *Droit Social*, 493-503.

Mosley, H. (1990), 'La Dimension Sociale de l'Intégration Européenne', *Revue Internationale du Travail*, No 2, 157-176.

Nagelkerke, A. (1994), 'Institutional Responses to Changing Conditions in European Systems of Industrial Relations', in J. van Dijck and J. Groenewegen (eds), *Changing Business Systems in Europe. An Institutional Approach*, Brussels: VUBPress, pp. 236-263.

Scorey, D. (1997), 'European Works Councils. Hidden in the Irish Mist. Ireland's "Transnational Information and Consultation of Employees" Act 1996', *Industrial Journal*, **2**, 85-193.

Sohn, D. (1994), 'Social Knowledge as a Control System: a Proposition and Evidence from the Japanese FDI Behaviour', *Journal of International Business Studies*, 2nd Quarter, 295-324.

Sparrow, P. and J.M. Hiltrop (1994), *European Human Resource Management in Transition*, New York: Prentice Hall.

Storm, M.L. (1995), 'De Europese Ondernemingsraad staat voor de Deur', *Fabrimetal Magazine*, No 3, March, 54-57.

Taylor, R. (1995), 'Entering into a new dimension', *Financial Times*, April 10.

Teague, R. (1989), *The European Community: The Social Dimension. Labour Market Policies for 1992*, London: Kogan Page.

UNCTAD (1994), *Transnational Corporations, Employment and the Workplace, World Investment Report 1994*, Geneva.

UNICE (1981), 'Position Paper', February 19.

Van Den Bulcke, D. (1984), 'Decision Making in Multinational Enterprises and the Information and Consultation of Employees: the Proposed Vredeling Directive of the EC Commission', *International Studies of Management and Organisation*, No. 1. pp. 36-60.

Van Den Bulcke, D. (1986), 'Autonomy of Decision Making by Subsidiaries of Multinational Enterprises', in J. Van Damme (ed.), *Employee Consultation and Information in Multinational Corporations*, London: Croom Helm, pp. 219-250.

Van Den Bulcke, D. (1993), 'European Economic Integration and the Process of Multinationalization', in Robson, P. (ed.), *Transnational Corporations and Regio-*

nal Economic Integration, Volume 9 of the United Nations Library on Transnational Corporations, London/New York: Routledge on behalf of the United Nations, pp. 163-172.

Van Den Bulcke, D. (1995), 'The European Works Council. A New Challenge for Multinational Enterprises', in R. Schiattarelli (ed.), *Challenges for European and International Business*, Proceedings of the 21st Annual Conference of the European International Business Academy, Volume 2, University of Urbino, Urbino, pp. 426-447.

Van Den Bulcke, D. and E. Halsberghe (1984), 'Employment Decision Making in Multinational Enterprises: Survey Results from Belgium', International Labour Office, Geneva.

Veersma, U. (1994), 'Workers' Rights and European Multinationals: towards European Industrial Relations', in J. van Dijck and J. Groenewegen (eds), *Changing Business Systems in Europe. An institutional approach*, Brussels: VUBPress, pp. 210-235.

Vitols, S. (1993), 'Les Comités d'Entreprises Européens – un aperçu', *Moniteur Européen de la Participation*, No. 6, pp. 59-61.

Yoshino, M. and V. Rangan (1995), *Strategic Alliances. An Entrepreneurial Approach to Globalization*, Boston: HBS.

11. Flexible Labour Markets and Employment Rights in the EU: Competitive Tendering, Business Transfers and the Revised Acquired Rights Directive

Stephen Hardy and Nick Adnett[1]

1. INTRODUCTION

European Union (EU) regulation of business transfers has since 1977 sought to safeguard employee's rights in the event of business reorganisations. The Acquired Rights Directive (ARD) was one of the first four social directives adopted under the 1974 Social Action Programme. This Directive provides prior consultation rights for employees who are to be transferred to another employer and protection of their pre-transfer terms and conditions of employment, pensions being an exception. Despite clarity in the purpose of the Acquired Rights Directive, much confusion in the law has prevailed in the following twenty years (Napier, 1993; More, 1995; Korner, 1996). Since 1985 the European Court of Justice (ECJ) has been required to provide nearly thirty rulings on the ARD and the European Commission has thought it necessary to issue a memorandum which attempts to clarify the law (European Commission, 1997). The confused legal position of workers affected by business transfers does not appear to have significantly restricted this type of business reorganisation. One feature of the growth of flexible labour markets in Europe has, as Hepple (1998) reports, been the record levels of intra-European merger and transfer activity since the mid-1990s. In part this activity reflects the impact of the single market, globalisation and changed production strategies, but in addition privatisation and the growth of other market-based reforms in the provision of public services have contributed to this trend.

The increased importance of business transfers together with continuing legal confusion, particularly regarding the scope of the ARD, induced the Member State governments at the 1993 Brussels Summit to agree to revise the ARD. The EU Commission's 1994 proposed revised ARD (Hardy and Painter, 1996) has been replaced by a second version, drafted in March 1997 and agreed by the EU Council of Ministers in July 1998. The 1998 newly revised Directive amends the definition of a transfer, by making implicit references to recent caselaw in the European Court of Justice (*Suzen versus...*, 1997), and permits EU Member States to allow negotiated changes to terms and conditions, as well as introducing joint liability and requiring the transferor to provide the transferee with 'adequate' information. The new ARD fell within the jurisdiction of Article 94 (ex Article 100) of the Consolidated Treaty of the European Community and required unanimous approval by the Council of Ministers. For this reason the diverse priorities of individual EU Member States needed to be respected in searching for an agreement which was acceptable to all.

In the following section our analysis commences with an assessment of whether, even, a revised ARD is compatible with the efficient functioning of modern flexible labour markets. The third section provides some new empirical evidence on the impact that the existing ARD has had on employment relations. The evidence relates to the consequences of the Compulsory Competitive Tendering (CCT) process introduced in the UK as part of the Conservative Government's policies to increase the role of market forces in those public sector services unsuitable for privatisation. An outline of the key changes in revised 1998 ARD is then provided and the changes analysed in relationship to the previous discussion and existing case law. In the conclusion, we seek to assess whether those revisions are likely to produce the clarity requested by national governments, the courts, contractors and their clients, trade unions and employees.

2. EMPLOYMENT RIGHTS AND THE FLEXIBLE LABOUR MARKET

In the 1990s the persistence of high unemployment and fears of deteriorating international competitiveness have generated widespread calls for greater flexibility in European labour markets. It has become conventional wisdom to argue that the EU has developed the wrong sort of labour market institutions and regulations for competitive success in the modern global economy.

Commonly the need for more flexible labour markets has been equated with the need to deregulate and return to the 'employment-at-will' policies of 'Anglo-Saxon' economics (Philpott, 1996). However, labour market flexibility has been used to describe a variety of, and sometimes mutually inconsistent, behaviour and outcomes. Labour market flexibility has usually been formally used to describe the ease with which both wages and employment can adjust to changing market conditions. The latter involves both external employment flexibility, the ease with which employers can adjust their number of employees, and internal employment flexibility, the ease of adjusting employee's pattern of working.

Assessing any harmful effects of labour market regulations first necessitates the distinction between regulations which merely add to labour costs and those that raise the costs of employment adjustments. In a competitive labour market regulations of the first type, such as mandatory sick pay and health and safety regulations, should lead to compensating wage adjustments leaving employment and productivity growth largely unaffected. Nickell and Layard (1997) suggest that the limited evidence available is supportive of this argument. However, our concern is with the ARD, an employment protection measure, which in contrast directly influences the costs of internal and external employment adjustments. Specifically the ARD is designed to reduce the ability of transferred businesses to generate short-term wage-bill reductions. As such, in common with other job security measures, we would anticipate that the ARD would tend to reduce the exit rate from employment into unemployment whilst causing the escape rate from unemployment into employment to fall as employers adjust hiring rates instead. Nickell and Layard (1997) report evidence which suggests that the combination of employment protection measures in Europe reduces short-term unemployment and raises long-term, but overall they have little net effect on unemployment.

Until recently most of the empirical analysis of employment protection measures was limited to their impact upon external employment flexibility and neglected their impact upon internal flexibility and hence productivity growth. It is only with the development of analyses of segmented and internal labour markets, and particularly the consequences of incomplete employment contracts and asymmetric information (Cartier, 1994 and Parkin, 1996) that economists have widened their analysis (Blank and Freeman, 1994). Within these frameworks employment protection measures assist in reducing excess hires and fires (Carter and De Lancey, 1997) and creating high average tenure which encourages socially advantageous investments in human and physical capital by employers and employees (Deakin and Wilkinson, 1994). Moreover, new technology has generated new economies of scale and scope, which together with the effects of increased competition in product markets have encouraged firms to adopt new employee management systems such as 'lean production' and Total Quality Management. Marsden (1996, 1997) and Brown and Rea (1995) point out that these systems also increase the importance of co-operative industrial relations and the need for rules and rule-making procedures to manage collective discontents. More generally, Wilkinson (1998) argues that institutions and regulations, such as the ARD, which create and strengthen high trust relations in the workplace promote operational and dynamic efficiency. Results reported in Levine and Tyson (1990) and Ichniowski *et al.* (1997) do indeed indicate that the role of participation in raising productivity growth is strengthened by a number of complementary factors including job security. In order to encourage employees to co-operate in adjusting employment practices to fast changing market conditions some restraints on entrepreneurial freedom, such as the transfer of acquired rights, may therefore be beneficial. Increased co-operation and an increased willingness to re-train amongst workers with both job and terms and conditions of employment security can therefore promote intra-organisation productivity improvements.

The above arguments generally neglect the inter-organisation and inter-sectoral changes usually viewed necessary for fast aggregate productivity growth. Hopenhayn and Rogerson (1993) argue that measures such as the ARD slow down the reallocation of labour from declining to expanding sectors. More recently Saint-Paul (1997) relates job security legislation to patterns of international specialisation. Countries with more employment protection are viewed as being more likely to specialise in mature goods towards the end of their product life cycle, implying less R&D and less learning-by-doing and therefore a lower long-run productivity growth rate than similar countries with lower levels of employment protection. These rival arguments indicate the need to resort to empirical evidence. Nickell and Layard (1997) fail to find evidence to indicate that stricter employment protection legislation lowers productivity growth. Indeed, they conclude that when employment protection measures are combined with policies which encourage worker participation, the evidence suggests that productivity growth increases. Bertola and Rogerson (1997) point out that notwithstanding Europe's much tighter employment security provision, its rates of job creation and destruction are remarkably similar to those in North America. However, they point out that there are other institutional determinants of labour market flows, such as the degree of wage compression, and that it may be misleading to concentrate upon a uni-dimensional interpretation of these flows.

In common with the existing literature we have so far ignored two important dimensions of this issue: uncertainty regarding the scope and requirements of employment protection law and incomplete compliance with that law. The theoretical case for selective employment regulation outlined above assumes that the legal framework is both understood and enforced. Perhaps surprisingly, this case has been eloquently stated by the British Business Services Association (BSA), an employers' organisation, in their evidence to the British Parliamentary Select Committee considering the revised ARD.[2] The BSA pointed out that:

> (I)nitially, contractors saw TUPE as an unwelcome intrusion in the contracting out process. TUPE's introduction was resisted by contractors mainly because it restricted their ability to reduce manpower levels and to offer different terms and conditions of employment. It lowered profit margins and raised operating costs. . . The BSA subsequently changed its view as the benefits of TUPE became more apparent. Many of the 'cowboys' who had depended upon cutting wages and benefits in order to have competitive bids were driven out of business. This improved the image of contractors who through the activities of some had developed the unsavoury reputation of offering poor quality service and being poor employers. (House of Lords (1998), p. 12).

Commenting specifically on the revised Directive the BSA's evidence argued that

> (u)ncertainty surrounding the transfer of undertakings must be eliminated quickly. A stable environment is necessary both from the point of view of clients, contractors, employees and government....Ensuring stability of employment for employees and doing what is best for them will ultimately prove best for companies and government. (House of Lords (1998), pp. 13-14.)

In the following section we report the results of our survey of employers and employees involved in business transfers resulting from the introduction of compulsory competitive tendering in the UK public sector. In the European context the UK is of particular interest for two main reasons. Firstly, the market-based reforms of the public sector introduced by the Thatcher Government have been widely followed throughout Europe. As a consequence terms and conditions of employment in this segment of the labour market have changed more rapidly than in most other segments. Secondly, notwithstanding the Thatcher Government's policies and the initial opt-out from the social chapter of the Maastricht Treaty, the British Courts have referred far more cases per year to the European Court of Justice (ECJ) involving social provisions than any other Member State (Stone Sweet and Brunell, 1998). We concentrate on the survey results concerning understanding of, and compliance with, the ARD.

3. COMPETITIVE TENDERING AND THE ARD: SURVEY RESULTS

Our main survey commenced in September 1995 and was intended to gather information on the experiences of employers and employees involved in business transfers occurring as a consequence of compulsory competitive tendering in the UK. This policy required certain services provided by local government and local health authorities to be opened up to a competitive process in which the existing in-house providers were supposed to compete on an equal basis (Adnett, 1998). The 300 employers and 300 employees contacted were chosen to provide a random sample of those involved in this process. The postal questionnaire was followed up by a small number of semi-structured interviews in February 1996. In the event, usable replies were biased in favour of large and medium-sized employers, whereas in the employee sample, union representatives accounted for over 40 per cent of respondents. Full details of the methodology employed are provided in Hardy *et al*. (1997) and more detailed results from the employer survey are in Adnett and Hardy (1998). Although the final overall response rate was 64 per cent, we limit our discussion here to the 149 employer and 137 employee respondents with direct experience of CCT.

In the following analysis we concentrate upon responses to detailed questions concerning the sample's most recent experience of a business transfer. Well over two-thirds of respondents were uncertain whether the ARD applied to that transfer, several stated that 'they did not know anymore'. As an alternative indicator of legal uncertainty, over two-thirds of these respondents reported being involved in litigation as a result of a business transfer. Concerning the extent of compliance with the consultation requirements of the ARD, over 40 per cent of employees claimed that they had not been consulted prior to the transfer taking place. In those transfers where employees reported a post-transfer reduction in pay this percentage was even higher. We now consider the other fundamental concern of the ARD: protecting the terms and conditions of employment of transferred employees. Table 1 summarises the responses, the employer and employee samples are not matched and we should not therefore anticipate that the detailed responses should be identical. The responses indicate widespread non-compliance with the ARD. Whilst the detailed responses from contractors suggest that the reductions were almost invariably less than 5 per cent, the response of employees indicate that they believed that the reductions, in basic hourly pay in particular, were often much greater. The differing overall perceptions of employers and employees regarding CCT transfers can be effectively summarised by two comments made in our follow up interviews. One employer remarked 'we are not all cost obsessed. But we thought, and were in fact told that, that was what transfers, and later CCT, was all about. Cost savings in order to save a business and jobs'. Whereas an interviewed employee exclaimed 'it can't be legal to steal our rights, can it?'.

*Table 11.1.   Percentage of respondents who reported decreases in employ-
              ment and specified terms and conditions of employment in latest
              business transfer*

	Employers	Employees
Number of Employees	60	74
Basic Hourly Pay	40	86
Holiday Pay	24	53
Sickness Pay	47	90
Overtime Pay	53	76

Note: Maximum sample size: 68 employers and 116 employees (respondents did not always
         answer each question).

We did attempt to explore the reasons why trade unions had failed to prevent such widespread non-compliance. Unions sometimes admitted that they had not been proactive in the early days of CCT, partly due to a lack of information and expertise at the local and regional level. Consultation rights of their members were often not protected and where consultation did occur unions were often by-passed. Overall, our research suggested that local union officials and union's national legal departments have often been overwhelmed by the number and complexity of TUPE cases. In some cases given their perceived unequal access to legal advice, unions traded-off their threat of litigation for concessions on employment levels and, in yet other cases, substantial number of workers preferred to collect redundancy payments rather than be involved in lengthy litigation with uncertain outcomes.

Our survey provides evidence consistent with many of the submissions made to the two recent House of Lords enquiries into the ARD (House of Lords, 1996 and 1998). Uncertainty regarding the applicability of the ARD to this type of business transfer was widespread. Workers transferred as a consequence of CCT were not in general benefiting from the rights to consultation and the safeguarding of their terms and conditions of employment supposedly established by the ARD. Unions sometimes lacked the expertise and sometimes the will to take the legal action necessary to enforce their member's rights. As a consequence those contractors willing to comply with the requirements of the ARD were at a competitive disadvantage in the tendering process. These findings indicate the inadequacies of the original ARD, especially in this area of changing employment practices. We next consider whether the revised ARD represents an effective response to these inadequacies.

4. THE REVISED ARD: DEVELOPMENT AND ASSESSMENT

The European Court of Justice's (ECJ) growing jurisprudence on the ARD since 1985, caused much tension amongst those EU Member States who initiated contracting out exercises. As Hardy and Adnett (forthcoming) have explained, it was the ECJ's conflicting rulings as to the scope of the ARD which engendered calls for reform. Eventually, the politico-legal debate surrounding the ARD at the EU level focused on reconciling the need for workplace flexibility with employment security. The newly revised ARD, as adopted in Council Directive 98/50 of 17th July 1998, in its Preamble notes that it seeks to amend the 1977 Directive in light of 'the impact of the internal market, the legislative tendencies of the EU Member States and the case law of the ECJ'. Whilst EU legislators intend to enforce some clarity within the legal framework governing business transfers (Hardy, 1998), their identification of the forces which have necessitated this revision suggests that this area of employment regulation and employee relations will remain vulnerable to future judicial interpretation and changing employment practices.

In the final text of the 1998 ARD, as agreed at the Luxembourg Social Affairs Council, the scope of the ARD is clarified by the fact that the test provided for the establishment of a business transfer is '(w)here there is a transfer of an economic entity which retains its identity, meaning an organised grouping of resources which has the objective of pursuing an economic activity, whether or not that activity is central or ancillary'. This is a clear and brief alternative to the suggestion of the House of Lords (1998) Select Committee, that the Directive ought to include a non-exhaustive list of factors drawn from a previous ECJ case, *Spijkers* (Hardy and Adnett, forthcoming). As such the 1998 revision is to be welcomed, as it resolves much of the controversy at EU level, but will still leave the national courts with much work to do in applying this new definition to the variety of transfer-type situations which can occur in reality. This newly revised Article 1 of the 1998 ARD marks a substantial defeat for the EU Commission who during the process of revision persistently sought to narrow the scope of the 1977 Directive. In particular, in its original revised Article 1 in 1994, the EU Commission proposed that the ARD be applied to transfers of economic entities which retain their identities. This distinction between the transfer of *economic entities* and *activities* has been understood to mean that under the original revision most of the business transfers which occurred throughout the 1980s and 1990s would have been excluded from the protection afforded by the ARD.

Ostensibly, the EU Commission's original proposal seemed to affirm the ECJ's tests applied in previous rulings (*Spijkers versus...* and *Redmond versus...*). Yet the ECJ in its judgements in these cases drew a distinction between the transfer of 'economic entity' transfers and a mere 'activity transfer'. However, this distinction was later blurred in the case of *Schmidt*, where the ECJ held that the contracting-out of cleaning involving one person amounted to a transfer protected under the directive. The *Schmidt* ruling in fact narrowed the semantic distinction between 'activity' and 'economic entity' business transfers. Clearly the recent *Suzen* decision brought this issue to the attention of the EU legislators. The danger behind separating out situations where activity-only business transfers are excluded from the ARD, whilst including business transfers amounting to economic entities, misleadingly supports the view that an activity alone cannot fall under the protection of the ARD. The new Article 1 puts an end to such vague and inequitable distinctions and effectively overturns the *Suzen* ruling.

Linked to the debate surrounding the revised scope of the ARD is treatment of fraudulent insolvency proceedings intended to deprive employees of the rights laid down in the ARD. Due to the current ARD's silence on business transfers caused by insolvency, the EU Commission proposed that the transfer of insolvent companies be protected by the new Directive. Under the revisions, EU Member States have been given a discretion as to whether to apply the individual employment protection provisions of the ARD to business transfers which take place in the context of insolvency proceedings, instituted with a view to the liquidation of the assets of the transferor under the supervision of a competent judicial authority. In essence these revisions mean that EU Member States have the discretion to provide that the transferor's debts, either in the form of arrears of payments, damages, or other liabilities, due before the business transfer or prior to the opening of insolvency proceedings, do not transfer to the transferee. This provision can be relied upon only if the affected employees are afforded the protection provided by EC 'Insolvency' Directive 80/897/EEC. EU Member States can allow the employer and employee representatives 'to change the terms and conditions of employment by an agreement concluded as a means of ensuring the survival of the undertaking'. In addition, EU Member States can also empower competent judicial authorities to alter or terminate contracts of employment or employment relationships existing at the date of the business transfer.

Perhaps of more significance is the new ARD's reforms in relation to the variation of terms and conditions of employment by an agreement concluded between employers and employees. Any such variation to the terms and con-

ditions of employment post-transfer presents many contentious legal implications. In seeking to settle these disputes, the new ARD allows EU Member
States to provide that an agreement between 'employee representatives' and
the employer, insofar as they enjoy sufficient independence to make such
agreements, to change terms and conditions of employment. Moreover, these
proposals will also determine whether and to what extent dismissals may take
place as a consequence of economic, technical and organisational reasons or
pre-insolvency proceedings. Following the ECJ's ruling in *Commission versus UK* (1994), the then British Government introduced Regulations which
provided for the designation of 'employee representatives' for the purpose of
consultation over transfers and redundancies. These Regulations leave employers with the choice of consulting a recognised trade union or 'non-union'
representatives elected by the workforce.

The scope for the variation of terms and conditions of employment has
been addressed in a number of EU and national cases. In a British context,
the case of *Wilson versus St Helens Borough Council*, the EAT held that:

> (I)t is true that there may be cases where an effective variation of the terms of em-
> ployment does take place subsequently either by express agreement or by agree-
> ment inferred from conduct...[but] the law, surprising though it may be to English
> legal tradition, is clear. If the operative reason for the variation is the transfer of
> the undertaking, then the variation will be invalid.

On appeal, the joined cases of *Wilson* and *Meade*, the Court of Appeal, allowing the appeal, held that the existence of a business transfer itself did not
justify a dismissal, unless the dismissal was for economic, technical or organisational reasons (ETO), as prescribed for in Regulation 8 of the TUPE
Regulations. For *Wilson*, this meant that for an Industrial Tribunal to find a
variation in terms and conditions justifiable after a business transfer, ETO
reasons would have to be found, not solely that a transfer had taken place. In
Meade, the outcome of the appeal meant that an agreement to employment
by a former employee of the transferor with the transferee on 'new' terms
and conditions was ineffective, albeit that an unfair dismissal claim could be
founded. In November 1998 the House of Lords overturned the *Wilson* decision and the case is expected to go to the ECJ.

Up until the decision of the House of Lords, these British cases appear to
be consistent with the ECJ's rulings in *Daddy's Dance Hall* and *Rask*. Most
notably, in *Daddy's Dance Hall* it was held that 'an employee cannot waive
the rights conferred upon him by the mandatory provisions of the Acquired
Rights Directive 77/187 even if the disadvantages resulting from his waiver
are offset from such benefits that, taking the matter as a whole, he is not
placed in a worse position'. The unlawfulness of transfer-related variations
appeared to be clearly established. Furthermore, in an EU context, the decla-

ration by the ECJ in *Merckx* that: 'A change in the level of remuneration is a substantial change in working conditions..., which provides that if the employment relationship is terminated because the transfer involves a substantial change in working conditions to the employee's detriment, the employer is to be regarded as responsible for the termination' (*Merckx*, 1996, p. 468). On the other hand, this British case law also makes it clear that the current ARD does allow for post-transfer variations, where agreement between the parties exists, but for reasons unconnected with the transfer. For instance, the UK's Court of Appeal in *Wilson* categorically states that employees who are genuinely dismissed for economic, technical or organisational reasons may be subsequently re-employed on different terms and conditions, and such will not warrant a breach of the existing law. The revised directive fails to clarify this economic technical, or organisational defence and further case law will be required before greater clarity is achieved.

Our survey found that where consultation did not occur prior to the transfer, post-transfer terms and conditions of employment were more likely to be altered. Whilst the original ARD required that information be given and consultation take place with employees' representatives, the new ARD seeks to add that such consultation takes place in 'good time' and with a view to 'reaching an agreement'. Since its amendments in 1994, the EU Commission has sought to ensure that any information exchanged between employers and employees, prior to the transfer, should be given in 'good time'. This revision was influenced by the arrangements set up under the auspices of the 1994 Working Time Directive. This harmonising piece of EU legislation promotes that any working time standards, such as hours of work, rest breaks, overtime and Sunday working, night work or holidays, are to be determined by collective bargaining where possible. Consequently, at very least, such activities require the consultation and participation of both employers and the workforce, and/or the workers' representatives. These revisions are clearly problematical to some EU member states, particularly the UK, where current national regulations fall short of this requirement.

The revised ARD also adds a transnational dimension to the information and consultation provisions of the Directive. This measure aims to cover cases where the decision leading to the transfer is taken by a decision-making centre, normally a Head Office or controlling undertaking, which is located elsewhere in the EU. This would parallel changes introduced by the Collective Redundancies Directive in 1992. Additionally, the revised Article 6(5) exempts undertakings where there are less than fifty employees. This proposal places a high exemption threshold, since most EU member states, other than the UK, have lower exemptions some at five and others at twenty, normally in line with their Works Councils' exemptions.

The 1998 revised ARD introduces new general provisions requiring EU Member States to provide suitable sanctions for employers who fail to fulfil the requirements of the Directive and to prohibit discrimination in applying the Directive. Newly proposed articles 7A and 7B introduce that any behaviour in response to the revised ARD should not entertain or cause discriminatory practices. Other new measures seek to implement sanctions 'effective and proportionate' to the breach, where employers fail to inform and consult employees about a transfer. These new measures cover two very important issues. Firstly, the potential for discriminatory practices, not only in terms of the applicability or otherwise of the Directive itself, but in terms of indirect gender discrimination. Such as was evidenced by the UK's Equal Opportunities Commission's study (Escott and Whitfield, 1995) highlighting the gender discrimination caused in contracting-out situations notwithstanding the ARD. Secondly, the issue of enforcement, not only in terms of remedies but also deterrence, is now opened by the EU Commission's adoption of a principle closely identified with the 1986 EU Merger Regulations.

As Cavalier (1997) suggests, the 1998 Amending Directive represents a victory for the European Parliament and EU trade unions, who together colluded to ensure that the underlying ethos of the original ARD, to safeguard employees' rights when subjected to business transfers, was preserved. Faced with political pressure from the EP and seemingly inconsistent legal guidance from the ECJ, the EU Council of Ministers were forced to act quickly in order to resolve the politico-legal frustration created by the outdated 1977 Directive. To that end, the EU legislators have now acted, seeking as we have seen to clarify the scope of the ARD and strengthen the consultation and enforcement requirements.

5. CONCLUSIONS

Both prevailing economic and political philosophies and the nature of European labour markets have changed significantly since the Acquired Rights Directive was introduced in 1977. We have presented evidence how the adoption of competitive tendering policies by member state's governments has left significant groups of previously public sector workers without the rights seemingly established by the ARD. Moreover, this uncertainty regarding the rights of workers affected by business transfers has directly contributed to a tendering process in which efficient contractors can be displaced by those more willing to risk the consequences of apparent non-compliance with EU employment law.

Our initial analysis has suggested that the establishment of clearly defined and enforced employment rights in a revised ARD can be made compatible with an efficient and flexible labour market. Regulatory measures which encourage mutually beneficial long-term employment relations, free from the risk of opportunistic behaviour, whilst promoting trust, co-operation and the continual updating of skills, are consistent with producing the desired increase in international competitiveness within the EU. The revised ARD produces an increase in clarity which will be widely welcomed. In strengthening consultation rights and requiring Member States to introduce sanctions for non-compliance it addresses some of the key deficiencies of the original ARD highlighted by our survey. However, as with any employment regulation, changing employment practices, including those originating from circumventive innovation, and unanticipated judicial interpretations suggest the need for continual monitoring.

NOTES

1. The authors wish to thank Richard Painter for his comments, participants in the survey and the Institute of Industrial and Commercial Law at Staffordshire University for their support of this research.
2. The British Government implemented the 1977 ARD initially in the form of the Transfer of Undertakings Protection of Employment) Regulations 1981(TUPE). It should be apparent from the following quotations that the BSA represent the largest companies in the business services industry within the UK.

REFERENCES

Adnett, N. (1998), 'The Acquired Rights Directive and Compulsory Competitive Tendering in the UK: An Economic Perspective', *European Journal of Law and Economics*, **6**, 69-81.

Adnett, N. and S. Hardy (1998), 'The Impact of TUPE on Compulsory Competitive Tendering: Evidence From Employers', *Local Government Studies*, **24**, 36-50.

Bertola, G. and R. Rogerson (1997), 'Institutions and Labor Reallocation', *European Economic Review*, **41**, 1147-1171.

Blank, R. and R. Freeman (1994), 'Evaluating the Connection between Social Protection and Economic Flexibility', in R. Blank (ed.), *Social Protection versus Economic Flexibility: Is There a Trade-off?*, Chicago: University of Chicago Press.

Brown, W. and D. Rea (1995), 'The Changing Nature of the Employment Contract', *Scottish Journal of Political Economy*, **42**, 363-77.

Carter, T. and P. De Lancey (1997), 'Just, Unjust and Just-Cause Dismissals', *Journal of Macroeconomics*, **19**, 619-28.

Cartier, K. (1994), 'The Transaction Costs and Benefits of the Incomplete Contract of Employment', *Cambridge Journal of Economics*, **18**, 181-96.

Cavalier, S. (1997), *Transfer Rights: TUPE in Perspective*, London: Institute of Employment Rights.

Commission versus UK (1994), IRLR 392 ECJ.

Daddy's Dance Hall (1988), IRLR 315 ECJ.

Deakin, S. and F. Wilkinson (1994), 'Rights vs. Efficiency? The Economic Case for Transnational Labour Standards', *Industrial Law Journal*, **23**, 289-310.

Escott, K. and D. Whitfield (1995), *The Gender Impact of CCT in Local Government*, EOC Report, EOC Discussion Paper Series, HMSO.

European Commission (1994), COM (94) Final.

European Commission (1997), COM (97) 60 Final.

EU (1977), Directive 77/187, Acquired Rights.

EU (1980), Directive 80/897, Insolvency Situations.

EU (1992), Directive 92/56, Collective Redundancies Amended.

EU (1994), Directive 93/104, Working Time.

EU (1998), Directive 98/50, Acquired Rights Revised.

Hardy, S. (1998), 'The Future of the Transfers Regime', in C. Bourn (ed.), *The Transfer of Undertakings and CCT in the Public Sector*, London: Dartmouth, pp. 181-202.

Hardy, S. and N. Adnett (forthcoming), 'Entrepreneurial Freedom versus Employee Rights: The Acquired Rights Directive and EU Social Policy Post-Amsterdam', *Journal of European Social Policy*.

Hardy, S. and R. Painter (1996), 'Acquiring Revised Rights?: Council Proposal to revise the Acquired Rights Directive', *Maastricht Journal of European and Comparative Law*, **3**, 35-46.

Hardy, S., R. Painter and N. Adnett (1997), 'TUPE and CCT Business Transfers: UK Labour Market Views', Survey No. 1, Institute of Industrial and Commercial Law, Staffordshire University, Staffordshire University Press, Stoke on Trent.

Hepple, B. (1998), 'The Legal Consequences of Cross Border Transfers of Undertakings within the EU', European Commission, DG V.

Hopenhayn, H. and R. Rogerson (1993), 'Job Turnover and Policy Evaluation: a General Equilibrium Analysis', *Journal of Political Economy*, **101**, 915-38.

House of Lords (1996), Select Committee on the European Communities, Transfer of Undertakings: Acquired Rights, Session 1995-96 5th Report, HMSO, London.

House of Lords (1998), Select Committee on the European Communities, Acquired Rights Revisited, Session 1997-98 22nd Report, HMSO, London.

Ichniowski, C., K. Shaw and G. Prennusshi (1997), 'The Effect of Human Resource Practices on Productivity: A Study of Steel Finishing Lines', *American Economic Review*, **7**, 291-313.

Korner, M. (1996), 'The Impact of Community Law on German Labour Law: The Example of the Transfer of Undertakings', European University Institute, Florence Working Paper Law No. 96/8.

Levine, D. and L. Tyson (1990), 'Participation, Productivity and the Firm's Environment', in A. Blinder (ed.), *Paying for Productivity*, Washington, DC: Brookings Institute, pp. 183-243.

Marsden, D. (1996), 'Employment Policy Implications of New Management Systems', *Labour*, **10**, 17-61.

Marsden, D. (1997), 'The "Social Dimension" as a basis for the Single Market', in J.T. Addison and W.S. Siebert (eds), *Labour Markets in Europe: Issues of Harmonization and Regulation*, London: Dryden Press, pp. 152-176.

Merckx versus Ford Motors (Belgium) (1996), IRLR 467 ECJ.

More, G. (1995), 'The Acquired Rights Directive: Frustrating or Facilitating Labour Market Flexibility', in J. Shaw and G. More (eds), *New Legal Dynamics of European Union,* Oxford: Oxford University Press, pp. 129-145.

Napier, B. (1993), *Market Testing, CCT and Business Transfers,* London: Institute of Employment Rights.

Nickell, S. and R. Layard (1997), 'Labour Market Institutions and Economic Performance', Centre for Economic Performance, University of Oxford, Institute of Economics and Statistics, Programme on The Labour Market Consequences of Technical and Structural Change., Discussion Paper No 23.

Parkin, R. (1996), 'Optimal Employment Security: The Benefits of Labor Market "Imperfections"', *Journal of post-Keynesian Economics,* **19,** 61-72.

Philpott, J. (1996), 'The Performance of the UK Labour Market: Is 'Anglo-Saxon' Economics the Answer to Structural Unemployment?' in T. Buxton, P. Chapman and P. Temple (eds), *Britain's Economic Performance,* 2nd edn, London: Routledge, pp. 340-366.

Rask versus ISS Kantineservice (1993), IRLR 133 ECJ.

Redmond versus Bartol (1992), IRLR 366 ECJ.

Saint-Paul, G. (1997), 'Is Labour Rigidity Harming Europe's Competitiveness? The Effect of Job Protection on the Pattern of Trade and Welfare', *European Economic Review,* **41,** 499-506.

Schmidt versus Spar und Leihkasse (1994), IRLR 302 ECJ.

Spijkers versus Gebroeders Benedix Abattoir CV (1986), 2 CMLR 296 ECJ.

Stone Sweet, A. and T. Brunell (1998), 'The European Court and the National Courts: a Statistical Analysis of Preliminary References, 1961-95', *Journal of European Public Policy,* **5,** 66-97.

Suzen versus Zehnacker Gebandereinigung GmbH (1997), IRLR 255 ECJ.

Wilkinson, F. (1998), 'Co-operation, the Organisation of Work and Competitiveness', ESRC Centre for Business Research, University of Cambridge, Working Paper 85.

Wilson versus St Helens MBC (1997), IRLR 505 CA.

F18
028

12. The International Co-ordination of Environmental Policy from an EU Perspective

Kristel Buysse, Chris Coeck and Alain Verbeke

1. INTRODUCTION

The past 25 years have seen a spectacular development of environmental regulation in response to growing environmental concerns. Numerous environmental actions have been initiated by national and sub-national governments. However, it has soon become apparent that in a world with strong inter-dependencies among nations, a unilateral and national approach to environmental regulation could lead to unsatisfactory outcomes. The European Union in particular has viewed the divergence of environmental policies between member states as an unwelcome development impeding the creation of a single market. Such concerns have provided the Union with a justification to develop its own environmental policies. The evolution of environmental policymaking at the Union level is described in the second section of this chapter.

One obvious argument in favour of international co-ordination of environmental policies is related to the transnational nature of many environmental problems. The polluting behaviour of one country damages other countries, yet the polluters of that country are at best forced to pay only for the damage inflicted in their own country. This leads to sub-optimal outcomes, and welfare gains can be realised when such externalities are internalised through the international co-ordination of environmental policies. This case of transboundary pollution will be analysed in the third section.

However, the need for more international and European co-ordination of environmental policies is most importantly the result of the ever increasing globalisation of the world economy and the closer economic integration of European Union member states. The argument that globalisation necessitates a co-ordinated environmental policy and that such a policy can contribute to a virtuous cycle with both economic and environmental benefits has not been well established yet. A broad literature exists, both theoretical as well as empirical and/or anecdotal, on the competitiveness effects of environmental regulation. The argument that unilateral environmental actions reduce national competitiveness is popular, though perhaps not well founded, and harmonisation of environmental policies, by imposing the same rules on everybody, can succeed in creating a perception of fair play. We shall analyse this argument more carefully in the fourth section. However, the main thesis is that co-ordinated environmental policies provide stronger incentives for innovations, positively contributing to economic growth and environmental protection. Local know-how, built up through innovative activities, attracts foreign direct investments from multinational enterprises (MNEs) with similar know-how. This stimulates the further development of local know-how, which in turn attracts more multinational activity. This reflects the virtuous cycle referred to above. A harmonised regulatory framework stimulates the expansion of MNEs and promotes free trade. Yet, unilateral environmental actions can disrupt free trade. The fifth section explains how a co-ordinated environmental policy contributes to the preservation of open borders and free trade, whereas the sixth section explains how it positively affects multinational operations. The seventh section discusses the impact of a co-ordinated environmental policy on the search for innovation activity.

The last section of the chapter focuses on a case study on the Belgian approach to environmental policy, which supports the argument in favour of more European co-ordination of environmental policy using the framework developed in this chapter.

2. THE EVOLUTION OF EUROPEAN ENVIRONMENTAL POLICYMAKING

The Treaty of Rome, signed in 1957, conferred no environmental regulatory authority upon the institutions of the European Economic Community. In this period, pollution was a pervasive problem, rooted in the process of industrialisation. It was only by the end of the 1960s that the environmental movement began to take hold in north-western Europe. This movement was instrumental in changing attitudes within the European Community member states. In 1972 all the member states endorsed the idea of a common European environmental policy at the Paris Summit Meeting of the Heads of State. The first Environmental Action Programme (1973-76) was approved in November 1973. Since then, several more Environmental Action Programmes have been drafted and implemented. The fifth and latest, called 'Towards Sustainability', was approved shortly after the signing of the Maastricht Treaty in February 1992 and runs until the year 2000. It marks a clear turning point in European environmental policymaking. This discussion will analyse European policymaking both before and after the Maastricht Treaty. But first, the institutional framework of European Union environmental regulation will be briefly described.

Institutional framework

As is well known, the European Commission has the power to propose laws. The Commission is subdivided into a number of Directorate Generals, each responsible for one sector of European policy (industry, competition, energy, environment, ...). As many legislative proposals encompass more than one sector, the final proposal may already be the product of a consensus between the concerned Directorate Generals. The power to enact laws is vested with the Council of Ministers[1], which votes on the proposals issued by the Commission.[2] Unanimity or qualified majority in the Council of Ministers is required for a proposal to become a law. Before 1992, the Council simply had to consult the European parliament in the process, but the Treaty of Maastricht of 1992 strengthened the role of the European Parliament by requiring that the Council co-operate with Parliament on the enactment of legislation. Finally, the Commission has the right to take a member state to the Court of Justice when a member is found not enforcing or complying with European legislation. The Court of Justice then issues a binding judgement. European environmental regulation most often takes the form of directives. Directives are binding as to the result to be achieved, but leave the method of implementation to the discretion of the member states.

The early period (1973-1992)

Although the concept of a common European environmental policy was endorsed in 1972, it was not until the Single European Act of 1986 that the legal foundation for such actions was laid. Earlier environmental initiatives were justified on the basis of two articles of the Treaty of Rome. The first was Article 100, which authorises the Council to issue regulation aimed at harmonising and unifying the laws of the member states that affect intra-European trade. Indeed, there was a concern that national environmental regulations, and in particular differing national environmental standards, would amount to the creation of new, non-tariff barriers to trade. Such concerns were reflected in the enactment of joint product standards aimed at avoiding environmental harm from the use of certain products, e.g. common standards on exhaust emissions from vehicles, noise levels of lawn mowers, or packaging and labelling of solvents. These joint standards could easily be justified as product harmonisation necessary for the completion of the internal market. Concerns that differing national process standards, for example differing emission standards on air pollution, could through their differential impact on the cost of production lead to unfair competition, provided the Community with a justification to harmonise process standards. The second article frequently used as a justification for European environmental policy-making was Article 235 of the Treaty of Rome, which authorises Community legislation, when necessary to achieve a Community objective and when other provisions of the Treaty fail to confer the requisite powers. The Community's objectives are summed up in Article 2 of the Treaty of Rome, and include among others 'a harmonious development of economic activities, a continuous and balanced expansion, . . . , an accelerated raising of the standards of living'. A broad reading of these objectives encompasses quality of life and aspects of human health. This provides the Community with some authority to issue several directives related to aspects of pollution and environmental protection that will not hinder intra-European trade, for example standards on the quality of bathing water or on the lead content in drinking water.

Prior to 1986, voting on all environmental directives required unanimity in the Council of Ministers. In 1986, the Single European Act (SEA) was made law and authorised the Community to enact environmental legislation on the legal grounds of Article 100 by qualified majority. In addition, Article 130s of the SEA authorised the Community for the first time to take legislative action in the environmental area; it also states that 'environmental protection requirements shall be a component of the Community's other policies' (Art 130r §2). Environmental legislation justified by Article 130 can be enacted only with the unanimous approval of all member states. On the other hand, under the provision of Article 130, member states retain the right to set stricter national environmental standards if they wish, which is not the case for joint environmental standards issued on the grounds of Article 100. Finally, the SEA requires the Council to co-operate with the European Parliament in the enacting of environmental regulation.

One feature of early environmental policy by the European Community was that it specialised in producing technical standards (product and process). Such a focus on command and control regulation was motivated by a desire to remove all barriers to trade and to promote fair competition. Hence even though some policies were concerned with protecting the environment, a large part of European environmental regulation was intertwined with

European economic policy, as environmental policy was often seen as contributing to the building of the single market.

Another feature of European environmental policy in this early period is that it followed national legislative initiatives in this area, rather than taking the lead. For example, an environmental leader, that is a member state with advanced environmental regulation in a particular sector, under pressure of its own national industry, would push the Commission to propose European legislation similar to its own. This then would arouse the opposition of other member states with less stringent environmental regulation in this area, so that the final piece of legislation would be the product of political bargaining at the Council between leaders and laggards. As an illustration of this procedure, The Large Combustion Plants directive (Dir. 88/609) can be cited. In 1983, Germany proposed a stringent Community regulation of SO_2 and NO_2 emissions, generated by fossil fuel-fired plants, boiler plants at petroleum refineries and other large plants. This proposal followed tight domestic regulation which had been enacted to counter the deterioration of German forests due to acidification. However, the German industry feared competitive losses as a result of such a regulation, and wanted to see its main international competitors subjected to similar regulations. The German proposal called for a uniform reduction of emissions of SO_2 by 60 % and NO_2 by 40 % by 1995, starting from a 1980 baseline. Great Britain, the largest source country of such gases opposed the plan vigorously. This induced a protracted period of intergovernmental negotiations at the Council of Ministers. The final settlement reflected a serious weakening of the initial proposal. The member states agreed to a non-uniform reduction of 20-40 % by 1993, 40-60 % by 1998, and 60-70 % by 2003 for SO_2 emissions.

Some critics argue that a common European environmental policy only results in a convergence towards the lowest common denominator. The Large Combustion Plant directive is only one of numerous cases in which the targets set forth in the directive were much less ambitious than those initially proposed. Yet it is worth pointing out that thanks to Community legislation, many lagging countries have committed themselves to numerous environmental standards which they would not enact without European initiatives. In our opinion, a more fundamental problem is the issue of member state non-compliance. In fact, the simple passage of Community legislation does not always ensure the effective enforcement of environmental standards by member states. Hence, even though the Community has enacted an impressive number of environmental directives, the number of infringements by member states on these directives is equally impressive. For a more thorough discussion of the enforcement problems, see Pfander (1996).

The Treaty of Maastricht and beyond

The Treaty of Maastricht of 1992 and the resulting Fifth Environmental Action Programme marked a clear turning point for European environmental policy. The Council of the European Union Environmental Ministers asked the Commission to assess the environmental dimension of the Europe 1992 project. The Commission's findings were devastating because they openly questioned the sustainability of the economic growth resulting from completion of the single market. The Council of Ministers swiftly invited the Commission to use its findings and insights as the basis for the Fifth Environmental Action Programme. This Programme was entitled 'Towards Sustainability', and proved to be much more ambitious than any of its predecessors.

The Maastricht Treaty gives a prominent place to the environment, which is explicitly mentioned in the *princeps* articles (Lévèque, 1996, p. 11). The promotion of sustainable growth respecting the environment is introduced in Article 2 as a Union mission. Environmental policy is added to the list of Community activities. Article 130, which was inserted by the SEA and relates to the integration of environmental protection into the Community's other policies, now reads: 'environmental protection requirements must be integrated into the definition and implementation of other Community policies'. The same article explicitly mentions the priority of pollution prevention and waste prevention at the source and the rational utilisation of natural resources, as well as the principle that the polluter should pay. Clearly, the Maastricht Treaty advances a more ambitious and proactive environmental policy at the community level than previously existed.

The implementation of more ambitious environmental programs necessitates a broadening of the range of instruments used. Following national trends in environmental regulation, the Treaty advocates the use of economic instruments to change the polluting behaviour of consumers and producers. They include tradable permits, fees, taxes, deposit-refund systems, user charges, stricter liability rules, etc. The Union also intends to play a proactive role in promoting self-regulation through the development of its Eco-Management and Audit Scheme (EMAS).[3] And finally, voluntary agreements between public authorities and enterprise coalitions where the latter agree to pollution reduction, are to be used more prominently. Examples of such voluntary agreements include the very recent agreement with European carmakers, which committed to a fuel-efficiency standard of 6 l/km for all new cars by the year 2008, and the voluntary agreements between industry and government in Germany and France regarding package recycling objectives.

The Treaty of Maastricht also changed the European fabric of environmental policy in two major ways. The first change is linked to the reform of the Community Institutions and rule-making procedure. One important reform is that most directives can now be approved by a qualified majority, including those based on Article 100. This makes it harder for a single member state to veto legislation. The Maastricht Treaty also transfers power from the member states (the Council of Ministers) to the other European institutions, and more particularly to the European Parliament by extending the 'co-decision-procedure'[4] to environmental concerns and policymaking. There are a few major exceptions to these new rules: namely provisions of a fiscal nature, measures significantly affecting a Member State's choice between different energy sources, and measures concerning town and country planning, land use and the management of water resources, which still require unanimous approval by the Council of Ministers and consultation of the European parliament only. However, the granting of more power to the Community institutions at the expense of national institutions was not very popular with member states. Therefore, to counterbalance this trend, the Treaty of Maastricht also puts more emphasis on the principle of subsidiarity. This principle authorises the Union to take action only if and insofar as the objectives of the proposed action can not be sufficiently achieved by the member states and can be better achieved by the Community. Applied to environmental policy, the subsidiarity principle legitimates Union initiatives in cases of transboundary pollution and green trade barriers, but also reserves a large role for national environmental regulation, thereby potentially reducing the role of the Union.

The second major change in policymaking was specific to environmental policy. Instead of the old top-down approach, the principle of 'shared responsibility' is introduced in environmental policymaking. The aim is to involve all concerned parties (industry, unions, academics, non-governmental organisations (NGOs), state governments, consumers, conservation organisations) in setting pollution targets and developing environmental plans and policies. It is hoped that the involvement of all stakeholders will lead to a broad endorsement of new environmental legislation and will facilitate the implementation and enforcement of such laws, thereby reducing the number of infringements on Union legislation. To overcome information barriers, the European Environmental Agency was created in 1993 with a mandate to disseminate information to all parties concerned in an effort to stimulate participation in the debate at all levels of society.

To illustrate the current dynamics of environmental policymaking in the European Union, the directive on the recycling and recovery of packaging waste (Dir. 94/62) can be used as an example. In 1991, Germany issued stringent environmental (recycling) regulation at the national level. The initial government proposal set an ambitious objective of 80 to 90 % recycling of packaging by 1995, as well as an obligation for retailers to take back packaging. After a short period of strong opposition, retailers and packagers united together to draw up a counter-proposal. The so-called Duales system emerged, whereby distributors were no longer required to take back their packaging and were instead allowed to rely on a fee-system paid to a consortium that would take care of reaching recycling targets. At the same time, the European Union also announced its intention to prepare a directive to set recycling targets for its member states. Worried that Germany would seek to influence the Community initiative, the French government swiftly proposed a recycling target of 75 % and reached a voluntary agreement with its national industry to set up a consortium (Eco-Emballage), similar to the German example. This move was aimed as a credible counter-proposal at the European level to the German system. A process of intense bargaining at the European level began between proponents of very ambitious recycling regulation on the one hand (namely Germany, Denmark and the Netherlands), and the others led by France and the UK. It culminated in a moderately ambitious Directive. This directive calls for recovery objectives of 50-65 % to be reached in five years in which a recycling component of 25-45 % is included. The difference between this example and the previous process of policy-design is that (1) industry was actively involved in setting targets and designing innovative methods to reach the targets, (2) regulations developed simultaneously in different countries as well as at different institutional levels, mutually influenced each other, (3) instead of an environmental leader imposing its own regulation on other member states, a race driven by the objective of pre-empting occurred between two member states to shape Union regulation.

The above analysis suggests that European Union member states have increasingly allowed environmental policymaking to be conducted at the Union level rather than the national level. This course of action builds upon high perceived benefits coming from international policy co-ordination as compared to the alternative of environmental policy formation at the national level. The economic foundations of international environmental policy co-ordination are described in the next sections.

3. TRANSBOUNDARY POLLUTION REQUIRES CO-ORDINATED ACTIONS

The problem with many environmental problems is that they are transboundary in their nature: economic activities in one jurisdiction cause damage to the environment of another state or jurisdiction. Take the North Sea as an example of transboundary pollution: the quality of the North Sea water depends on the polluting behaviour of all states bordering it. Pollutants such as toxic waste are discharged into the North Sea either directly or indirectly through the transportation of those pollutants by rivers that flow into the North Sea. Hence, the economic activities of many states have an impact on the North Sea water quality. Similarly, many states are affected by the quality of the North Sea waters, namely all those that depend on the tourism industry that has developed along the shores and on fishing.

Game theory may be a useful tool for analysing problems of co-operation in a transnational context. In a non-co-operative solution a state does not consider the damage inflicted by its own pollution on other states when determining how much pollution it will allow to be generated on its own territory. This is a typical case of a negative externality, whereby the non-co-operative outcome will result in too much pollution being generated.

In a co-operative approach, all states co-ordinate their policies in order to achieve the best overall outcome. This requires that all externalities be internalised so each state sets its pollution levels according to the rule that the cost of preventing the last unit of pollution in each country should be equal to the sum of the marginal damages inflicted by that country on all countries, the own country included. In other words, when deciding on pollution levels in each country, abatement costs should be balanced against the totality of damage costs, rather than the individual damage costs. This leads to more pollution abatement in the co-operative outcome as compared with the non-co-operative outcome.

It is clear that an overall welfare improvement can be attained by international co-operation on global environmental problems. This also explains why voluntary international agreements on environmental protection, such as the 'Montreal Protocol on Substances that Deplete the Ozone Layer', have been successfully concluded. But participants gaining from international co-operation can earn even higher returns by free-riding, that is by not increasing abatement levels in the anticipation that all other participants will increase their abatement levels according to the agreement. While saving themselves the costs of increased pollution abatement, they still enjoy some of the benefits resulting from better pollution control abroad.

The challenge for international environmental agreements is that they must effectively incorporate a stick or carrot into their design that deters free-riding, if not they are unlikely to be self-enforcing. Barrett (1994) investigated under which conditions international environmental agreements are likely to be self-enforcing, using two different theoretical specifications[5], and analysed his findings in the light of the Montreal Protocol. His conclusion is that self-enforcing international environmental agreements (IEAs) with a large number of signatories emerge only when the difference in net benefits between the co-operative and non-co-operative outcome is small. When the gains are large, the free-rider problem is so pervasive that no agreement can be enforced. Hence, not all international environmental problems can be resolved through IEAs.

Although there may be overall gains to internationally co-ordinated environmental policies, it does not automatically follow that each co-operating state gains. This is because the costs and benefits from pollution control are usually not uniformly distributed. For example in the case of North Sea pollution, it is well known that a high concentration of nutrients in the water stimulates algae growth, which adversely affects the size of the fish population. Algae growth is strongest in front of the Danish coast. Moreover, some countries depend more on fisheries as a source of income, and will therefore gain more from cleaner sea waters. Other countries have more polluting industrial activities on their territory and will experience higher costs following a move towards cleaner production. Such a-symmetries often necessitate the use of side payments from winners to losers to make all states involved agree to an internationally co-ordinated environmental policy. This in turn requires the existence or creation of an international institution with the power to enforce policies and compensation payments. The main reason why the European Union has been successful in soliciting the unanimous support of all member states necessary to enact stringent environmental regulation is that it had the power to link environmental policy with funding for regional development programs. For example, the Cohesion Fund was set up inter alia to provide Spain, Portugal, Greece and Ireland with financial assistance for the implementation of strict environmental standards. This approach was crucial to overcome their opposition to stringent environmental policies at the Union level.

4. HARMONISATION OF ENVIRONMENTAL REGULATION GUARANTEES FAIR COMPETITION

Competitiveness reflects the ability of an industry and an economic system to sell products in the domestic and international market. This ability depends on the costs at which this industry or economic system can produce a product of a given quality, relative to the costs of competitors. Conventional economic thinking suggests that environmental policy entails economic costs both at the level of the firm and at the macro-level. Environmental standards force firms to adjust their production processes to comply with these standards. This requires better control of emissions released during production, the installation of additional capital to treat waste and pollution before it is disposed off, the accelerated depreciation of highly polluting equipment which needs to be replaced by cleaner technologies. The need to invest in environmental protection can crowd out other, potentially more profitable investments. Uncertainty about present and possible future regulation may inhibit investment altogether. In addition, the operation and maintenance of pollution control equipment requires additional labour but does not necessarily contribute to sales volume or profitability. Similarly, the necessity to comply with environmental regulation absorbs managerial and administrative resources, again with no effect on sales or market share. In sum, environmental standards raise operating costs at the firm level. Expenditures related to pollution abatement and control for selected OECD countries amounted to 1 to 2 % of GDP in 1992 (Adams, 1998, p. 90). Investment expenditures on pollution abatement and control comprised 3 to 4 % of gross fixed capital formation in 1992 in selected OECD countries (Adams, 1998, p. 91).

Environmental taxes also have the effect of raising firms' operating costs because they make firms pay for the use of scarce environmental resources. Whereas environmental standards induce compliance but provide no incentives to move beyond compliance, taxes represent a permanent incentive to reduce the consumption of scarce resources on which taxes are levied. It is also generally accepted that environmental taxes represent the most cost-effective policy instrument for achieving environmental quality targets.

Environmental regulations in many industrialised countries combine command and control measures with economic incentives such as environmental taxation, user charges, tradable permits, and deposit-refunds systems. In particular the imposition of taxes on top of command and control measures may make environmental protection very costly for the industry. The effects of environmental regulation are higher production costs for all, with pollution-intensive and natural resource-based industries/firms experiencing the most adverse impacts. However, higher production costs do not automatically translate into reduced sectional competitiveness as measured by changes in net exports. Such losses in competitiveness occur only under certain conditions, namely when:

(1) The products affected by environmental regulation are tradable, and the trade intensity of the product (= ratio of exports plus imports to production) is high. High trade intensity limits the ability of firms to pass on higher production costs to consumers. This condition is likely to be satisfied in the case of a small open economy such as Belgium, or more specifically the Belgian regions which enact environmental regulations.

(2) The size of the tax and the stringency of the regulation is high relative to the most important trading partners. In fact, effects on competitiveness only arise when environmental policies in different countries impose different compliance costs on competing firms, which occurs for example when the variation in tax rates across countries is high.

Hence, stringent environmental regulation may reduce the competitiveness of the industries producing the pollution-intensive goods. However, econometric studies have failed to establish a clear relationship between the stringency of environmental regulation and industrial competitiveness. Jaffe *et al.* (1995) surveyed all direct and indirect empirical evidence with reference to this subject. They allowed for a broad definition of competitiveness, analysing studies that related the impact of environmental regulation to one of the following competitiveness indicators: changes in net export patterns, shifts in the locus of production of pollution-intensive goods, changes in the attractiveness of a country as a locus for foreign direct investment, productivity at the sectoral and macro-economic level. The impact of environmental regulation is most commonly measured by the environmental compliance cost burden on firms or industries. Empirical estimates failed to find a statistically significant, negative relationship between the total costs of abatement and net exports at the industry level. In addition, there is very little empirical support for the 'pollution-haven' hypothesis, which predicts that costly environmental regulation will prompt an outward flow of foreign direct investments of the most polluting industries. There is some evidence that environmental regulation contributes to a productivity slowdown, but its impact on economic growth was again negligible. Hence Jaffe *et al.* concluded that 'overall, there is little evidence to support the hypothesis that environmental regulations have had a large adverse impact on competitiveness, however that elusive term is defined.' (Jaffe *et al.*, 1995, p. 157).

Several elements may contribute to explain these findings. The limited ability of available data to measure differences in the stringency of environmental regulation and in compliance cost burdens borne by competing firms that are subject to different regulations represents a major problem in all of the studies surveyed. Another reason why the differences in the stringency of environmental laws and regulations of different jurisdictions are not adequately identified by the data is because these differences are usually not very large, at least not within the sample of OECD countries. Since 1972, the EU has issued many directives regarding the quality of water and air. Hence environmental policy enacted by the member states is meant to meet the same quality standards, ruling out large variations in policies. However, to the extent that effluent taxes have been imposed, taxation rates have remained relatively low.

In spite of the empirical evidence, the belief is commonly held that uncoordinated environmental regulations can distort competition, although the direction of the distortion is difficult to predict on theoretical grounds (Barrett, 1992; Ulph, 1996).[6] As noted earlier, concerns about unfair competition justified European Union policy aimed at harmonising process standards (e.g. the Large Combustion Plant directive). Similar considerations are reflected in the current debate on carbon dioxide taxes. There is a belief that the imposition of such a tax has the potential to cause disruptions in trading patterns.

Finland, Norway, Sweden, Denmark and the Netherlands have introduced a carbon/energy tax, but they all offered some form of exemption to their most energy-intensive industries, thus explicitly recognising the existence of possible competitiveness effects (OECD, 1994, p. 169). To mitigate such effects, some have lobbied for the introduction of a carbon/energy tax at the Community level. But the Commission's proposal of 1992 to introduce a $10/barrel failed to mobilise the required unanimous approval from its member states, and received widespread opposition from many industrial lobbies and the energy sector in particular. In the end, the proposal on the introduction of a carbon/energy tax has been transformed into a non-binding guideline.

At the same time, many business leaders are also worried that the unilateral imposition of high effluent taxes or stringent standards will benefit foreign rivals at their own expense. Belgian companies, for example, have used this argument to put pressure on the government to refrain from unilaterally enacting even more stringent regulations in the near future, or to lobby for other concessions. The business community is more likely to accept stringent environmental policy as a legitimate instrument for environmental protection when initiated by the European Union as part of a program that aims to harmonise environmental standards and effluent taxes among member states. This is because a harmonised environmental policy does not appear to alter the conditions of competition within the EU, where the majority of rivals are located.

5. HARMONISATION OF ENVIRONMENTAL POLICIES SAFEGUARDS FREE TRADE

If the effects of national environmental protection measures on competitiveness appear ambiguous, their trade effects are quite clear. Indeed, national environmental policies sometimes employ trade restrictions to enforce environmental protection, as the following examples will illustrate.

In the early 1990s, the US imposed a total ban on the imports of tuna fish from Mexico. The US government was very concerned about the protection of dolphins, and argued that the current methods of catching fish as practised by Mexico killed and injured more dolphins than the maximum allowed under US regulations. An import ban was thus justified because Mexico did not meet US standards of environmental protection. In response, Mexico challenged the US action before the GATT, charging protectionism. A GATT dispute settlement panel ruled against the US, stating that nations may not restrict trade on the basis of the process under which specific products are manufactured or harvested. This ruling came under severe criticism of environmental organisations, which saw the GATT rulings on free trade as a direct threat to environmental protection.

Another well known recent case resulted from the Danish bottling regulations. The Danish law requested that all beer and soda be sold in packaging materials that can be returned and reused. In addition, packaging materials were subject to approval by the Danish government. Metal-containing packaging materials were not allowed. If a producer sold beer or soda in re-usable packaging material which had not been approved by the Danish government, then this producer was entitled to a sales volume of no larger than 3,000 Hl a year. This restriction as well as the ban on beer and soda cans had the effect of erecting non-tariff barriers to trade. Prompted by the UK and France, the European Commission carefully investigated the Danish regulation with regard to the bottling of beer and soda in March 1997 and ruled that it violated the Directive (94/62) of December 1994 on packaging materials.

The above examples show how national environmental standards may interfere with the principle of free trade. They also suggest that it can be difficult to find the right balance between safeguarding the benefits of liberalised trade on the one hand, and the promotion of environmental protection and conservation on the other hand in the settlement of environmental trade disputes. But most importantly, the settlement of international trade disputes occurring each time when a jurisdiction attempts to impose its environmental protection laws on other jurisdictions involves high transaction costs, so disputes are better avoided altogether. The formulation of a global environmental policy, and in particular the promotion of more internationally agreed environmental standards through multilateral negotiations under the auspices of an international organisation like the WTO offers a solution. This coordinated approach to environmental regulation has been adopted by the European Union, as reflected in its Environmental Action Plans. The European Union explicitly recognises the need for more environmental protection, but is also aware that national environmental protection laws may distort the process of economic integration, which is driven by trade liberalisation and corporate integration. The European Union now uses two broad principles to resolve such conflicts. First, environmental protection measures should not discriminate between foreign and domestically produced goods. Second, there should be no other policy which could achieve the same environmental objectives with less discrimination or trade distortions.

6. CO-ORDINATED ENVIRONMENTAL POLICY AND MNE BEHAVIOUR

The linkage between environmental regulations and the strategies of multinational enterprises (MNEs) is undoubtedly a subject that merits more research attention. MNEs dominate most pollution-intensive industries such as chemicals, petroleum and heavy manufacturing. Environmental regulations may require MNEs to develop green firm-specific advantages (FSAs) (Rugman and Verbeke, 1998a). The question should then be answered whether specific green FSAs can be developed and used within individual countries (as a response to pressures for national responsiveness), or whether these FSAs can be used globally, i.e., in a nonlocation-bound fashion.

Recent research has led to the conclusion that environmental regulations at present appear to have little effect on the FSA configuration and the location decisions of MNEs. In turn, this suggests that MNEs design their production processes according to best global practices. MNEs operate in accordance with the most stringent environmental regulations prevailing in the relevant countries where they operate (Magretta, 1997). This is consistent with Levy's (1995) empirical results on the environmental performance of MNEs. He found that a higher degree of multinationality is associated with superior environmental performance, probably because external pressures from international environmental regulations increase more rapidly than the firm's bargaining power. For these firms international environmental policy co-ordination may lead to substantial scope economies. MNEs perhaps have the most to gain from international policy co-ordination in a context where domestic firms may attempt to use environmental policy as a tool to obtain shelter against foreign rivals. For example, Vogel and Rugman (1997) reviewed 10 cases of environmentally related trade disputes between Canada and the United States and found that in nine of these cases environmental regulations were used to obtain shelter. This occurred in two ways : (1) by imposing discriminatory policies against imports as part of environmental regulations; (2) by enforcing product standards that either completely restrict or place a significantly higher cost burden on foreign producers. Often, shelter is disguised as an environmental conservation measure (Rugman and Soloway, 1997).

Given that MNEs usually try to avoid the creation of shelter because of the retaliation danger and the fact that 'fragmented' environmental policies reduce the potential to gain economies of scope, it is not surprising to see their active involvement in many policy initiatives at the international level, even when the enforcement of compliance is weak, see Rugman and Verbeke (1998b). In addition, international business theory suggests that international environmental policy co-ordination may increase foreign direct investments if it is perceived by firms as a reduction of government induced transaction costs associated with operating in national markets.

7. CO-ORDINATED ENVIRONMENTAL POLICIES STIMULATE INNOVATION ACTIVITIES

In addition to thinking of pollution as an externality, some economists also view pollution as a consequence of (poor) technology choices and our current mode of economic development (Goodstein, 1995; Beck, 1992). In this view, lasting solutions to environmental problems should be found in the adoption of new technologies and the marketing of new products that consume fewer scarce natural resources and are ecologically sustainable.[7] However, it may be difficult for firms to replace the entrenched polluting production technologies by cleaner technologies. The introduction of cleaner technologies requires high initial investments in research and development and tooling (Goodstein, 1995). Moreover, other factors such as low reversibility of environmental investments or uncertainty about both the costs and benefits associated with such investments may also discourage the development of cleaner technologies. See Rugman and Verbeke (1998a) for a more thorough review of the issues.

The introduction of cleaner production technologies and environment friendly products, i.e. environmental innovations, is important for economic reasons as well. First, many environmental innovations are likely to reduce the compliance cost burden on firms. Environmental regulation forces firms to pay for the pollution they cause and for the scarce natural resources they consume. Environmental innovations cause pollution and the usage of scarce resources to fall, thus allowing for cost savings. Lower production costs improve the competitive position of a firm. Secondly, environmental innovations leading to the introduction of new products with superior characteristics, from an environmental perspective may enable firms to strengthen their competitive position through green product differentiation. In either case, firms develop green capabilities which can be used to gain a competitive advantage in a world of growing environmental concerns.

Given that the benefits of environmental innovations are potentially large, it is important for environmental regulation to induce firms to move beyond compliance and to engage on this new path. Porter and Van der Linde (1995, p. 110) have identified several ways in which government policy could stimulate innovative activities :

(1) environmental regulation should focus on clear goals and flexible approaches, leaving it to the industry to find the most cost-effective ways of reaching them;

(2) government policy should encourage continued improvement and innovation through the use of economic incentives (e.g. taxes and tradable permits), the promotion of voluntary agreements and the dissemination of information (e.g. through demonstration projects);

(3) there should be a co-ordination of environmental regulation between industry and regulators and among regulators themselves at different levels (local, regional, national, supranational) to avoid inconsistencies.

The last condition contains a plea for better international co-ordination of national (regional) environmental policies. The development of environment friendly technologies and products necessitates large upfront investments in research and development and marketing. These huge sunk costs suggest the existence of scale economies. Firms are more likely to innovate when there is a potentially large market for their new approaches. The harmonisation of environmental standards and effluent tax rates contribute to create such a large market. For example, when a firm develops a new technology that enables it to comply with local environmental regulation in a cost-effective way, the technology will prove to be equally cost-effective in all other countries which have very similar regulations. The case of carbon/energy taxes is again instructive here. Such taxes raise the cost of fossil fuel energy, thus providing firms with an incentive to develop and switch to alternative energy sources like biomes or solar energy. However, firms located in a jurisdiction where no carbon/energy taxes are levied, will not switch to an alternative energy source unless it is cheaper than untaxed fossil fuel energy there (which is unlikely). Hence, if only a handful of countries levies a carbon/energy tax the market for alternative energies will be small and innovations in this field discouraged. In this respect, a European-wide introduction of a carbon/energy tax would have been preferable to the current situation whereby only Scandinavia and the Netherlands levy a tax.

Other indirect ways in which a harmonisation of environmental policies stimulate innovations and the development of green core competencies are through their beneficial impact on free trade and through their incentive effects for multinationals. Both of these issues were discussed above.

8. CASE STUDY: ENVIRONMENTAL POLICIES TOWARDS WATER POLLUTION IN BELGIUM

Although environmental protection is a policy area in which the European Union is particularly active, member states still enjoy considerable autonomy in designing their own environmental policies. Some member states have unilaterally introduced additional instruments to regulate environmental pollution. The purpose of this section is to highlight costs which may result from an uncoordinated use of regulatory instruments. The Belgian experience is particularly instructive as the majority of environmental legislation is enacted at the sub-national (regional) level and regions do not seem to coordinate their policies.

Institutional background

The constitutional reforms of 1980 and 1988 have led to the delegation of important legislative powers to the three regions of present-day Belgium, which now enjoy autonomy in the setting of economic policy, the promotion of international trade and investments, and the enactment of environmental policy among others. The current division of competencies between federal and regional governments implies that legislation on social security contributions, income and corporate taxation is enacted by the national government and applies to all firms operating on Belgian territory with no regional variations. Regional governments can use their economic, trade and environmental policy as strategic tools when engaging in regional competition, but when doing so they of course need to respect all European Union directives on competition policy.

Environmental regulation in each of the regions is characterised by a sectoral approach to environmental issues. That is, each source of pollution (water, air, solid waste and noise) is covered separately by a set of laws. A variety of instruments is used by all regions: emission standards (water and air), taxes (waste water effluents, waste disposal, packaging materials), user charges (water, municipal waste) and deposit refunds. Standards and tax rates are set by the regional governments. Because only the impact of the environmental regulation of water resources on corporate behaviour has been studied by scholars for both the Flemish and Walloon region, this section focuses on a review of the regulation of water pollution in the Flemish region and Wallonia, and its effects on industry.

In both regions, firms are required to apply for a permit if they plan to engage in activities (as defined by the law) that will abstract water from public water distribution networks and/or discharge waste water into public waters. In order to obtain a permit, a company must submit a request with the regional public authorities in charge of environmental protection. The approval of such a request is conditional upon the firm meeting a number of environmental standards that aim to safeguard a minimum quality of the natural environment and to prevent pollution. Most standards refer to the discharge of pollutants into water and air. In Flanders, all environmental quality standards have been incorporated in the Decision of the Flemish Executive of January 7, 1992, also known as VLAREM II. In contrast, the legal situation is far more complex in Wallonia, where the relevant standards for water quality are covered by more than 60 decrees, many applying only to specific industries. This makes it extremely difficult to compare the stringency of the environmental standards demanded by each region.

In addition to these command and control measures, Flanders and Wallonia also levy water usage charges and taxes on water pollution. The user charges apply to both households and firms, and the current rate is 16 BEF/m^3 in Wallonia and 59.9 BEF/m^3 in Flanders. Waste water effluent taxes were introduced in both regions in 1990. For large consumers of water,[8] the amount of taxes due is given by the product of the pollution load contained in the discharged waste water and the effluent tax rate. The pollution load is calculated using a formula which takes into account the following factors:

(1) the volume (in litres) of industrial waste water discharged during a typical day in the month of peak industrial activity in the year prior to tax collection;

(2) the content of substances in suspension;

(3) the biochemical and chemical oxygen consumption by the waste water;

(4) the content of heavy metals, such as lead, chrome, copper, mercury, zinc, cadmium;

(5) the content of phosphorus and nitrogen compounds;

(6) the volume of drained cooling-water and the difference in temperature between the cooling water and the receiving surface water;

(7) the source from which the water is taken, and more specifically whether this source is different from the source in which the industrial waste water is drained.

Since the beginning of 1994, the formulas used by Flanders and Wallonia have been very similar, with only the weights assigned to the different heavy metals differing slightly. Prior to 1994 however, the Walloon formula did not include the concentration of any heavy metals, phosphorus or nitrogen compounds.

For large consumers of water, the calculation of the tax base uses actual measurements of waste water quality, carried out by the relevant public agencies. Sometimes, direct measurements are impossible and an alternative method based on industry-specific conversion coefficients must be used. No direct measurements of water pollution are carried out for small consumers of water. Given the very large number of small consumers (including all households), this would be very costly, if not technically impossible. Therefore, small consumers of water are taxed on their annual water consumption, which can easily be measured.

Table 12.1.   *Evolution of the tax rate per pollution unit in
the Belgian regions (in BEF)*

	Tax rate in Flanders	Tax rate in Wallonia
1991	600	360
1992	600	360
1993	600	360
1994	615	360
1995	628	360
1996	956	360
1997	975	360

Source: Vlaamse Milieumaatschappij (VMM), Direction Générale des
Resources Naturelles et de l'Environnement

The major difference in environmental policy between the two regions is situated in the applicable tax rates on water pollution. Table 12.1 summarises the evolution of the tax rate in both regions since 1991. As can be seen, Wallonia has never changed its tax rate on water pollution, although it moved to a more stringent definition of the tax base in 1994 when it copied the Flemish formula for calculating the pollution load. In contrast, Flanders has raised the tax rate gradually, with a big jump in 1996.

To conclude, both regions are increasingly relying on effluent taxes as an instrument for changing the polluting behaviour of the firms on their territory. Tax rates are particularly high in Flanders, where they are used for budgetary purposes as well.[9] This has reduced their perceived legitimacy, as explained below.

Critical assessment of the regional policies towards water pollution

In the above discussion of transboundary pollution problems, it was noted that pollutants are often transported through rivers and canals, causing pollution generated in one region (country) to have an adverse effect on the water quality in another region (country). In particular, it appears that the water quality of some Flemish rivers and canals is adversely affected by the pollution generated in Wallonia. For example, the source of the Scheldt is in Northern France, this river crosses the Belgian border and flows through Wallonia (the province of Hainaut) and Flanders successively. Likewise, the city of Liège in Wallonia and the city of Antwerp in Flanders are interconnected by the Albert Canal, one of the main dumps for industrial waste. This clearly represents an asymmetric problem of transboundary pollution: pollution of the Walloon waters causes much more damage to the Flemish waters than the reverse does. In other words, there is an interregional externality inflicted by the upstream region (Wallonia) on the downstream region (Flanders). The current regional approach to environmental policy fails to internalise such externalities.

The current situation of lower tax rates in Wallonia gives rise to occasional complaints that efforts to reduce the pollution of rivers and canals in the Flemish region are frustrated by the polluting behaviour of the Walloon industry, which does not face the same incentives to cut back its pollution. Co-ordination of environmental taxation schemes, resulting in equal tax rates for all regions, would be more effective and welfare-improving, but Wallonia may not gain in the absence of compensation payments made by Flanders.

The current regional differentiation in environmental taxation has not yet caused an explicit outcry from Flemish companies that the extra costs imposed on them as a result of a more stringent environmental taxation scheme has given their Walloon competitors an unfair advantage. Nor has this question received much attention in academic circles. However, the impact of regional environmental policies towards water resources on corporate environmental management and industrial pollution has already been studied in depth and this research at least implicitly suggests that policy problems resulting from a lack of policy co-ordination may arise (see Gallez, 1998; Coeck *et al.*, 1995; Verbeke and Coeck, 1997).

Wallonia. A recent study by Gallez (1998) investigated the impact of the environmental policy aimed at the protection of water resources on corporate environmental behaviour in Wallonia. The purpose of this study was to determine the importance of the different environmental instruments as a motivating factor for a number of environmental actions taken at the corporate level, as opposed to actions taken in response to other environmental pressures.

The main conclusion of the study is that almost half of the corporate environmental actions can be attributed to the Walloon government's environmental policy, the other half being a result of other pressures such as competition, consumer demand, international regulation and environmental movements. However, government regulation tends to disproportionly stimulate curative measures such as better housekeeping and modifications in the production process. In contrast, actions related to final products and inputs are mainly motivated by factors other than the Walloon environmental policy on water resources. This suggests that government policy, although effective in inducing some changes in pollution behaviour, does not stimulate innovative green thinking such as for example the use of life cycle analysis in environmental management, or green product differentiation. It was found that firms are most responsive to the conditions that need to be satisfied in order to obtain a water permit. This is a typical command and control measure, which as explained above, does not provide additional benefits for innovative firms to move beyond compliance.

Flanders. Coeck *et al.* (1995) investigated the responsiveness of firms' pollution behaviour to environmental taxation in Flanders. They estimated a linear regression which explained the relative evolution in pollution volume as a function of the level of taxation, the average elimination costs and the relative evolution in production. The authors predicted that the relative reduction in pollution volumes would be largest for firms which had a high level of taxation, or a low average elimination cost, or a negative relative evolution in production. The exercise however did not yield economically meaningful results. One explanation for this is probably that the data covered a short period only, i.e. 1991-93, and the selected sample only included the large production units for which the pollution volume could be measured directly.

Another explanation is based on subsequent research by Verbeke and Coeck (1997), which suggested that the present policy of environmental taxation is not perceived as a legitimate instrument of environmental protection. As mentioned above, the waste water effluent tax in the Flemish region is a 'revenue-generating' tax, as its revenues are used to finance the MINA fund (see endnote 9). This has created a suspicion within the Flemish business community that the environmental taxes are levied by the Flemish authorities primarily for budgetary purposes. The fear exists that if firm behaviour is too responsive to the imposition of environmental taxes, resulting in drastic cuts in the pollution volumes, the government will merely raise effluent tax rates in response to a reduced tax base. Obviously, such speculations reduce the incentive effect of taxation.

In sum, both studies suggest that neither in Wallonia nor in Flanders environmental regulation has produced significant changes in the polluting behaviour of firms. The focus of many managers is on compliance with current regulations. A possible explanation for this narrow focus is that environmental taxes in Wallonia are too low to provide a strong incentive for firms to move beyond compliance, whereas in Flanders, the incentives are weakened by the perception that environmental taxes are actually revenue taxes. Co-ordination of environmental policy is recommended. The optimal policy would raise effluent tax rates in Wallonia, thereby resulting in a stronger incentive effect, while it would also increase the legitimacy of the effluent taxes in Flanders by making them appear less like a revenue tax. Moreover, such a policy would also contribute to internalising the externalities caused by water pollution in Wallonia.

9. CONCLUSION

The main conclusion of this chapter is that the co-ordination of environmental policy at the European and international levels offers a unique opportunity to simultaneously achieve economic growth driven by free trade and foreign direct investments, and substantial environmental protection. The harmonisation of environmental regulation in the European Union has caused the poorer member states to rise to the level of environmental protection prevailing in the richer ones. It has also partially prevented unilateral environmental regulations by member states from having a strong influence on individual firms, industries and the environmental quality of neighbouring States.

However, many member states have recently introduced additional instruments – mainly economic incentives – to regulate environmental pollution, and a harmonised use of such instruments at the level of the European Union is still in its early stages. A case study on the regulation of water pollution in Belgium was used to highlight some of the possible costs associated with an unco-ordinated use of economic incentives, in particular environmental taxes. In Belgium, water pollution through rivers is mainly a problem of asymmetric spillovers from the upstream region (Wallonia) to the downstream region (Flanders). However, the effluent taxes on water pollution, issued unilaterally by each region in 1990, do not internalise such externalities. A more strongly co-ordinated policy seems desirable but may need to be combined with side payments in order to be acceptable. Such a proposal would currently not gain much political support in Belgium where the more general issue of inter-regional transfer payments (e.g. as regards social security) has been the subject of a major debate between the Walloon and Flemish regions. The transboundary nature of water pollution is however not unique to Belgium, but common to all European countries. This problem of transboundary water pollution has already been addressed at the level of the European Union mainly by issuing common environmental quality standards. Yet, a broadening of the regulatory instruments used by the European Union is necessary, as has recently been recognised by the Union itself.

This chapter has also suggested that innovative 'green' thinking can contribute to sustainable economic growth through the development of a sector for environment friendly technologies and products. The European Union has endorsed this idea in its fifth Environmental Action Programme, and has adjusted the process of European environmental policymaking accordingly. The recent directive to encourage the re-use of packaging materials, which has developed in co-operation with industry, can be considered a step in the right direction. Yet, we found little evidence of green thinking in the Belgian case, suggesting that environmental policy in Belgium has not contributed much to green thinking or to the adoption of a long term perspective by business leaders on the economic opportunities generated by a green approach. A better co-ordination of environmental policy at the national level can provide an incentive for behavioural change. The European Union can also contribute to a change in attitude of managers vis-à-vis the environment both directly through its regulatory efforts and indirectly through competitive pressures from the single market.

Finally, this chapter suggests that the European Union is increasing its co-operation with industry to develop new environmental regulations. As a result of this trend, recent environmental initiatives have taken the form of voluntary agreements. Many industrial sectors are dominated by a limited number of multinational enterprises. These firms can be expected to play an increasingly important role in shaping future European environmental policy. It was argued that most multinational enterprises would benefit from a European approach to environmental policy. However, the impact of European versus unilateral environmental regulation on MNE operations requires further in-depth research.

NOTES

1. In the case of environmental regulation, it is the Ministers of the Environment of each Member State that vote on the Commission's proposals.
2. In practice, many proposals are the result of Commission consultation with the Council representatives, implying a consensus at the time when matters come before the Council for a vote (Pfander, 1996, p. 64).
3. EMAS was initially intended to be mandatory, but later an agreement was made with industrialists to leave the individual companies the choice about whether or not to adopt the scheme (see Lévèque, chapter 8 for a detailed discussion).
4. Under this procedure, the European Parliament must also vote on each proposal by the Commission, and the outcome of such a vote is binding for the Council of Ministers. In other words, a proposal rejected by the European Parliament (a majority of MPs voting against) cannot become a Directive.
5. One specification of Barrett's model solves jointly for the number of signatories, the terms of the agreement and the actions of non-signatories; the other solves the IEA as an equilibrium to an infinitely repeated game which is renegotiation-proof.
6. Barrett demonstrated that the use of environmental policy for strategic purposes, that is setting weak environmental standards with the hope of gaining a competitive edge is very deceptive, sometimes leading to results opposite to expectations.
7. Ecological sustainability is defined here as a situation whereby the rate at which pollution is generated does not exceed the rate at which pollution can be absorbed by nature.
8. In Flanders, a firm is considered as a large consumer of water if it consumes at least 500 m^3 annually.
9. In Flanders, tax revenues are earmarked for the MINA fund (Milieu en Natuur Fonds), which was set up by the Flemish Regional Government to finance a broad range of environmental projects.

REFERENCES

Adams, J. (1998), 'Environmental Policy and Competitiveness in a Global Economy: Conceptual Issues and a Review of the Empirical Evidence', in OECD, *Globalisation and Environment,* Paris, pp. 53-100.

Barrett, S. (1993), 'Strategic Environmental Policy and International Competitiveness', in OECD, *Environmental Policies and Industrial Competitiveness,* Paris, pp. 158-165.

Barrett, S. (1994), 'Self-Enforcing International Environmental Agreements', *Oxford Economic Papers,* **46**, 878-894.

Beck, U. (1992), 'From Industrial Society to the Risk Society: Questions of Survival Social Structure and Ecological Enlightment', *Theory, Culture and Society,* **9**, 97-123.

Coeck, C., R. S'Jegers, A. Verbeke and W. Winkelmans (1995), 'The Effects of Environmental Taxes: An Empirical Study of Water and Solid Waste Levies in Flanders', *Annals of Public and Cooperative Economics,* **66**, 479-497.

Gallez, C. (1998), *Impact des Instruments Environnementaux sur le Comportement des Entreprises: Application à la Politique de Protection de l'Eau en Région Wallone,* Louvain-la-Neuve: CIACO.

Goodstein, E. (1995), 'The Economic Roots of Environmental Decline: Property Rights or Path Dependence?', *Journal of Economic Issues,* **29**, 1029-1044.

Jaffe, A.B., S.R. Peterson, P.R. Portney and R.N. Stavins (1995), 'Environmental Regulation and the Competitiveness of U.S. Manufacturing: What Does the Evidence Tell Us?', *Journal of Economic Literature,* **33**, 132-163.

Lévèque, F. (ed.) (1996), *Industry, Competitiveness and the Policy Process,* Cheltenham, UK and Brookfield, US: Edward Elgar.

Levy, D.L (1995), 'The Environmental Practices and Performance of Transnational Corporations', *Transnational Corporations,* **4**, 44-67.

Magretta, J. (1997), 'Growth through Global Sustainability: An Interview with Monsanto's CEO, Robert B. Shapiro', *Harvard Business Review,* **76**, 78-88.

OECD (1994), *Managing the Environment: the Role of Economic Instruments,* Paris.

Palmer, K., W.E. Oates and P.R. Portney (1995), 'Tightening Environmental Standards: the Benefit-cost or No-cost Paradigm?', *Journal of Economic Perspectives,* **9**, 119-132.

Pfander, J.E. (1996), 'Environmental Federalism in Europe and the United States: A Comparative Assessment of Regulation Through the Agency of Member States', in J.B. Braden, H. Folmer and T.S. Ulen (eds), *Environmental Policy with Political and Economic Integration,* Cheltenham, UK and Brookfield, US: Edward Elgar.

Porter, M.E. and C. Van der Linde (1995), 'Toward a New Conception of the Environment-Competitiveness Relationship', *Journal of Economic Perspectives,* **9**, 97-118.

Rugman, A.M. and J.A. Soloway (1997), 'Corporate Strategy and NAFTA: When Environmental Regulations are a Barrier to Trade', *Journal of Transnational Management Development,* **3**, 231-251.

Rugman, A.M. and A. Verbeke (1998a), 'Corporate Strategies and Environmental Regulations: an Organizing Framework', *Strategic Management Journal,* **19**, 363-375.

Rugman, A.M. and A. Verbeke (1998b), 'Multinational Enterprises and Public Policy', *Journal of International Business Studies*, **29**, 113-136.

Ulph, A. (1996), 'Strategic Environmental Policy, International Trade and the Single European Market', in J.B. Braden, H. Folmer and T.S. Ulen (eds) *Environmental Policy with Political and Economic Integration,* Cheltenham: Edward Elgar, pp. 235-256.

Verbeke, A. and C. Coeck (1997), 'Environmental Taxation: A Green Stick or a Green Carrot for Corporate Social Performance?', *Management and Decision Economics*, **18**, 507-516.

Vogel, D. and A. Rugman (1997), 'Environmentally Related Trade Disputes between the United States and Canada', *American Review of Canadian Studies*, **27**, 271-292 .

Zito, A.R. (1997), 'The Evolving Arena of EU Environmental Policy: the Impact of Subsidiarity and Shared Responsibility', U. Collier, J. Golub and A. Kreher (eds), *Subsidiarity and Shared Responsibility; New Challenges for EU Environmental Policy,* Baden-Baden: Nomos Verlaggesellschaft, pp. 11-34.

13. Services of General Interest: a Challenge for European Economic Integration

Anne-Marie Van den Bossche and Sandra Coppieters

1. INTRODUCTION[1]

The Treaty of Amsterdam, signed on October 2, 1997, marks a new step in the process of European integration. For the topic under consideration, this third major revision of the original EEC-Treaty[2] is of particular importance, in that for the first time it includes 'services of general economic interest' in the Principles of the European Community, as laid down in Part One of the EC Treaty. Even though these services had not been entirely outside the ambit and scope of the EC-Treaty before this explicit mentioning, and despite the fact that the actual significance of the explicit reference is debatable, their being listed among, inter alia, the tasks of the European Community (Article 2, new Article 2);[3] the activities of the Community (Article 3, new Article 3); or even, the extremely important principle of non-discrimination on the basis of nationality (Article 3, new Article 12), does amount to a genuine 'upgrading'.[4]

Article 7d (new article 16) reads as follows: 'Without prejudice to Articles 77, 90 and 92, and given the place occupied by services of general economic interest in the shared values of the Union as well as their role in promoting social and territorial cohesion, the Community and the member-states, each within their respective powers and within the scope of application of this Treaty, shall take care that such services operate on the basis of principles and conditions which enable them to fulfil their missions'. In addition to the Article itself, the Conference adopted a specific declaration, which stresses that '[The] provisions of Article 7d of the Treaty establishing the European Community on public services shall be implemented with full respect for the jurisprudence of

225

the Court of Justice, inter alia as regards the principles of equality of treatment, quality and continuity of such services'.[5]

The purpose of this chapter is to indicate how the liberalisation policy of the European Union has influenced services of general economic interest, why such services are a challenge for European economic integration and provide some insight into how this challenge has been met until now.

2. HISTORICAL BACKGROUND

The late nineteenth century was a turning point for society in terms of the public services. From then on the absolute economic liberal model was abandoned and replaced by a more interventionist model. State intervention was justified by both economic and social objectives and was supported by renowned economists.[6] The action of public authorities mainly concerned those services/sectors that were considered essential to the economic life of the community. The reasons for intervening were quite diverse and ranged from a lack of private interest because of intensive capital requirements or lack of/uncertainty as to profitability (Dehousse and Van den Hende, 1996), and a need to secure the supply of certain basic products/services, to the need to join infrastructures in order to realise economies of scale. The overall incapacity of the market to meet social objectives such as reducing inequality and accessibility also inspired this new economic model (C.E.E.P., 1995; Rapp, 1995). Traditionally sectors such as communication, energy, transport, etc. were considered as services of general economic interest. The way these services are organised and perceived legally vary from member-state to member-state (C.E.E.P., 1995; Vandamme, 1997). Generally speaking in countries with a Latin legal tradition the notion is a very strong legal concept, sometimes even an constitutional right, while countries with a more Anglo-Saxon or Germanic tradition either do not know the concept, or do not give it any particular legal connotation.[7]

From the 1980s onwards, the necessity of a public sector as a means to respond to the market's deficiencies was put into question. Economists and lawyers criticised the appropriation of benefits by particular categories and the possible risk of being held ransom by the operator of the supervisory administration or regulator. This criticism led to the demand for more competition and the separation between operator and regulator. Complaints about inefficient service provision and high prices and important technological changes supported this demand for change.[8] Private parties showed increasing interest in providing certain services themselves. In some cases, there is evidence of the emergence of a potential *and* a willingness to raise money for the development and maintenance of certain infrastructures. At the same time, however, the approach clearly differed.

While some member-states, the Scandinavian countries and the United Kingdom mainly, were eager to adapt their public services to a more liberal model, thus allowing more competition in these sectors, improved access to services of a better quality and price and even privatising some of these sectors, others, and in particular Latin countries (France, Belgium, Italy, Spain, Portugal and Greece) chose to hang on to their classic model of one single operator to provide the service of general interest. This comes as no real surprise, as these are precisely the countries where the notion of the public sector is a strong legal concept.[9]

To date, just how to cope with these differences has been a genuine challenge for European economic integration (see Dubois, 1997). The key question, then, is which direction to take and how far Union action should go to successfully deal with the challenge of more demanding consumers in terms of choice, quality and price[10]; more demanding companies in terms of better price deals resulting from worldwide competition; the impact of new technologies on the economic profile of the 'classical monopoly' sectors and the introduction of new services; and the differing rate of modernisation of certain countries and certain sectors.[11] The debate is however not limited to legal issues. Political and strong emotional considerations are never far away. Particularly in countries which are strongly bound to the public sector, the attempts to liberalise are considered an attack on the 'sacred' public services, one of the basic elements of 'European civilisation'.[12]

This attitude definitely blurs the real question whether there is a conflict between the concept of services of general interest with Union law to start with. It does, moreover, not really contribute to identifying the real issues. [13]

3. THE CONCEPT OF SERVICE OF GENERAL INTEREST AND COMMUNITY LAW

As already indicated, the Treaty of Rome did contain some indirect references to the notion of public sector. Article 37 E(E)C (new Article 31) prescribes the elimination of state monopolies of a commercial character, while Article 77 E(E)C (new Article 73) allows certain state aids in the transport sector if they represent certain obligations inherent in the concept of public service.[14] For the topic under consideration, however, the most important one is Article 90 E(E)C (new Article 86).[15] This article submits public undertakings and undertakings to which member-states have granted exclusive or special rights to the provisions of the Treaty, unless this obstructs the performance of the particular tasks assigned to them. It therefore not only deals with competition rules, but also with the provisions on free movement of goods, of services or the freedom of establishment etc.

Since the European Economic Community aimed at establishing a Common Market,[16] it comes as no surprise that initially, primary attention was given to free movement of goods and the abolition of all barriers to trade; hence, the regular use of Article 37 EC (new Article 31) to do away with state trading monopolies.[17] Article 90 EC (new Article 86) on the other hand remained for a very long time 'in a genuine state of hibernation'[18] and accordingly remained unused for many years. Not only economic criticism, but more importantly the ambition to create a Single Market, prompted a change of heart.[19] The transition from a common market to a single market implied that the Community's main concern was no longer confined to goods, but also turned to services such as public services. Sheltering access to and eliminating competition in these services was no longer tolerable, since they endangered not only the competitiveness of the European industry, but also economic and social cohesion within the Community.[20]

Gradually the Commission started to make use of its powers under Article 90, par 3, EC (new Article 86, par 3). From a legal point of view, this paragraph is of particular importance, in that it explicitly allows the Commission to take legislative action on its own (without the intervention of the European Parliament and the Council of Ministers).[21] A first legislative action concerned the adoption of a directive, envisaging to realise more transparency in the financial relations between public undertakings and member-states.[22] Later came the Telecommunications directives.[23] From 1985 onwards, the Commission in addition used its powers to specifically condemn member-states for breach of Article 90 EC (new Article 86).[24] To get a full picture and be properly informed about the need for change in some vital sectors of general interest, such as the telecom sector, postal sector or the energy sector, the Commission also launched a series of Green Papers.[25] Finally, Article 90 EC (new Article 86) started to be invoked in proceedings before national courts, the first of which led to preliminary rulings of the Court of Justice in the Corbeau and Almelo cases.[26,27]

Tackling the problems surrounding services of general interest implied a careful and scrupulous investigation. The Commission opted to proceed on a sector by sector basis, to establish which ones should be liberalised, and if so, to what extent. Different options exist in this respect: total liberalisation, partial – and therefore – guided liberalisation, or maintenance of the status quo. Total liberalisation would have come down to a 'big bang'. The result would have been a total and immediate opening up to competition, leaving the provision of all services of general interest entirely to private operators and the logic of a free market economy. From a pure competition policy point of view, this is certainly the best solution. It would, however, at the same time entail serious problems for less profitable or unprofitable services such as services in less developed or remote areas for which total exposure to the market forces would imply either the elimination of those services or substantial price rises. In the European

Community, this option has never been seriously considered.[28] In its Communication on services of general economic interest[29] – the first encompassing declaration on the principles ruling Article 90 EC (new Article 86) – the Commission almost solemnly declared that services of general economic interest are an important element in the European model of society, in that they further the fundamental EC objectives of solidarity and equal treatment within an open and dynamic market economy.[30] This statement of principle was, however, immediately complemented by emphasising on the importance of finding the right balance between the demands of the internal market and free competition on the one hand, and the objectives of general interest, on the other.

This balance was found in the concept of safeguarding the universal service, which implies the provision of a service of good quality at reasonable prices affordable to all. In order to secure the financial viability of the universal service provider the Commission has allowed certain services to be reserved. This option represents a perfect balance between opening the market and at the same time protecting what was considered essential for the European citizen. A well defined concept of universal service therefore 'protects against the risk that market forces on their own might exclude certain groups of users or users in certain regions from being able to access new services'.[31] At the same time, however, it should be clear that this balance is a delicate one. 'Too narrow a vision of universal service and citizens may be kept out of full participation in society. Too broad a vision and the competitive forces which are the principal driver of better services, lower prices and greater innovation will be held back as new players in the market will be deterred from entering the market'.[32]

It must be stressed that the political support from both the Council of Ministers (read: the member-states) and the European Parliament strongly differed from sector to sector. Whereas consensus was quite easily reached on the need to – gradually – liberalise the telecommunication sector, politically speaking, the postal sector seems to be a totally different matter. Only very recently, the first prudent and gradual steps could be taken in this sector.

It may already be clear from the foregoing, that the European notion of liberalisation should not be confused with the notions of 'complete opening up to competition', or even 'deregulation'. The equation might be correct in some parts of the world, notably the United States, but in Europe, liberalisation goes hand in hand with significant regulation of essential economic sectors.[33] Liberalisation 'à l'Européenne' is first and foremost concerned with the abolition of exclusive rights which give rise to legal monopolies.[34] By abolishing the legal monopoly, regulatory entry barriers disappear, so that market entry becomes possible and new entrants can start operating in the sector. Liberalisation is therefore an important and necessary element for opening up a sector to effective competition, although it can never be a sufficient element in itself, because the abolition of exclusive rights does not automatically prevent an undertaking with a dominant position from exploiting its competitive advantage as former monopolist and abusing this market power to prevent competition and the emergence of potential competitors. The only way to do away with such practices and to guarantee effective competition, is the strict application of the competition rules.[35] The Commission has always remained very attentive in this area, and has taken action against the former monopolists whenever necessary.

Before taking a closer look at the liberalisation process in two sectors: the telecommunications sector and the postal sector, which constitute clear examples of finished versus only starting liberalisation, it is necessary, briefly, to devote some attention to a number of definitions and to clear up any confusion in terminology, including that for public services, services of general interest, services of general economic interest – which are sometimes used and presented as synonyms, despite clear differences in meaning. The Commission's Communication on the services of general interest proves very useful in this respect.[36] While the term *service of general interest* refers to both market and non-market services, the term *service of general economic interest* is confined to market services, in fields such as transport networks, energy or communications.[37] Both types of services share a common feature: that they are subject to specific *public service obligations*. These then are obligations imposed by the public authorities on the body rendering the service, with a view to promoting or facilitating the performance of the general interest role and can be applied at regional or at national level. The resulting basic operating principles of general interest services therefore are fourfold: continuity, equal access, universality and openness. The term *public service* itself is used in a double way. It either refers to the body providing the service (the operator) or to the general interest role assigned to it and for which public service obligations may be imposed.[38] A last concept of crucial importance in the area under consideration is the concept of *universal service*, which is to be understood as 'a defined minimum set of services of specified quality which is available to all users independent of their geographical location and, in the light of specific national conditions, at an affordable price'.[39] The essence of this concept is its evolutionary nature. The object of the resulting obligations, is to make sure that everyone has access to certain essential services of high quality at prices they can afford.[40] Universal service obligations, therefore, act as the absolute minimum at the European level,[41] which can be complemented at the national levels by general interest duties, provided, of course, that the means used comply with Community law.[42]

Finally, attention should be drawn to the fact that, because of Article 222 EC (new Article 295),[43] 'Community policies on the liberalisation of regulated public services do not require the privatisation of public enterprises, although many former public monopolies have been sold to the private sector, especially those in the field of telecommunications (e.g. British Telecom, the Dutch KNP, the Spanish Téléfonica)'.[44,45]

4. LIBERALISATION IN PROGRESS: THE HESITANT CASE OF THE POSTAL SECTOR

In June 1992 the Commission launched its Green Paper on the development of the single market for postal services.[46] In this document the Commission highlighted the differences between the member-states in postal services provided, access and quality of service. It argued that these differences created market distortions for those sectors who rely heavily on postal services for advertising purposes, or distribution of magazines and periodicals for instance. At the same time, they could also create potential market distortions for the postal sector itself when exclusive rights were larger than necessary to secure the universal postal service. In the long run this could even endanger the economic and social cohesion within the Community. The Commission pleaded for the *establishment of the universal postal service* to secure the continuation of the public service mission of the postal administration in good economic and financial conditions. To achieve these objectives the Commission discussed four general options. The first option mentioned (complete liberalisation of the postal sector) was at the same time dismissed because of fears that it would lead to the loss of the universal service at prices affordable to all. In addition it was not at all certain that private operators would even be interested. Total harmonisation (option 2) and mere maintenance of the status quo (option 3) were considered undesirable. The last and preferred option consisted in the further opening up of the market while at the same time strengthening the universal service. To achieve this goal, common objectives for universal postal services needed to be defined at Community level, thereby allowing the establishment of reserved services in order to safeguard the financial viability of the universal service provide while, at the same time, improving the quality of service.

After consultation with the interested parties, the Commission prepared a Communication on a guideline for the development of the community postal services.[47] Overall there seemed to be a consensus on the need for Community action and the main approach of the Commission. The Commission suggested that it draw up a series of proposals for directives on the definition of the universal service and the reserved sector, on the quality of postal services and on commercial harmonisation and technical standardisation and also proposed to take action concerning access for community operators to third markets. The European Parliament, however, urged the Commission to draw up one single legislative proposal based on Article 100A of the Treaty (new Article 95).[48] Due to differences in opinion on the definition of the universal postal service and the timetable for liberalisation, it took over two years before the Commission could present its proposal for a directive on common rules for the postal sector.[49] In the Communication accompanying this proposal the Commission called for the adoption of a complementary Notice on the application of the competition rules to the postal sector.[50] While the Directive – to be adopted by the Council of Ministers in co-decision with the European Parliament – was intended to harmonise the regulatory framework, the Commission Notice would provide the postal operators with more clarity on the application by the Commission of the Treaty competition rules. This would allow the establishment of a universal postal service and a gradual liberalisation and opening-up of the postal market to increased competition.

The proposed Directive called for the establishment of a *minimum mandatory universal postal service* to be provided throughout the Community to all citizens. This universal service covered both national and cross-border services and had to include at least the collection, transport and distribution of addressed mail items and addressed books, catalogues, newspapers and periodicals up to 2 kg and addressed postal packages up to 20 kg and services for registered items and insured items. In order to secure the financial viability of the universal service, a list was added enumerating those services which could be reserved to the national postal operators.[51] Domestic mail, the price of which is less than five times the public tariff for an item of correspondence in the first weight step and weights less than 350 grammes, was included in this list. The distribution of incoming cross-border mail and direct mail, for its part, could only be reserved until the end of the year 2000. It was the Commission's intended prerogative to decide on the continuation of this reservation after the year 2000. The competence to further liberalise the domestic mail services was in the hands of the European Parliament and the Council. The Commission would submit a report on this issue not later than the first half of the year 2000.

The reactions to these proposals were very diverse and predicted the resistance which the proposals would have to endure both at the level of the Council (read: the member-states) and the European Parliament. Only thanks to the devotion of the Irish Presidency, an agreement on both Community instruments was finally reached in December 1997.[52] The result, however, was disappointing for many. Compared to the original proposal of the Commission, the ultimate text only envisages a very small-scale liberalisation of the postal sector. According to the Directive, the universal service involves the permanent provision of a postal service of specified quality at all points in the national territory at affordable prices for all users, covering both national and cross-border services. The minimum facilities only cover services for postal items up to 2 kilograms, postal packages up to 10 kilograms and services for registered and insured items. However, national authorities may increase this weight limit for postal packages to any weight not exceeding 20 kilograms, while member-states must ensure the delivery of postal packages received from other member-states weighing up to 20 kilograms.[53] Domestic mail and cross-border mail and direct mail continue to be reserved, and the decision-making power on further liberalisation is attributed to the European Parliament and the Council. Before l January 2000 they have to decide on the further gradual and controlled liberalisation, which has to be effective no later than the year 2003.[54] Compared to the original proposal, this means that the prospect of full liberalisation is postponed by three years. Clearly the political climate was not ready for a further liberalisation of the postal sector. Moreover, since the Directive expires on 31 December 2004,[55] some member-states argue that from 2005 on only national legislation will apply (which amounts to claiming exclusive competence to decide on further liberalisation/reservation), while the Commission has argued that it will make use of Article 90 (new Article 86).

While the Directive is intended to provide more certainty to the member-states when granting exclusive rights, the postal Notice is clearly aimed at the postal operators themselves, as it wants to offer them more clarity on the application of the competition rules to their behaviour and on the conditions under which state aid can be lawfully granted to them. The Notice emphasises that the holder of exclusive or special rights automatically has a dominant position on the relevant market.[56] Not offering the service or offering an inefficient service not adapted to technological developments, would therefore amount to abusing this position. Moreover, the dominant enterprise is under an obligation not to engage in exclusionary practices which would further diminish the remaining competition in the market.[57]

The Notice clearly acknowledges that member-states are free to define general interest services or to grant exclusive rights in order to provide these services.[58] When doing so, they are, however (and of course), bound by Article 90 EC (new Article 86).[59] While in its first paragraph, this Article envisages the abolition of exclusive or special rights, the second paragraph allows a derogation from the application of the Treaty rules. The Commission confirms that when a postal service of general economic interest falls within the limits of the reserved area as defined in the Directive, these rights are presumed to be justified under Article 90, par 2, EC. This presumption can be rebutted if factual evidence shows that the restrictions of competition flowing from these special or exclusive rights are not necessary to avoid the obstruction of the performance of the particular tasks assigned to the postal operator or if the development of trade is affected to such an extent as would be contrary to the interests of the Community.[60] The Commission expressly refers to the existing case law on this subject.[61]

The Notice deals in some detail with the conditions for application of Article 90, par 2, EC in the postal sector.[62,63] Specifically with respect to the further granting of reserved exclusive rights for the supply of postal services, the Notice allows the member-states to subject the provision of these services to declaration procedures or class licenses or even individual licensing procedures. In the Commission's view, these procedures must fulfil the qualitative requirements of being transparent, objective and non-discriminatory. At the same time, the member-states have to establish that the services can only be provided by the granting of special or exclusive rights. Put differently, there may not be less restrictive means of achieving the desired result. Finally, compliance with the proportionality principle also demands that the grant of exclusive or individual rights be balanced with the general interest. Prohibiting self-delivery to ensure the financial viability of the public postal network is therefore a clear example of a non-proportionate measure.

Specific attention is devoted to the need for an independent regulatory body and effective monitoring of the reserved services together with the need to ensure the transparency of accounting.[64] Finally, equal and free access to the postal network is put forward as an essential requirement. The public postal operator does not, however, have to accept postal items which are fraudulently conveyed to another member-state in order to circumvent the postal monopoly.[65]

As far as direct mail is concerned, the present degree of liberalisation clearly differs from member-state to member-state, which leads to a number of problems. The Commission is aware of these, and therefore envisages adopting a case by case approach, instead of specifying the obligations of the member-states in a general way. For the time being, member-states may in any case maintain certain existing restrictions or introduce licensing systems to avoid distortions or destabilisation of revenues. Similar rules apply to the sector of distribution for inward cross-border mail. For items falling within the scope of the reserved services, member-states may lawfully maintain restrictions to avoid traffic diversion. As far as clearance, sorting and postal items are concerned, the maintenance of existing restrictions is allowed to stimulate the operator to which the member-states have granted special and exclusive rights to restructure. Such restrictions can, however, only relate to items falling within the scope of the existing monopolies.[66]

Reading the directive and the Postal Notice together, it is safe to say that the actual state of liberalisation of the postal sector is fairly limited. The – mainly political – resistance has therefore gained the upper hand. The resistance in this area is in sharp contrast with the attitude taken towards the liberalisation of the telecommunications sector, which – from a legal point of view – can be described as complete.

5. LIBERALISATION IN PROGRESS: THE DIFFERENT CASE OF THE TELECOMMUNICATION SECTOR

Initially the EC policy on telecommunications was aimed at the establishment of common development lines. As early as 1986 a directive was adopted on the mutual recognition of type approval for terminal *equipment*.[67] However the liberalisation process really began to run its course after the 1987 Green Paper on the development of the common market for telecommunications services and equipment.[68] Directive 88/301 liberalised the market for terminal equipment. For the liberalisation of telecommunication *services,* on the other hand, the Commission opted for a more gradual approach. Initially, the liberalisation process only concerned value-added services and data services.[69] Directive 90/388[70] did not therefore cover public voice telephony,[71] telex services,[72] mobile radiotelephony, paging services and satellite services. The scope of the directive was then gradually extended, starting with the liberalisation of satellite communications.[73] Then came the abolition of the restrictions on the use of cable television networks for the provision of already liberalised telecommunications services[74] and shortly after that, the liberalisation of mobile and personal communications.[75] The last hurdle to the implementation of full competition in telecommunications markets was taken with the adoption of Directive 96/16 and the opening up to competition of public voice telephony and telex services.[76]

The era of full liberalisation of all telecom services therefore started on the 1st of January 1998.[77] Directive 96/19/EC does, however, allow a temporary exception[78] for member-states with either less developed (such as Greece, Spain, Ireland and Portugal) or very small networks (such as Luxembourg). In accordance with this provision Luxembourg,[79] Spain,[80] Portugal,[81] Ireland[82] and Greece[83] have indeed been granted additional implementation periods. As a result, the telecommunications sector will be fully open to competition in all member-states no later than the year 2000.[84]

A striking feature is the attention devoted to the need to guarantee the provision of a universal telecommunications service. Initially launched by the Commission in its 1987 Green Paper,[85] the concept was gradually and consistently defined and developed.[86] From the outset, it was believed that the concept of universal service 'is improving the level of service currently found in the Community and operates as a guarantee that the [resulting] advantages would be widely spread and that the interests of the consumers are actively promoted'.[87] The current concept of universal service 'corresponds to the obligation to provide access to the public telephone network and to deliver an affordable telephone service to all users reasonably requesting it'.[88] Universal service therefore includes the following elements: the right for users to obtain a connection to the fixed universal public telephone network[89] (i.e. one having general geographic coverage)[90], for telephone, fax and data communications[91] within the shortest time-scale possible,[92] and to connect and use approved terminal equipment situated on the user's premises, in accordance with national and Community law; the right to adequate and up-to-date information on access to and use of the fixed public telephone network and voice telephony service; set and published targets for the supply-time and quality of service; the guarantee that service offerings continue for a reasonable period of time after termination, which moreover can only take place after consultation with users affected;

compensation and/or refund arrangements in case of insufficient service quality levels;[93] the guarantee that published tariffs[94] and supply conditions cannot be changed overnight and without prior agreement of the national regulatory authority;[95] the possibility to obtain itemised billing on request;[96] the availability of regularly updated directories of subscribers to the voice telephony service[97] and enquiry and emergency services[98] and the provision of public payphones meeting the reasonable needs of users, in terms of both numbers and geographical coverage.[99] Next to these elements, which are of particular importance for end-users, more specific rules deal with service providers and special network access,[100] interconnection[101] and cost accounting principles to be adhered to.[102]

The affordability of the universal service was also highlighted. This implies that, throughout the territory, prices for 'initial connection, subscription, periodic rental, access and the use of the service', are reasonable and affordable.[103] Even though such affordability was considered to be 'crucial to the extension of telecommunications service to every citizen',[104] the Commission did not, however – in line with the principle of subsidiarity – find it necessary to suggest harmonised rules in this respect, but limited itself to indicating two possible options for the financing of the universal service.[105] This can be ensured either by payments into an independent universal service fund, which would then make payments to operators actually providing the universal service, or by payments directly made to operators providing universal service as an additional payment to the commercial charges for inter-connection with their network.[106] When establishing a mechanism for sharing the cost of universal service, member-states have to take due account of the principles of transparency, non-discrimination and proportionality in setting the contributions to be made.[107] At the same time, it was made very clear, that any such financing scheme should not disproportionately burden new entrants and accordingly insulate the dominant telecommunications organisations from competition.[108] Moreover, the funding mechanisms adopted should seek only to ensure that market participants contribute to the financing of universal service, and not to other activities which are not directly linked to the provision of the universal service.[109]

Fully aware of the evolutionary nature of the concept of a universal service, the Commission pointed to the need for regular monitoring[110] of its application in the telecommunications sector as early as 1996.[111] A first survey of 'the scope, level, quality and affordability of universal service', and enquiry into 'the need, in the light of the [then] prevailing circumstances, for adaptation of the scope of universal service at a European level, bearing in mind the need for predictability for investment decisions',[112] was scheduled for January 1, 1998, and a second review has been announced for the end of 1999. On 25 February 1998, thus only a little later than planned, the Commission adopted its first monitoring report on the universal service in the Telecommunications sector. According to the Commission, the current system works quite well in that service levels, price and quality have gradually but continuously improved. At present there seems, therefore, no need for change or alternations. With respect to the evolution of tariffs, the report states, that despite the re-balancing of tariffs, consumers are better off in real terms, although for lower usage sub-scribers this is not always the case because fixed costs have remained stable or have risen. At the same time, however, an increasing tendency could be detected towards the provision of special low users-schemes in order to spread consumer benefits.[113] A particularly interesting finding, is that only a small number of member-states[114] have found it necessary to introduce specific schemes for the sharing of any costs related to universal service obligations.[115]

The conclusion therefore seems indeed to be, that '[I]n establishing a frame-work for full communications liberalisation from 1998 onwards, the European Community has established measures to safeguard universal service and in-crease consumer rights. European Union legislation guarantees service and quality levels', while at the same time it strives towards 'the right balance between establishing effective competition – as a means to greater innovation and choice and in particular services and prices which correspond to customers' needs – and extending benefits to all customers'.[116] Yet the evolution is not complete and further developments will be monitored closely to make sure that the benefits of competition and choice extend 'to all citizens irrespective of income and location'. Future monitoring will in particular concentrate 'on areas which appear to be of greatest concern including households without telephone service, affordability and related consumer protection issues; the situation of low income and disabled users, the state of affairs at a regional level and, in the context of the growing use of Internet, the situation for schools, hospitals and libraries'.[117]

CONCLUSION

Public service obligations are not at all at war with European integration and free market principles. The European Union has deliberately opted for a liberali-sation with a human touch through the development of the concept of universal service and universal service obligations which can be imposed on operators offering services which are considered to be of general economic interest. The fact that in the fully liberalised telecommunications sector the majority of member-states have not made use of the possibility of establishing specific schemes for the financing of these universal service obligations, clearly shows that the opening-up of the sector to competition does not lead to unjustified burdens being imposed on universal service operators. It is therefore submitted that this element of European civilisation[118] is clearly not in danger.

NOTES

1. The References contain a list of legislation and Commission documents referred to in this article. In the footnotes, only the shortened references will be used.
2. The first being the 1986 European Single Act, the second the 1992 Maastricht Treaty.
3. The Treaty of Amsterdam will enter into force, once ratified in all the member-states. This will also lead to a re-numbering of the articles. For the sake of clarity, throughout the text reference will be made to both the present and the new number of Treaty Articles (in brackets).
4. In an article written before the signing of the Treaty of Amsterdam, Kovar concluded that 'the requirement to find a *juste* equilibrium between satisfying collective needs of a society characterised by solidarity and market efficiency *deserves* such upgrading' (Kovar, 1996, p. 533; own translation).
5. Declaration no.13 on Article 7d of the EC-Treaty.
6. Such as J.S. Mill, A. Marshall, A.C. Pigou, J.M. Keynes, . . . See on this also C.E.E.P.,1995 and Vlachos, 1996.
7. On this see Durand, 1996; for France see Kovar (1996).
8. On this see Delacour, 1996.
9. See for an extensive analysis see C.E.E.P., 1995.
10. See on this C.E.E.P., 1992.
11. COM(96) 443 final, p. 13.
12. See for instance Rapp (1995). This author also affirms that 'Public service operators have been the deliberate victims of European deregulation policies and have become Europe's bad conscience' (own translation) (p. 354). For the C.E.E.P. the 'public service cannot be considered as an *ordinary* commodity or service, and robbing it of its originality would be to degrade it' (own emphasis) (C.E.E.P.,1992, p. 18).
13. See on this Buendia Sierra 1996; along the same lines, Kovar (1996) and Dubois (1997).
14. With Koen Nomden, it must be mentioned that '[T]his article has only played a marginal role in recent Community policy on the liberalisation of regulated public services', NOMDEN, K., 'Reconciling liberalisation and public service obligations' (Nomden, 1997, p. 6).
15. This article reads as follows: '1. In the case of public undertakings and undertakings to which member-states grant special or exclusive rights, Member-states shall neither enact nor maintain in force any measure contrary to the rules contained in this Treaty, in particular those provided for in Article 6 and Articles 85 to 94. 2. Undertakings entrusted with the operation of services of general economic interest or having the character of a revenue-producing monopoly shall be subject to the rules contained in this Treaty, in particular to the rules on competition, in so far as the application of such rules does not obstruct the performance, in law or in fact, of the particular tasks assigned to them. The development of trade must not be affected to such an extent as would be contrary to the interests of the Community. 3. The Commission shall ensure the application of the provisions of this Article and shall, where necessary, address appropriate directives of decisions to Member States.'
16. Art. 2 EC reads 'The Community shall have as its task, *by establishing a common market . . .*'
17. It suffices here to indicate with Kapteyn and Verloren van Themaat. (1990, p. 407) that 'any organisation through which a Member State, de jure or de facto, either directly or indirectly, supervises, determines, or appreciably influences imports or exports between member-states is equated with a state trading monopoly'. The most important ones were mineral oil, tobacco products and alcohol. See on Article 37 EC also Constantinescu *et al.* (1992).
18. Expression used in the *Collection des Juris-Classeurs*, Fascicule 580, no. 3 (own translation).
19. See C.E.E.P. (1995), Rapp (1995), Fournier (1996) and Dubois (1997).
20. According to UNICE (1998, p. 15), 'the relative failure so far of the Single Market programme in fully opening up many service sectors to greater competition, has a negative effect on industrial competitiveness and limits the development of new employment opportunities. Accelerating liberalisation, elimination of highly distorting state aids and wide-ranging

regulatory reform in these areas must become a priority for the completion of the Single Market'.

21. This at the same time partly explains why the Commission has for a long time been quite reluctant to make use of this competence. Member-states did not particularly like the idea of being 'put aside' in the legislative process.
22. Directive 80/723. On this directive see Delacour (1996).
23. See on this infra, para 26 et seq.
24. Decision of 24 April 1985, 'Greek Insurances', *OJ* 1985, L152/25; Decision of 22 June 1987, 'Canary Islands', *OJ* 1987 L 194/28; Decision of 20 December 1989, 'Dutch Courrier-services', *OJ* 1990 L 10/47; Decision of 1 August 1990, 'Spanish Courrier-services', *OJ* 1990 L 233/19; Decision of 28 June 1995, 'Brussels Airport', *OJ* 1995 L 216/8; Decision of 4 October 1995, 'GSM Italy', *OJ* 1995 L 280/49 and Decision of 18 December 1996, 'GSM Spain', *OJ* 1997 L 76/19.
25. COM(87) 290 final; COM(88) 238 final; COM(89) 334 final; COM(91) 476 final.
26. Judgement of 19 May 1993, 'Corbeau', C-320/91 [1993] ECR I-2536. See for a brief description of this postal case C.E.E.P. (1995) and Nomden (1997).
27. Judgement of 27 April 1994, 'Almelo v. Ysselmij', C-393/92 [1994] ECR I-1508. See for a brief description of this electricity-case C.E.E.P. (1995) and Nomden (1997).
28. Buendia Sierra (1996); Kovar (1996).
29. COM(96) 443 final.
30. Idem, p. 1. Along the same lines, p. 3, 'Services of general interest are a key element in the European model of society'.
31. COM(1998) 101 final, p. 9. Although specifically dealing with universal service in the telecommunications sector, this statement is of general application.
32. COM(96) 73 final, p. 8. Although made in respect of universal service in the telecommunications sector, this statement is of general value.
33. See Buendia Sierra (1996) and Dubois (1997). This point of view is strongly backed by the Council, the European Parliament, the Economic and Social Committee and the Committee of the Regions. See for a statement along these lines for the telecommunications sector, COM(96) 73 final, p. 3. According to the Commission, 'this regulatory approach has been chosen in part to avoid inefficient and distortionary practice by new entrants, but also to ensure that all citizens of the Union have access to certain services of high quality at prices they can afford', COM(1998) 101 final, p. 20.
34. See Deacon (1997).
35. Along the same line - specifically dealing with telecommunications - Deacon (1997). See also 'Guidelines on the application of EEC competition rules in the telecommunications sector' and COM(96) 649 final.
36. COM(96) 443 final, p. 2. See also, Kovar (1996).
37. COM(96) 443 final, p. 2 and 7.
38. *Ibid.*
39. This is the standard definition in Community legislation. See f.i. Directive 97/33/EC, Article 2, sub g); COM(1998) 101 final, p. 8. See for more information on this concept in the postal and the telecommunications sector, infra III and IV.
40. COM(96) 443 final, p. 7 and 28.
41. Delacour (1996).
42. COM(96) 443 final, p. 30, 'There is nothing to prevent the Member-states from defining additional general interest duties over and above universal service obligations, provided that the means used comply with Community law'.
43. This article reads: 'This Treaty shall in no way prejudice the rules in Member-states governing the system of property ownership'. As a result, it is 'of no consequence whether an enterprise is publicly or privately owned when it comes to applying Community law' (Nomden, 1997, p. 6).
44. See Van Miert (1997) and Dubois (1997). At the same time, however, UNICE (1998), is of the opinion that 'privatisation of most non-core public sector activities and enterprises, and

the contracting-out of market services should be pursued and stepped up. In most European countries, privatisation of public utilities and services with a commercial character (posts, telecommunications, transport, energy, banks) would not only help to improve public finances but, most importantly, would contribute to raising competitiveness through better quality of services and lower costs for business' (p. 27).

45. Nomden (1997) 6. According to KOVAR (1996) 494, 'competition pressure on public services almost logically leads to reconsidering their status' and 501 'Privatization is not actually required by Community law, but it would be wrong to deny that it does contain some kind of stimulus to engage in this direction' (own translation).
46. COM(91) 476 final.
47. COM(93) 247 final.
48. European Parliament (1993). The choice of this legal basis would at the same time guarantee the involvement of the Parliament in the legislative process, whereas action on the basis of Article 90 would not do so, *cf. supra.*
49. COM(95) 227 final.
50. SEC(95) 0830.
51. Article 8-9, COM(95) 227 final.
52. Directive 97/67; SEC(97) 2289/4.
53. Article 3 Directive 97/67.
54. Article 7, Directive 97/67.
55. Article 27, Directive 97/67.
56. para. 2.6, SEC(97) 2289/4.
57. para. 2.7-2.9, SEC(97) 2289/4.
58. para. 6.1, SEC(97) 2289/4.
59. See for the text of this paragraph, supra, footnote 20.
60. para. 8.3, SEC(97) 2289/4.
61. Judgement of 23 April 1991, 'Höfner v. Macrotron', C-41/90 [1991] ECR I-1979; Judgement of 10 December 1991, 'Merci', C-179/90 [1991] ECR I-5889.
62. Chapter 8, title (i)-(iii), SEC(97) 2289/4.
63. See for a general description of the conditions for applying Article 90/2 see C.E.E.P. (1995) and Kovar (1996).
64. Chapter 8, title(iv) and (vi), SEC(97) 2289/4.
65. Chapter 8, title(vii), SEC(97) 2289/4.
66. para. 8.4 to 8.6, SEC(97) 2289/4.
67. Directive 86/361.
68. COM(87) 290 final. For an extensive analysis see Dony (1996).
69. Directive 90/388.
70. See Article 1, para 2, Directive 90/388 and recitals 1 and 18.
71. Voice telephony is defined as 'the commercial provision for the public of the direct transport and switching of speech in real-time between public switched network termination points, enabling any user to use equipment connected to such a network termination point in order to communicate with another termination point' see Article 1 , indent 7 Directive 90/388.
72. Telex service is defined as 'the commercial provision for the public of direct transmission of telex messages in accordance with the relevant 'Comité Consultatif International Télégraphique et Téléphonique' (CCITT) recommendation between public switched network termination points, enabling any user to use equipment connected to such a network termination point in order to communicate with another termination point' see Article 1, indent 8, Directive 90/388.
73. Directive 94/46.
74. Directive 95/51.
75. Directive 96/2. According to Article 1, par 1, indent 10, mobile and personal communications services are defined as 'services other than satellite services whose provision consists, wholly or partly, in the establishment of radio-communications to a mobile user, and makes use wholly or partly of mobile and personal communications systems'.

76. Directive 96/19.
77. See on the transition period, Article 2, para. 2, subpara. 4 , Directive 96/19.
78. Article 2, para 2, 3rd part, Directive 96/19.
79. According to Commission decision 97/568, till 1 July 1998.
80. According to Commission decision 97/603, till 30 November 1998.
81. According to Commission decision 97/310, till 1 January 2000.
82. According to Commission decision 97/114, till 1 January 2000.
83. According to Commission decision 97/60, till 1 January 2000.
84. For a clarifying chart indicating the requested and granted derogations, see *Agence Europe*, 19 June 1997.
85. COM(87) 209 final.
86. For an extensive analysis see Dony (1996).
87. COM(96) 73 final, p. 3. Along the same lines, Recital 8, Directive 97/33, 'Whereas obligations for the provision of universal service contribute to the Community objective of economic and territorial cohesion and territorial equity'.
88. COM(96) 73 final, p. 3 and 21.
89. Article 3, Directive 95/62; Recital 4, Directive 96/19.
90. Recital 4, Directive 96/19.
91. COM(1998) 101 final, p. 10.
92. Article 7, Directive 95/62; Recital 4, Directive 96/19.
93. Articles 3 to 7, Directive 95/62.
94. See for the basic principles of transparency and cost orientation of these tariffs, Article 12, Directive 95/62. Article 14 deals with discounts, low-usage schemes and other specific tariff provisions. See on this, also Directive 97/51, Annex I, sub 3. Harmonised tariff principles.
95. Article 8, Directive 95/62.
96. Article 15, Directive 95/62.
97. COM(96) 73 final, p. 5; Article 16, Directive 95/62; Recitals 17-18 and Article 1, para 6, Directive 96/19; COM(1998) 101 final, p. 10.
98. Recital 17 and Article 1, para 6, Directive 96/19; COM(1998) 101 final, p. 10.
99. COM(96) 73 final, p. 5; Article 17, Directive 95/62; COM(1998) 101 final, p. 10.
100. Article 10, Directive 95/62.
101. Article 11, Directive 95/62. See on inter-connection, also Recitals 11-16 and Article 1, para 6, Directive 96/19. In 1997, Directive 97/33 was adopted specifically dealing with 'interconnection in telecommunications with regard to ensuring universal service and interoperability through application of the principles of Open Network Provision'.
102. Article 13, Directive 95/62; Article 1, para 6, Directive 96/19.
103. Recital 21, Directive 96/19. Along similar lines, COM(1998) 101 final, p. 10.
104. COM(96) 73 final, p. 6. At p. 21, the Commission put forward that 'affordability is at the heart of the framework for universal service for telecommunications'.
105. See for the calculation of the cost of universal service obligations for voice telephony, COM(96) 608 final. See also Annex III to the Directive 97/33.
106. COM(96) 73 final, p. 5-6, p. 2; Article 4c Directive 95/62; Article 5, para 2, Directive 97/33; COM(1998) 101 final, p. 10.
107. Article 5, para 1, Directive 97/33.
108. Recital 19, Directive 96/19.
109. Recital 19 and Article 1, para 6, Directive 96/19; Recital 8, Directive 97/33.
110. Also called for by the European Parliament. See Beres Report on Universal Service for telecommunications in the perspective of a fully liberalised environment, 21 November 1996, PE 218.932.
111. Reference to such monitoring is omnipresent in COM(96) 73 final.
112. COM(96) 73 final, p. 22.
113. COM(1998) 101 final, p. 2, 13-16 and 19-20.
114. Not entirely surprising, one finds here the countries of the *Latin* tradition, France, Italy, Spain, Portugal, Greece (and Ireland), COM(1998) 101 final, p. 18.

115. COM(1998) 101 final, p. 3, 10 and 17-18.
116. COM(1998) 101 final, p. 23.
117. COM(1998) 101 final, p. 24.
118. *Cf. supra*, para 7.

REFERENCES

Buendia Sierra, J.L. (1996), 'Services d'intérêt général en Europe et politique com-
munautaire de concurrence', *Competition Policy Newsletter*, **2**, 14-22.
C.E.E.P. (1992), *Updating the Concept of Public Service*, Brussels, C.E.E.P.
C.E.E.P. (1995), *Europe, Competition and Public Service*, Brussels, C.E.E.P.
COM(87) 290 final (1987), 'Green Paper on the development of the common market for
telecommunications services and equipment'.
COM(88) 238 final (1988), 'Commission Working Document on the internal energy
market'.
COM(89) 334 final (1989), 'Communication from the Commission: Towards the
completion of the internal market for natural gas'.
COM(91) 476 final (1991), 'Green Paper on the development of the single market for
postal services'.
COM(93) 247 final (1993), 'Communication from the Commission to Council and
Parliament guidelines for the development of community postal services'.
COM(95) 227 final (1995), 'Proposal for a European Parliament and Council Directive
on common rules for the development of Community postal services and the im-
provement of quality of service'.
COM(96) 73 final (1996), 'Communication from the Commission on universal service
for telecommunications in the perspective of a fully liberalised environment'.
COM(96) 443 final (1996), 'Communication from the Commission on services of
general economic interest in Europe'.
COM(96) 649 final (1996), 'Draft communication from the Commission on the applica-
tion of the competition rules to access agreements in the telecommunications sector.
Framework, Relevant markets, Principles'.
COM(98) 101 final (1998), 'Communication from the Commission to the Council, the
European Parliament, the Economic and Social Committee and the Committee of the
Regions. First monitoring report on universal service in telecommunications in the
European Union'.
Constantinescu, V., R. Kovar, J.P. Jacque and D. Simon (1992), *Traité Instituant la
CEE. Commentaire Article par Article*, Paris: Economica, pp. 199-211.
Deacon, D. (1997), 'Comments on 'the Coherence of the EU Policies on Trade, Compe-
tition and Industry Case Study : High Technologies', http://europa.eu.int/search97cgi.
Decision 97/114 (1997), 'Decision of the Commission of 4 December 1996 concerning
the grant of additional implementation periods to Ireland for the implementation of
Commission Directives 90/388/EC and 96/2 as regards full competition in the tele-
communications sector', *Official Journal*, L41/8.
Decision 97/310 (1997), 'Decision of the Commission of 12 February 1997 concerning
the grant of additional implementation periods to Portugal for the implementation of
Commission Directives 90/388/EC and 96/2 as regards full competition in the telecommunications market', *Official Journal*, L133/19.

Decision 97/568 (1997), 'Decision of the Commission of 14 May 1997 concerning the grant of additional implementation periods to Luxembourg for the implementation of Commission Directive 90/388/EC as regards full competition in the telecommunications market', *Official Journal*, L234/7.

Decision 97/603 (1997), 'Decision of the Commission of 10 June 1997 concerning the grant of additional implementation periods to Spain for the implementation of Commission Directive 90/388/EC as regards full competition in the telecommunications market', *Official Journal*, L133/19.

Dehousse, F. and L. Van den Hende (1996), 'La Place des Services Publics dans la Conférence Intergouvernementale', in M. Dony (ed.), *Les Services Publics en Europe: entre Concurrence et Droits des Usagers*, Brussels, ULB, pp. 37-55.

Delacour, E. (1996), 'Services Publics et Concurrence Communautaire', *R.M.C.*, 501-509.

Directive 80/723 (1980), 'Directive of the Commission of 25 June 1980 concerning transparency in the financial relations between Member States and public undertakings', *Official Journal*, L195/35; afterwards changed by Directive 85/413 (1985), *Official Journal*, L 229/20 and Directive 93/84 (1993), *Official Journal*, L254/16.

Directive 86/361 (1986), 'Directive of the Council of 24 July 1986 on the initial stage of the mutual recognition of type approval for telecommunications terminal equipment', *Official Journal*, L217/21.

Directive 88/301 (1988), 'Directive of the Commission of 16 May 1988 on competition in the markets for telecommunications terminal equipment', *Official Journal*, L131/73.

Directive 90/388 (1990), 'Directive of the Commission of 28 June 1990 on competition in the markets for telecommunications services', *Official Journal*, L192/10.

Directive 94/46 (1994), 'Directive of the Commission of 13 October 1994 amending Directive 88/301/EEC and Directive 90/388/EEC in particular with regard to satellite communications', *Official Journal*, L268/15.

Directive 95/51 (1995), 'Directive of the Commission of 18 October 1995 amending Directive 90/388/EEC with regard to the abolition of the restrictions on the use of cable television networks for the provision of already liberalised telecommunications services', *Official Journal*, L256/49.

Directive 95/62 (1995), 'Directive of the European Parliament and the Council of 13 December 1995 on the application of Open Network Provision to voice telephony', *Official Journal*, L321/6.

Directive 96/2 (1996), 'Directive of the Commission of 16 January 1996 amending Directive 90/388/EEC with regard to mobile and personal telecommunications', *Official Journal*, L20/59.

Directive 96/19 (1996), 'Directive of the Commission of 13 March 1996 amending Directive 90/388/EEC regarding the implementation of full competition in telecommunications markets', *Official Journal*, L74/13.

Directive 97/33 (1997), 'Directive of the European Parliament and the Council of 30 June 1997 on interconnection in telecommunications with regard to ensuring universal service and interoperability through application of the principles of Open Network Provision', *Official Journal*, L199/32.

Directive 97/51 (1997), 'Directive of the European Parliament and the Council of 6 October 1997 amending Council Directives 90/387/EEC and 92/44/EEC for the purpose of adaptation to a competitive environment in telecommunications', *Official Journal*, L295/23.

Directive 97/67 (1997), 'Directive of the European Parliament and the Council of 15 December 1997 on common rules for the development of the internal market of Community postal services and the improvement of quality of services', *Official Journal*, L15/14.

Dony, M. (1996), 'Le Cadre Juridique Communautaire dans le Secteur des Télécommunications', in M. Dony (ed.), *Les Services Publics et l'Europe : entre Concurrence et Droits des Usagers*, Brussels, ULB, pp. 165-191.

Dubois, J. (1997), 'L'Approche de la Commission Européenne face à la Liberalisation et aux Obligations de Service Universel', in IEAP, *Managing Universal Service Obligations in Public Utilities in the European Union*, Maastricht, IEAP, pp. 17-25.

Durand, C.F. (1996), 'Service Public Européen et Politique Industrielle ou la Promotion de l'Intérêt Général et du Service aux Citoyens', *Revue du Marché Commun*, No. 396, 211-221.

European Commission (1991), 'Guidelines on the application of EEC competition rules in the telecommunications sector', *Official Journal*, C233/2.

European Parliament (1993), 'Resolution on the Single Market for Postal Services', *Official Journal*, C194/397.

Fournier, J. (1996), 'Les Services Publics et le Droit Communautaire', in M. Dony (ed.), *Les Services Publics et l'Europe: entre Concurrence et Droits des Usagers*, Brussels, ULB, pp. 7-16.

Kapteyn, P.J.G. and P. Verloren van Themaat, P. (1990), *Introduction to the Law of the European Communities after the Coming into Force of the Single European Act*, Deventer: Kluwer Law and Taxation Publishers.

Kovar, R. (1996), 'Droit Communautaire et Service Public: Esprit d'Orthodoxie ou Pensée Laïcisée', Revue Trimestrielle de Droit Européen, **32**, 215-242 and 493-533.

Nomden, K. (1997), 'Reconciling Liberalisation and Public Service Obligations', in IEDAP, *Managing Universal Service Obligations in Public Utilities in the European Union*, Maastricht, IEDAP, pp. 5-16.

Rapp, L. (1995), 'La Politique de Libéralisation des Services en Europe, entre Service Public et Service Universel', *Revue du Marché Commun*, no. 8, 352-357.

SEC(95) 0830 (1995), 'Draft Notice from the Commission on the application of the competition rules to the postal sector and in particular on the assessment of certain state measures relating to postal services', *Official Journal*, C322/3.

SEC(97) 2289/4 (1998), 'Notice from the Commission of 17 December 1997 on the application of the competition rules to the postal sector and on the assessment of certain state measures relating to postal services, *Official Journal*, C39/2.

UNICE (1998), *Benchmarking Europe's Competitiveness: from Analysis to Action*, January 1998.

Vandamme J. (1997), 'Les Différentes Conceptions des Entreprises et Services Publics en Europe', in IEDAP, *Managing Universal Service Obligations in Public Utilities in the European Union*, Maastricht, IEDAP, pp. 27-38.

Van Miert, K. (1997), 'La Conférence Intergouvernementale et la Politique Communautaire de Concurrence', *Competition Policy Newsletter*, **3**, 1-5.

Vlachos, G. (1996), *Droit Public Economique Français et Communautaire*, Paris: Armand Colin.

Index

Abrams, R. 15
Acquired Rights Directives (EU) 183,
    184, 185, 186, 187, 188–94
Adler, F.M. 121
Adnett, N. 188, 190
air pollution, regulations 203
Akhtar, M.A. 11, 15
Amsterdam, Treaty of 225–6
Ansic, D. 13
ARD *see* Acquired Rights Directives
Ardeni, P. 11
Argimón, I. 68
Arize, A.C. 15, 16, 17, 18–19
Assery, A. 15
asymmetric shocks 28, 29–30, 31–2, 35,
    44, 58–9, 60–61

Bailey, M.J. 15
Baillie, T.R. 106
Bajo, O. 69
Balassa, B. 121
Baldwin, R. 1, 13
Barnum, C. 96
Barrett, S. 207, 210
Barro, R. 70
Barry, F. 51, 52, 53, 54, 57
Baumol, W. 70
Bayoumi, T. 2, 58, 60
Beck, U. 214
Beechler, S. 173
Belgium
    attitudes to EMU 91, 92, 93, 94
    political structure 216
    trade 124, 125, 128, 129, 130–31
    water pollution policies 215–20
Bellace, J. 158, 160, 161, 177
Benelux
    trade 123, 129–31

see also Belgium; EEC; EU;
    Netherlands
Bertola, G. 186
bilateralism, in trade 127, 128, 129, 131
Bird, A. 173
Blanchard, O. 57
Blank, R. 185
Blanpain, R. 158, 160, 161, 165, 166
Bockelmann, H. 10
Bodnar, G. 11
Boothe, P. 16, 106
Borio, C. 10
Bradley, J. 57
Bradley, S.P. 144
Brett, J. 174
Brewster, C. 173, 177
Britain *see* United Kingdom
Brittan, L. 175
Brodsky, D.A. 16
Brooks, R. 16, 17
Brown, W. 186
Brülhart, M. 59
Brunell, T. 187
Buigues, P. 51, 138
Burgoyne, C.B. 86, 97
business transfers 183–4, 185, 186–7,
    188–94
    see also take-overs

Campa, J. 57
Campbell, I. 9
Canova, F. 71
capital mobility, and the EMU 78–9
Caporale, T. 16
Capron, H. 150
Caracostas, P. 138
carbon taxes 210–11, 215
Carley, M. 160

245

multinational enterprises
  in cohesion countries 52, 57
  decentralisation in 171–3, 174
  and environmental regulations 213–14
  EU policies 175–7
  and exchange rate variability 21
  human resource management 173–4,
    176, 177
  industrial relations 173, 174–5, 176
  information provision in 172, 173–4
  networks in 172–3, 174
  structure 172–5
  transfers within 21
  see also European Works Councils

Nagelkerke, A. 174
Napier, B. 183
Narula, R. 139, 140, 142
national differences *see* cultural
  differences; non-nationalism
national economic pride, measures 92–3,
  95, 96, 97, 98
Netherlands
  attitudes to EMU 91, 92, 93, 94
  trade 124, 125, 128, 129, 130–31
networks 172–3, 174
  see also technological alliances
Nicholson, N. 21
Nickell, S. 185, 186
Nicolini, J.P. 69
non-nationalism, measures of 92, 93, 95,
  96–7, 98
North Sea, pollution in 206–7, 208

Ó Gráda, C. 50
Obstfeld, M. 57
Ogilvie, J.C. 90
open-mindedness *see* self-confident
  open-mindedness
organisational change, and labour market
  flexibility 185–6
O'Rourke, K. 50

Painter, R. 184
Park, J.Y. 11
Parkin, R. 185
Pavitt, K. 136, 139, 142
Pecchenino, R.A. 106
Peel, D.A. 15
Pentecost, E. 11

Pepermans, R. 86, 87, 96, 98, 99
Perée, E. 11, 12, 16, 17, 18
personnel management *see* human
  resource management
Peterson, J. 136, 137, 138, 149
Pfander, J.E. 203
Philpott, J. 185
Pitchford, R. 86
Plasschaert, S. 21
political economy 13–14, 20
pollution control
  costs 208–9, 214, 215
  instruments 204, 209, 215, 216,
    217–18, 219–20
  see also air pollution; environmental
    regulations; transboundary
    pollution; water pollution
Porter, M.E. 139, 143, 214
postal services 231–4
power distance
  in national cultures 86, 87, 94, 95, 97
  see also centralisation;
    decentralisation
Pozo, S. 16
Prewo, W.F. 121
price differentials, and the EMU 35, 51
productivity
  and employment protection 185–6
  in exchange rate models 107–8, 109
progressive non-nationalism *see* non-
  nationalism
protectionism
  and environmental regulations
    211–12, 213
  and exchange rate variability 13–14
  and road transport markets 41
Psacharopoulos, G. 75
psychological constructs *see* cultural
  differences
Pu, Y. 3, 106, 107, 108, 112, 117
public services
  and competition 228–30, 231–2, 233
  and economic integration 227
  EU policies 225–6, 228–30
  government provision 226–7
  see also postal services;
    telecommunications
Pugh, G. 13, 17, 19, 20
purchasing power parity, in exchange
  rate models 104, 106, 107